DOUBLE READING

DOUBLE READING

Postmodernism after Deconstruction

JEFFREY T. NEALON

Cornell University Press

ITHACA AND LONDON

First published 1993 by Cornell University Press.

International Standard Book Number 0-8014-2853-X
Library of Congress Catalog Card Number 93-636

Printed in the United States of America

Librarians: Library of Congress cataloging information
appears on the last page of the book.

⊗ The paper in this book meets the minimum requirements
of the American National Standard for Information Sciences—
Permanence of Paper for Printed Library Materials, ANSI Z39.48-1984.

Contents

Acknowledgments

I have a great many people to thank for their assistance with this project. Among them, certainly, Paul Jay, Pamela Caughie, and Paul Davies are first and foremost.

The idea for this book first began to take shape in 1987 at the Collegium Phaenomenologicum in Perugia, Italy. I thank all the participants in the Collegium, though I owe a particular debt to Rodolphe Gasché, whose work has made mine possible, and to John Sallis, who, I can say without bombast, taught me how to read. I wish also to acknowledge a long-standing obligation to John Boly, David Krause, and Jack Wenke—the triumvirate that set me on the course that leads to this book. Thanks to John Protevi and Michael Naas, whose careful comments have substantially improved this work, and to John McGowan for a close and helpful reading. Andrew Lewis did a splendid job editing the manuscript, and Joe Sullivan prepared the index. Finally, thanks to Charles Bernstein for generously taking time out to discuss his work with me.

Also, I gratefully acknowledge the material support furnished by the Arthur J. Schmitt foundation, and the support—material and otherwise—offered by my parents, Thomas and Jean Nealon. But, in the end, this project would have remained impossible without Sherry Brennan, who knows better than anyone that "all thoughtful people are impatient, with a restlessness made inevitable by language."

An earlier version of Chapter 2, "The Discipline of Deconstruction," appeared in *PMLA* 107 (1992): 1266–79. Reprinted by permission of the copyright owner, The Modern Language Association of America. An earlier version of Chapter 3, "Exteriority and Appropriation: Foucault, Derrida, and the Discipline of Literary Criticism," appeared in *Cultural Critique* 21 (1992): 97–120. © 1992, Oxford University Press, Inc. Used with permission. A section of Chapter 4 appeared as "Thinking/Writing the Postmodern: Representation, End, Ground, Sending" in *boundary 2* 20 (1993).

For permission to include material published by them, grateful acknowledgment is also due the following: Fiction Collective, for permission to quote from *The Endless Short Story* by Ronald Sukenick, copyright © 1986 by Ronald Sukenick. Harvard University Press, for material from *A Poetics* by Charles Bernstein, copyright © 1992 by Charles Bernstein. Penguin USA, for text from *Gravity's Rainbow* by Thomas Pynchon. Copyright © 1973 by Thomas Pynchon. Used by permission of Viking Penguin, a division of Penguin Books USA Inc. United Kingdom rights to reprint from *Gravity's Rainbow*, copyright © 1973 by Thomas Pynchon; reprinted by permission of Melanie Jackson Agency. Roof Books, for permission to quote from *Progress* by Barrett Watten, copyright © 1985 by Barrett Watten. Sun & Moon Press, for permission to use material from Charles Bernstein, *Content's Dream* (Los Angeles: Sun & Moon Press, 1986), pp. 59, 75, 82–83, 246. © Charles Bernstein, 1986. Reprinted by permission of the publisher. A passage from "China" by Bob Perelman is reprinted by permission of the author. The quotation "Yes and no (what else?)" by Barbara Johnson is reprinted by permission of the author.

J. T. N.

If rationality is the issue today, is it merely to conjure up the alleged lack of philosophical argumentation and discursive consistency? Is it not, rather, because thinking has discovered a new sort of finitude which requires not the abandonment of the traditional forms and claims that constituted it, but their displacement within operations of thought whose calculated economy obeys a "rationality" of its own? To pose the question of rationality with regard to the postmodern is then, perhaps, to recover a sort of thinking which, although it presupposes a displacement of all essential forms constitutive of thought in the tradition of thinking, is more of the order of the philosophies concerned with the "richer" concept of reason.

—RODOLPHE GASCHÉ
"Postmodernism and Rationality"

("we keep coming
back and coming back . . . "
to the vision of dis-
placement at the site of
enactment, procurement,
debasement, trans-
substantiation, fulmination,
culmination . . .)

—CHARLES BERNSTEIN
"Artifice of Absorption"

DOUBLE READING

1 / "In the Interests
of Professionalism"

Despite the tendency of the semiotic process to be open-
ended and relatively indeterminate, determination takes
place all the time, has always taken place, and will always
take place, over and above the efforts of individual thinkers.
. . . The problem then becomes that of defining the conditions under which such a violent arrestation—in other
words: institution—takes place.
                              —Samuel Weber
                              Institution and Interpretation

Given the incredible amount of critical work done on the subject, a study of postmodernism and deconstruction requires as much
justification as introduction. A good deal of literary critical ink has
recently been spilled over each of the topics and writers I consider
here: certainly Derrida, Foucault, Heidegger, and Pynchon are not
new names to the discipline of literary criticism; and even "Language" poetry, although it may be a new name to some, has likewise
been well commented upon. In fact, so much work has been done
on these topics and authors that *simply* to add to the bibliography
seems not only pointless, but also in some sense irresponsible—
irresponsible insofar as it surreptitiously feeds a growing institutional framework without questioning the processes of (that) institution or their consequences. Hence I take a different tack.
Throughout, I emphasize the role(s) of the discipline of literary criticism—and, by extension, the roles of the university—in the production and control of meaning, while simultaneously trying to
recognize and account for my own status as a literary critic and as

a person who teaches and studies literature within an institution. This twofold emphasis will necessarily entail, throughout, my engagement with what Jacques Derrida has called "a double gesture," the attempt to think the necessary, indispensable work of the university "even while going as far as possible, theoretically and practically, in the most directly underground thinking about the abyss beneath the university" ("Principle of Reason" 17). This double gesture will, I hope, allow me to investigate important questions about postmodern literature and literary theory, but also to examine the problems raised by the institutionalized nature of my own work.

Scholarly work of all types should attempt to take into account the functions of institutionalization, but doing so seems especially important when one is discussing the literary manifestations of "postmodernism" and "theory"—the two generic categories into which this work most easily fits, and the two topics it most closely treats. First, and most obvious, there quite literally would be no categories "postmodernism" and "theory" if it were not for a disciplinary apparatus that classifies phenomena in order to study them—a process that, as Michel Foucault points out, actually creates what a discipline wishes to study by securing its proper object, its field of study.[1] The very act of creating an institutionalized field of study labeled "postmodern theory" engenders a twofold problem: postmodern literature and theory—if one can speak of their "generic" forms and put aside for the moment the potentially questionable nature of that opposition—tend to emphasize the "open-ended and relatively indeterminate semiotic process" that Samuel Weber points out in the passage that serves as the epigraph to this chapter (*Institution and Interpretation* 20–21). The process(es) of institution, however, tend to emphasize the "inevitable" closure of limits, the importance of determinate or determining institutional programs of decision making or standard setting. In other words, although the *discursive* claims and manifestations of postmodernism emphasize the irreducibility of meaning and the inevitability of various kinds of indeterminacy, the processes of the institution and the functioning of the apparatuses of professionalism seem, for the most

---

1. See Foucault's *Archaeology of Knowledge*, 31/44. Here and throughout this work, wherever a translation and an original are both cited, I cite the translation page number first.

part, to remain undisturbed. One sees this especially (and ironically) in theoretical writing, where—to return to Weber's vocabulary—"individual thinkers" of indeterminacy often suffer "violent arrestation" at the hands of both "competing" theorists and well-meaning followers. Competing theorists are likely to "violently arrest" a theoretical text in order to reduce it to a determinate, criticizable, or surpassable position. Sympathetic followers are more likely to arrest it by transforming it into an interpretative grid, an aid to producing determinate readings.

One might conclude from this paradox that the practice of criticism simply has not caught up with the theory. What usually follows such a conclusion is either some discussion concerning how to close the gap between theory and practice or a declaration that such a gap is "inevitable."[2] I prefer to point out instead what tends to be overlooked in such discussions, the surreptitious forwarding of a certain institutional interest in determination *itself*, an interest in arresting what purports to be an open-ended process in the service of "professional," institutional ends. As Paul Bové points out in *Intellectuals in Power*, even the most trenchant oppositional criticism can be made to legitimate the hegemonic functions of the university through "the endless repositioning of intellectuals vis-à-vis other intellectuals in their battles for social rewards" (224). Determining the adequacy of competing critical positions tends to leave contemporary theorists in the uncomfortable position of moral judge or arbiter above the fray of mere opinion—a role, as Bové puts it, that "is essentially a legitimation of the status quo of intellectual life" (223). Such determination and critical jousting can, in other words, protect certain hegemonic power structures (both theoretical and institutional) while seeming to criticize or undermine them.

In "The Profession of Theory,"[3] David Kaufmann summarizes the problems of institutionalization and theory when he writes that,

2. One sees the former proposition played out in any number of primers, from books as disparate as Eagleton's *Literary Theory* and Norris's *Deconstruction: Theory and Practice*. The latter "anti-theory" mode is found in the work of the "new pragmatists." See Mitchell's *Against Theory*.

3. It is important to note that Kaufmann's essay was originally published in a very noticeable place within the profession: an issue of *PMLA* titled "The Politics of Critical Language."

despite the many important questions it poses, "recent theory . . . has precipitated the latest in a century-long history of pseudocrises that have functioned to protect the institutionalization of literature in the academy. . . . Theory—like its discontents—helps keep the world safe for lit. crit." (523). Theory's automatic co-optation, of course, creates a dicey problem for anyone who wants to take account of the forces and problems of institutionalization vis-à-vis literary crit-icism. In the face of this insight—that simply criticizing a power structure may actually help it to perform its work—the question becomes how to think against a structure when one is irreducibly *within* that structure, when there is no pure space "outside" from which one can criticize or judge. Or, to rephrase the problem, how does one think "practice" when it can no longer simply be governed (or have its results guaranteed) by a determinate or determining "theory"? The question becomes, in Reiner Schürmann's words, what happens "once 'thinking' no longer means securing some ra-tional foundation upon which one may establish the sum total of what is knowable, and once 'acting' no longer means conforming one's daily enterprises, both public and private, to the foundation so secured" (*Heidegger on Being and Acting* 1)? This, I argue, is *the* question of the postmodern: insofar as almost any notion of the postmodern is characterized by the absence of a pure, grounding "rational foundation," how to proceed without this grounding pu-rity becomes crucial for a time or place we would call postmodern. It is also my contention throughout this work that the question of the postmodern is irreducibly both a systematic (philosophical or theoretical) and an institutional (pragmatic or worldly) question. I take up the "systematic" aspects of this question beginning with Chapter 2 in an examination of Derrida and literary criticism, and focus primarily on the "institutional" questions in this chapter— though the distinction will, I hope, become more and more dubious as I proceed. In Chapter 3, I continue to examine literary criticism as an institutional system in relation to Foucault's texts. I hold in reserve the question of theories of the postmodern until Chapter 4, at which time I also broach the question of postmodern literature. Chapters 5 and 6 deal with the institutional and systematic problems raised by postmodern texts, specifically Thomas Pynchon's *Gravity's Rainbow* and "Language" poetry. The Conclusion takes up ethics and politics "after" deconstruction.

The Ultimate Frustration of the Institution

There is an initial tension between the "interests" of institution-alization and those of postmodernism and theory. Namely, insti-tutionalization tends to undermine the openness that much postmodern theory calls for. As Kaufmann continues in "The Profes-sion of Theory," the upshot of this paradox is that "literary academ-ics are confronted by a series of interesting but ultimately frustrating aporias" (528), paramount among them the realization—similar to Bové's, just mentioned—that theory has "militated against the ten-dencies of [academic] specialization at the same time that it has acted as their agent" (528). Kaufmann goes on to sum up the dilemma that these aporias pose for the critic: "To practice theory is to help the very divisions and forms of domination that theory seeks to overcome. By the same token, however, to give up critical, truly critical thought in the academy would be to strangle such thought in the only cradle it has left and to sacrifice what we still have of our best hopes" (528). Kaufmann has eloquently stated the disci-plinary and institutional consequences surrounding what I call the question of the postmodern: how does an oppositional critic proceed when no "outside" position can be secured, when theorizing in an attempt to undermine a system or institution runs the risk of actually "help[ing] the very divisions and forms of domination that theory seeks to overcome"? Certainly one cannot simply "give up critical, truly critical thought in the academy," but how does one make thought or action *truly* critical if the category that would ground such a criticism—truth—has been withdrawn? Kaufmann—like so many others who formulate the question of the postmodern—has no answers to these "ultimately frustrating aporias," precisely be-cause they are, in his eyes, *ultimately frustrating.* As he puts it, "What remains, then, is hardly the stuff of heady perorations: the desire for an integrity that will sell itself neither cheaply nor easily and the hardened edge of an irony that, in the words of one of our less fashionable poets, 'will not scare' " (528). What remains, in other words, is an impasse: the desire to recuperate a grounding integrity "must constantly fail" (528)—dashed by the hardened (though, he seems to suggest, ultimately frivolous) edge of a theoretical irony that posits the impossibility of such a ground.

Kaufmann's assessment of the paralysis in which literary criticism finds itself is quite similar to Paul de Man's in "Shelley Disfigured," his essay on *The Triumph of Life* written for *Deconstruction and Criticism*. Toward the end of the essay, de Man takes stock of "our present critical and literary scene":

> It functions along monotonously predictable lines, by the historicization and the aesthetification of texts, as well as by their use, as in this essay, for the assertion of methodological claims made all the more pious by their denial of piety. Attempts to define, to understand, or to circumscribe romanticism in relation to ourselves and in relation to other literary movements are all part of this naive belief. *The Triumph of Life* warns us that nothing, whether deed, word, thought, or text, ever happens in relation, positive or negative, to anything that precedes, follows or exists elsewhere, but only as a random event whose power, like the power of death, is due to the randomness of its occurrence. It also warns us why and how these events then have to be *reintegrated into a historical and aesthetic system of recuperation that repeats itself regardless of the exposure of its fallacy.* (68–69, my emphasis)

De Man's focus here is "systematic," whereas Kaufmann's is primarily "institutional" (though already this distinction becomes problematic, since each depends on the other and both on a ground that seems to be eroding). But although de Man clearly has an agenda different from Kaufmann's, they share a concern about the state of literary criticism in the absence of a transcendental ground and reach strikingly similar conclusions: in the absence of a "beyond" that could ground it, criticism is doomed to a "recuperation that repeats itself regardless of the exposure of its fallacy," destined to follow "monotonously predictable lines," endlessly concerning itself with Kaufmann's "interesting but ultimately frustrating aporias." In short, both Kaufmann and de Man claim that the determinate and determining practice of criticism can never "catch up with" the indeterminacy posited by literary theory, that the impasse cannot be resolved, and that we are left with no choice but to go on *as if* the problems, fallacies, chiasmi, and aporias revealed by theory could be put aside. They both seem to grant the undisplaceable *imminence* of an inevitable, nihilistic impasse for the discipline of literary criticism—an impasse that locates itself at the site of the question of the postmodern.[4]

This widely recognized and discussed impasse, however, has certainly not curtailed the production of literary criticism and theory—quite the contrary. In fact, an entire theory industry has grown up around literature departments in the past twenty years, and with this industry has come the increasingly specialized professionalization of theory and interpretation. As Kaufmann points out, the impasse at or in which literary criticism finds itself has not had the cooling effect that one would expect on the profession(alization) of literature studies; rather, the impasse has fueled this most frustrating of Kaufmann's aporias—and given rise to a plethora of symposia, journal articles, and books (such as this one) in which "specialists" attempt to diagnose criticism's illness.

The institutional metaphor of medicine is, in some sense, unavoidable here, as is an implicit comparison of the two disciplines.[5] Although medical care and technology have certainly improved in the last twenty years, the discipline has also become more specialized; and although medicine has certainly had liberating effects (saving and improving the quality of patients' lives), it has also begun to exercise a certain kind of insidious control, a kind of "discursive" control, as, for example, more and more tests as well as second and third opinions become "necessary."[6] Medical care generally improves as more specialized tests and more layers of interpretation

4. It should be noted that de Man tends to see this impasse itself as a new rigor that "refuses to be generalized into a system" ("Shelley Disfigured" 69), but my point here is that this undecidable de Manian impasse becomes generalizable when it grants the imminence of the present system. De Man here does not attempt to *displace* what he feels is an empty opposition between aestheticism and historicism, but focuses on the undecidability brought about by this opposition in Shelley's *Triumph,* and then argues that this "process differs entirely from recuperative and nihilistic allegories of historicism" (69). I'm not so sure: I have no problem with arguing that undecidability is inescapable, but it seems precisely a "nihilist allegory" to grant the simple inevitability of the system that engenders this undecidability by arguing that this process is destined always and everywhere to fall short (which is why for de Man it is "historically more reliable than the products of historical archeology" [69]). See Chapter 2 for a more detailed discussion of this topic as it pertains to Derrida's very different notion of undecidability and history.

5. See Weber's "Vaulted Eye: Remarks on Knowledge and Professionalism," where he makes several striking comparisons between medicine and teaching—which, along with the law, are the "exemplary professions" (45).

6. This is, of course, not to mention the more obvious problem that medicine and the academy share: access (rather, the lack of access) for the underprivileged.

are added to the process of diagnosis, but these tests and these layers of interpretation, both of which are applications of recently developed "progressive" methodologies, can lead to frustrating interpretative or diagnostic impasses. Of course, "progress" in the discipline of literary criticism certainly never saved or even necessarily improved the quality of anyone's life outside the discipline, but I think the comparison remains apt: literary criticism, like medicine, has seen an unprecedented rise in specialization in the last twenty years, and although this rise most certainly has opened it up (one could say "improved" it), it has also brought along with it a different kind of control, a "discursive" control that, because it is difficult to recognize, often goes unanalyzed. I make this seemingly outlandish and digressive comparison between the disciplines of literary criticism and medicine to emphasize that, for either discipline, *it is neither possible nor desirable to regress to some pre-specialized "golden age."*

It would obviously be ludicrous to deny that human sciences such as medicine have "progressed"—that a cancer patient, for example, is not better off today than he or she would have been twenty, thirty, or fifty years ago. It would be equally ludicrous either to attempt to recuperate a picture of the literary critic as a folksy generalist whose stubborn individualism would keep him or her out of an institutional setting, or simply to apologize for the disciplinary progress that professional specialization seems to allow. On the one hand, it would be disingenuous of me *simply* to criticize or undermine a profession to which I "belong" and in which I work, but, on the other hand, it would be intellectually dishonest of me *simply* to accept a status-quo vision of professional life. It is rather incumbent upon me to ask how and why it is that this process of institutionalization and professionalization can *seem* inevitable. Kaufmann may be correct when he asserts, "Professors of literature can neither submit to professionalization nor resist it" (528), but even this statement begs certain questions: questions about submission and resistance from within, about the seemingly totalizing conditions of this institutional specialization, about how and why institution leads to a paralyzing impasse for those who would want to study or disrupt it—questions about, in other words, the institutionalization of theory and the institutionalization of the question of the postmodern.

Kaufmann's model is certainly not the only version of the disciplinary role of theory within the university. Jonathan Culler, in *Framing the Sign: Criticism and Its Institutions,* puts forth a much more positive picture of contemporary theory within the academy. He characterizes theory as "anti-disciplinary, challenging not only the boundaries of disciplines, on whose legitimacy the university structure seems to depend, but also these disciplines' claims to judge writing that touches their concerns. In practice, 'theory' contests the right of psychology departments to control Freud's texts, of philosophy departments to control Kant, Hegel, and Heidegger" (24–25). For Culler, theory, rather than adding to a kind of discursive disciplinary control, precisely disperses such controls by questioning the "disciplines' claims to judge writing that touches their concerns." For Culler, theory does not secure and protect a disciplinary knowledge, but rather subverts "the articulation of knowledge" (25), leading to "changes which repeatedly transgress university boundaries" (25) and open up the disciplines. This is certainly a more positive picture of the role of theory in the university, but it does not seem to silence Kaufmann's objections. Indeed, it seems to forward precisely what Kaufmann sees as an overenthusiasm concerning the "liberating" role of theoretical discourse, as well as surreptitiously broaching the "unwanted" professionalization of thinking that inevitably comes with the institutionalization of theory.

In fact, Culler's discussion turns out to be a sort of homage to the institution of theory, which is odd, given the way he traces the rise of literary professionalism. For example, in discussing the importance of the refereed journal in bringing about the institution of theory, he writes:

> One can argue that the system of publication exists not just to accredit professionals (a system of degrees would do that) but to distinguish those accredited from providers of services (such as nurses and school teachers), to accredit them as participants in an autonomous enterprise—a quest for knowledge—where in principle projects are not imposed by outside forces but flow from the

critic's own curiosity or from the so-called 'needs' of the field itself.
(29)

Although Culler is here simply *summarizing* the rise of literary professionalism, this passage certainly sounds like the beginnings of a
theoretical and ideological *critique* of the professionalizing role of
journals: they serve to "distinguish" literary professionals from mere
"providers of services," and foster what could only be called a mystifying and theoretically indefensible portrait of the critic as a kind
of individualist genius whose "projects are not imposed by outside
forces" or institutions but rather "flow from the critic's own curiosity" in the name of "an autonomous enterprise," a seemingly
disinterested "quest for knowledge."[7]
   Indeed, Culler's summary of the rise of professionalism continues
in such a way that a sort of demystifying reading of literary criticism's
professionalist fictions seems both necessary and imminent. For example, still summarizing, Culler quotes Christopher Jencks and
David Riesman's *Academic Revolution:* "Professionalism, [they write],
is 'colleague-oriented rather than client-oriented' " (29). Culler does
not comment on this quotation, though one expects him to, if for
no other reason than that such a claim—that literary criticism exists
outside a commodity system—is especially specious in the context
of his own discussion of the professional centrality of journals, which
rather obviously have to be "client-oriented" in order to compete
for a shrinking theory dollar in an increasingly competitive market.[8]
Likewise, when Culler notes that "in the academy, professionalism
ties one's identity to an expertise and hence to a field in which one
might be judged expert by one's peers" (29), it seems precisely the
prolegomena to a sort of neo-Foucauldian argument—perhaps like
the one sketched out by Kaufmann—concerning the processes by
which the supposedly "liberating" discourses of theory lead to a

---

7. For just such an ideological critique of the role of the critic, see Said's book *The World,
the Text, and the Critic*, especially the introduction, "Secular Criticism."
   8. Cf. Weber's discussion of Burton Bledstein's work on "the culture of professionalism":
the professional seeks to define his or her services as having "predominantly a *use-value*,
not an exchange value. It is precisely in the effort to distinguish himself from the busi-
nessman, on the one hand, and from the worker, on the other, that the professional finds
it necessary to cultivate the professional ethos and 'culture' . . . " (*Institution and Interpretation*
27).

proliferation of other (more insidious) means of control, the process by which "professionalism ties one's identity to an expertise."[9]

Culler, however, produces no such critique. Rather, he celebrates professionalism in precisely those terms it seemed he was sure to undermine: "The connection between criticism and the continuing professional evaluation on which promotions, grants, and prestige depend may thus generate a more specialized yet more innovative criticism than would some other arrangement. The need to make an 'important new contribution' is built into the American academic system" (29–30). Here Culler puts forth exactly the benign vision of the university that it had seemed he was setting up to be criticized: he characterizes the academy as a place of innovation, where an "important new contribution" is graciously rewarded by "promotions, grants, and prestige." Specialization, he argues, is necessary to produce "a more innovative criticism." He may consider it self-evident, but the "innovative criticism" that he imagines as the end (product) of literary studies remains quite problematic. What he posits here seems to be precisely a version of the "critic-as-autonomous-genius" paradigm. Also, the imperatives of disciplinary self-protection (veiled in the terminology of progress) and the commodity fetish implied by emphasizing the "new and improved"—as well as how critical "innovation" protects, promotes, and generates specialization—seem to be buried under a very rosy picture of personal freedom within the theoretical university. (In fact, one might note that Culler's vision of the theoretical humanities seems uncannily similar to the—supposedly outdated—vision of the academy in which the ends of a disinterested, appreciative Arnoldian criticism generate, protect, and promote the generalist—an irony to which I will return.)

Culler continues to explain the virtues of this professionalism:

Professionalism makes a critic's career depend upon the judgments of experts in his or her own field: deans, departments, publishers and foundations have, *in the interests of professionalism,* increasingly relied on peer reviews in decisions to hire and promote, to publish books and articles, and to award grants. *While reducing capricious-*

---

9. See "The Repressive Hypothesis," in *The Foucault Reader,* 301–29. Also, as I think will become clear, I am *not* attempting to make an argument for Kaufmann as a Foucauldian.

ness and favoritism in important decisions, this *progress of profession-alism shifts power* from the vertical hierarchy of the institution that employs a critic to a horizontal system of evaluation. (30, my emphases)

It seems that Culler here names not only a subversion of disciplinary knowledge strategies as the consequence of theory's professional-ization but also a shift of disciplinary power's axis from vertical to horizontal—though, of course, the shifting of power becomes a goal in itself when one argues, as Culler does, that power cannot be simply undermined or subverted, that there is no simple liberation from institutions or power.[10] But what seems anomalous here is precisely Culler's forwarding of a kind of liberation that comes "in the interests of professionalism." The "system of evaluation" that grows out of this shift helps in "reducing capriciousness and fa-voritism," a formulation that continues the liberationist metaphor that he develops throughout his discussion of the "progress of professionalism." But in *shifting* axes, one does not necessarily—or even primarily—*reduce* capriciousness or favoritism or in any way escape these undesirable by-products of the workings of an insti-tution. In fact, given the polarization of theoretical camps in recent years, one could argue that specialization has *increased* capricious-ness and favoritism rather than vice versa.

But, to get back to the "original" question, what is the status or role of theory in this rise of professionalism? As he continues, Culler concretely ties his professional-progress metaphor to the question of theory in an astonishing way: "We must assert the value not just of specialization but of professionalization also, explaining how *pro-fessionalization makes thought possible* by developing sets of questions, imposing norms which then have to be questioned and thereby promoting debate on key problems" (54, my emphasis). Profession-alism here finds its apotheosis in Culler's argument not simply as an improved system of evaluation or even as a bolstering of critical ends but *literally as a transcendental ground—as that which "makes thought possible."* I find this formulation absolutely chilling, and not simply because of the ominous consequences it seems to have for

10. See his discussion of Foucault in *Framing the Sign,* 62–68.

the hopes of nonprofessionals to think at all, but because thought or knowledge seems to be named here solely in terms of its nineteenth-century disciplinary manifestation, as "*developing* sets of questions, *imposing* norms, and thereby *promoting* debate on key problems."[11] Professionalism, as Culler defines it here, seems less what makes thinking possible than what makes the ends of thinking controllable—by deciding what sets of questions will be addressed, what norms imposed, and what problems deemed key. Here theory is made, quite literally (and paradoxically, given Culler's original formulation of the role of theory) into the *discipline of professionalism*— into a kind of metadiscipline that takes the other disciplines as its object, and organizes them under its classifications and rules.

For Culler, then, theory is a kind of new ground of the humanities (a new ground that protects and promotes the ends of professionalism) because it affords the professional the "critical or self-critical space within which *discoveries* and critiques take place" (54, my emphasis). The language of the so-called hard sciences fits well here with Culler's call for innovation.[12] And it is perhaps here that an irony I noted earlier becomes most apparent: if the project of the humanities is to be a kind of scientistic innovation, then of course specialization is unavoidable; but this logic of the ends of the humanities is uncannily similar (in that it is dialectically opposed) to the Arnoldian paradigm that makes necessary the generalist. In fact, Culler sets up his argument in direct opposition to this generalist paradigm. He writes of the decision before us today:

> One can distinguish two general models at work. . . . The first makes the university the transmitter of a cultural heritage, gives it the ideological function of reproducing culture and the social

11. Of course, Culler maintains that "the rights of the amateur should be asserted, for the amateur's perspective has special value"; he rightfully asserts that at one time or another, we are all amateurs "as we move from one field to another." However, in Culler's view, the amateur's work has such "special value" only insofar as it assists, corrects, or augments the specialist's work: "cross-disciplinary amateurism" "generates new insights, as well as errors that can lead specialists to rethink what needs to be said to prevent them" (*Framing the Sign* 54).

12. See Weber, who quotes Marx on the capitalist/imperialist paradigm of the language of "progress": " 'The conquest of each new country signifies a new frontier' . . . [and] each new frontier signifies only a new country to be conquered" (*Institution and Interpretation* 148).

order. The second model makes the university a site for the production of knowledge, and teaching is related to that function: in early years students are taught what they need to know in order to progress to more advanced work; in later years, they follow or even assist their teachers' work at the frontiers of a discipline. (33)

There are several problems with Culler's formulation of the decision before us. First, he has simply inverted the Arnoldian paradigm of the generalist: for the generalist, the tradition is the repository of real knowledge (*epistémè*), whereas theory is the realm of mere ideology (*doxa*). But Culler, without examining the dubious terms of this opposition, rearranges them to favor the specialist, who is now involved in the "production of knowledge," whereas the generalist is assigned the "ideological function of reproducing culture and social order." Certainly the ideology/knowledge opposition is ripe for deconstruction, and Culler even goes on to give us the ammunition to do so: how, we might ask, does teaching students "what they need to know to progress to more advanced work" escape the "ideological function of reproducing culture and social order"? Likewise, if students' goals are to get to the point where they may "*follow or even assist* their teachers' work at the frontiers of a discipline," one might ask how professionalist teaching escapes a paternalistic, appreciative model or fosters innovation? In any case, it seems that the theoretical professionalism that Culler calls for serves to conserve or protect—just as strongly as the paradigm it seeks to displace by inverting—the most traditional imperatives of the discipline.[13] And Culler admits that professionalism may have its problems, but he feels that they are outweighed by "its compensating strengths—an encouragement of innovation, for example—and one must remind oneself of the alternatives which the opponents of professionalism promote: a vision of the humanities as repository of known truths and received values, which a dedicated non-professional corps of workers present to the young" (55). So, in the end, Culler sees professionalism as the only defense against a slide back to the bad old days of higher education as ideological indoctrination, carried

---

13. See Kaufmann's discussion of the Arnoldian strain of contemporary theory in "Profession of Theory," 523–24.

out by functionaries for the state's interests, "a dedicated non-professional corps of workers."

For Culler, then, professionalism is inevitable—it is absolutely necessary to avoid what he sees as the disastrous outcome of its denial. And, it should be noted, he is by no means the only high-profile theorist who is also an apologist for professionalism: Stanley Fish, writing from a new-pragmatist perspective that is particularly abhorrent to Culler,[14] comes to a similar conclusion about the necessity, value, and inevitability of professionalism.[15] About the hesitation that some of the contributors to *The New Historicism* express about the disciplinary consequences of their theoretical work, he writes, "Whatever the source of the malaise, I urge that it be abandoned and that New Historicists sit back and enjoy the fruits of their professional success, wishing neither for more nor less. In the words of the old Alka-Seltzer commercial, 'try it, you'll like it'" ("Commentary" 315). Fish proposes professionalism as a possible cure for the "malaise"—the impasse—of a literary criticism robbed of its transcendental ground. Even if professionalism is not exactly the cure, he suggests, at least it will allow the critic to forget or soothe the consequences of totalizing overindulgence.[16] And although Culler's professionalism cannot simply be conflated with Fish's sloganeering, "don't-worry-be-happy" brand, they do both name professionalism as a valuable and necessary cure for the impasse of literary criticism. It is also interesting that they do so from opposing sides of what would seem to be a ragingly discordant deconstruction/new historicism debate (which I will discuss at some length in Chapter 3). What is particularly intriguing here, however, is that through Culler's and Fish's discussions of

14. Culler vehemently attacks the new pragmatism, "whose complacency seems altogether appropriate to the Age of Reagan" (*Framing the Sign* 55). It is curious, however, that he seems finally to envision the future of literary studies as a kind of Rortian conversation: "The future is perhaps best imagined as an ongoing debate" (56).

15. Fish's "thesis"—reiterated in a series of essays on professionalism—is roughly the following: "My contention is that anti-professionalism, insofar as it imagines a position of judgment wholly uncontaminated by professional concerns, is incoherent, since in order to be heard as relevant, a critique must already be implicated in the assumptions and goals that define the profession" ("Reply to Gerald Graff" 125). This is precisely the dilemma to which the Derridean "double gesture" speaks and why this gesture is, to use a problematic but appropriate word, necessary.

16. Alka-Seltzer's other famous slogan, after all, was "I can't believe I ate the whole thing."

the necessity of professionalism it seems we are back—by an extremely circuitous route—to Kaufmann's assertion that theory's professionalism can neither be affirmed nor denied in any consistent manner: its affirmation can be denied as an untheoretical acceptance, whereas even its denial—insofar as it comes irreducibly from *within*—can be shown to be a surreptitious affirmation. As a cure for criticism's malaise, then, professionalism seems also to be a poison: professionalism as *pharmakon*.

The Institutional Pharmakon

Pharmakon is one of Derrida's well-known "undecidables." In his analysis of the discourse on writing in Plato's *Phaedrus*, Derrida notes that Plato's text uses the same word—*pharmakon*—to characterize writing's seemingly dual and contradictory position vis-à-vis memory (see *Dissemination* 61–172). Socrates tells the story of two gods, Theuth, the inventor of writing, and Thamus, a ruler. Theuth comes to Thamus with his "elixir [*pharmakon*] of memory and wisdom" (*Phaedrus* 274E); Thamus responds, "You, who are the father of letters, have been led by your affection to ascribe to them a power opposite of that which they really possess. For this invention will produce forgetfulness in the minds of those who learn to use it. . . . You have invented an elixir [*pharmakon*] not of memory but reminding" (275A). The undecidable opposition inscribed in the very word *pharmakon*—an "elixir of memory and wisdom" that also gives rise to "forgetfulness in the minds of those who learn to use it"—leads to a puzzling impasse in Plato's text: how can an "elixir" of "letters" be a "cure" for wisdom if it is also a "poison"? How can writing both aid and subvert memory? Indeed, Plato himself here depends on this *pharmakon*, writing a didactic story that Socrates remembers he "heard of the ancients" (274C). The nagging question becomes: how can a pure knowledge be upheld or attained at all when following the necessarily discursive logic of knowledge leads inexorably to an impasse, to depending on that which should by rights be exiled to the realm of *doxa?*

The "systematic" situation of undecidability outlined here (the "cure" of knowledge also brings, at the same time and through the same word, the "poison" of writing) quite closely resembles the "institutional" situation of the profession of theory: the cure of theory brings with it the poison of professionalism. In the language of deconstruction, perhaps one could say that the postmodern academy is in the position of Plato's *pharmakon:* undecidable, caught at or in what seems like an impasse. This impasse becomes all the more frustrating for the discipline of literary criticism because it seems to be a *necessary* outcome of critical thinking itself: the thinking that is to uncover *epistémè* uncovers only impasse. That this impasse can likewise be "explained" by critical thinking only adds to the slippage, leaving us inexorably, repeatedly within or at the impasse, blankly staring down Kaufmann's "ultimately frustrating aporias." The only tool we seem to have at our disposal to neutralize the impasse, critical thinking that could lead to critical action, is implicated as/in the "cause" of the impasse itself.

And it is interesting that this institutional impasse is likewise inscribed in Plato's text.[17] Thamus continues on the poison of letters: "You have invented an elixir [*pharmakon*] not of memory but reminding; and you offer your pupils the appearance of wisdom, not true wisdom, for they will read many things without instruction and therefore will seem to know many things, when they are, for the most part, ignorant and hard to get along with, since they are not wise, but only appear wise" (275A–B). The descent from knowledge to mere opinion that comes with writing likewise creates, by making students "ignorant and hard to get along with," an institutional impasse. In some sense, we postmoderns would want to cheer on this supposed amateurish "ignorance" in our students, thinking of it instead as a healthy and necessary skepticism concerning a received tradition. But there is a chiasmic reversal here; this necessary skepticism must be *learned* from a corps of professional teachers and scholars. We are back, again, at Kaufmann's impasse: in the university, theory—as truly critical thought—can neither be taught nor abandoned; and, as Fish writes, "Anti-professionalism is professionalism itself in its purest form" ("Anti-Professionalism" 106).

So we are left with Derrida's question, "If the *same* premises lead

---

17. Cf. Barbara Johnson's discussion of pedagogy and *Phaedrus* in *A World of Difference*, 83–85.

to evaluations that are apparently contradictory, what does that tell us about the system of reading and hierarchization at work?" ("Age of Hegel" 21). It is at this point, then, that it becomes necessary to rethink the path that led to this impasse, to find some way to rethink the impasse, some way to think opposites together—theory and academy, poison and cure, thinking and acting—without falling into the spuriousness of simply neutralizing the differences within some "beyond," but likewise without giving in to the status quo of impasse: "to avoid both *neutralizing* the binary oppositions . . . and simply *residing* within the closed field of these oppositions, thereby confirming it" (Derrida, *Positions,* 41). In other words, it is at this point that the double reading and writing of deconstruction becomes necessary. Necessary because deconstruction attends precisely to this impasse, but as other than simply impasse or stagnation. Necessary because there seems to be no simple ground beyond these oppositions, but a difference, a displacement, a double bind *between* them—an "outside" or double that disrupts their functioning rather than guarantees it. As Derrida puts it, "A repetition without identity—one mark inside and the other outside the deconstructed system, should give rise to a double reading and a double writing" (*Dissemination* 4). For Derrida, one move in this double reading is thematizing or "critical," a repetitive reading of sorts done necessarily from within the confines of the system or institution. The second move of this reading or writing, however, goes back over itself, questions its own motives, attempts to attend to what was excluded—systematically or institutionally—in the first move. For Derrida, a double reading or writing tends to a kind of outside, not a stable ground but rather an exteriority that "can no longer take the form of the sort of extra-text which would arrest the concatenation of writing" (5). This is what Derrida calls "out-work," the nondialectical "work" of the outside, the "work" of the undecidable. I will, as I promised, take up the "systematic" aspects of double reading/writing in the following chapters, but I would like here to outline the *institutional* "necessity" of a deconstruction.

The text that takes up this question of deconstruction and the academy most trenchantly is Weber's *Institution and Interpretation,* a deconstructive analysis of the work of the academy and the functioning of disciplines—and one that is notable in that it does not look primarily to Derrida's GREPH work for its institutional focus.[18] Though Weber at times criticizes Derrida's inattention to institutional matters, he performs a kind of double reading, based, it seems, very much on Derrida's "systematic" work, of the functioning of the academic disciplines. According to Weber, the basic problem surrounding professionalism, especially within the university, is not that the liberating intentions of the disciplines have been or are inexorably destined to be betrayed by the limitations of institution, but rather that the disciplines fail to continue to ask themselves ground questions, fail to attend to what is *excluded* in or through their analyses. As Weber writes, the academy has built itself on "instituted areas of training and research which, once established, could increasingly ignore the *founding limits and limitations* of the individual disciplines" (32, my emphasis). Disciplines can posit innovative ends or lament unintended outcomes only if practitioners "ignore the founding limits and limitations" of the discipline—because those foundings are themselves *impure* (exclusionary and arbitrary) and therefore cannot hope to lead to pure ends. According to Weber, any discipline must cover over its founding problems, limits, and exclusions in order to perform its analyses. Disciplines do so most often precisely by appealing to the "advance of knowledge" or the liberation that they are supposed to bring about: in short, disciplines—of whatever type—do not ask ground questions, they ask end questions. Ground questions lead to what disciplines read as an impasse because such ground or "foundational" questions can upset the easy obtaining of an end: if a discipline seriously examines its ground, it will indeed "inexorably" reach an impasse, precisely because the exclusions that work to constitute a discipline—its objects, its methodologies—are *groundless.*

Deconstruction, however, reads this impasse—this withdrawal of ground—as the closure of a way of thinking: after the closure or withdrawal of a transcendental mode of thinking, any attempt to think with transcendental categories will, of course, lead to an im-

18. See, for discussions of Derrida's GREPH [*Groupe de recherches sur l'enseignement phi-losophique*] work, Ulmer's *Applied Grammatology,* Culler's *On Deconstruction,* and Fynsk's "Decelebration of Philosophy."

passe, the postmodern refusal—or inability—to guarantee the success of transcendental thinking.[19] But, at the same time, there is no *pure* (nonarbitrary and nonexclusionary) resting-place after closure. Hence the necessity of the double logic, a logic that works both inside and outside the categories of the closure, both inside and outside the academic institutions that have based themselves on these categories. We need, in other words, to "answer" the question of the postmodern, but, because of this double bind, the answer cannot be singular. Derrida writes:

> Two logics, then, with an incalculable effect, two repetitions which are no more opposed to each other than they repeat each other identically and which, if they do repeat each other, echo the duplicity that constitutes all repetition: it is only when one takes into "account" this incalculable double-bind of repetition . . . that one has a chance of *reading* the unreadable text which follows immediately, and to read it *as unreadable*. (*Post Card* 352/373–74; translation modified by consulting Weber, *Institution and Interpretation*)

With the closure of metaphysics, something comes to thought that cannot be read or understood in the terms of that thought, something such as the "perfectly logical" impasse of knowledge and its institutions, the fact that one set of data can lead to two conclusions that radically exclude each other. This "unreadable" text does, however, follow a "logic," though not a determinate (and therefore not a simply *in*determinate) one; it "follows" the dual logic of the "incalculable double-bind of repetition." And it is only when one takes this logic into "account" (though, obviously, there is no simple accounting possible here)[20] that one has a chance of *reading* at all. Thus it is only when one recognizes the logic of the impasse of unreadability that one has the chance of accounting for the unreadable as something other than the dialectical, non-sensical opposite of the readable. Likewise, it is only through recognizing the determinate/determining logic that leads to the impasse of an institution or discipline—literally recognizing a way of thinking and acting that *inex-*

---

19. See my much more detailed discussion of this point in Chapter 4.
20. Cf. Weber, *Institution and Interpretation:* "If 'account' . . . is inscribed within quotation marks, it is to indicate that the double bind cannot simply be taken into account" (97).

orably leads to nihilist reversals and hence to inaction—that one can attempt to account for this impasse as other than simple paralysis or stasis, other than a simple obstacle to be overcome. It is this "logic," which I call the logic of the postmodern, inasmuch as it "answers" what I have called the "question" of the postmodern, that I attempt to investigate and articulate throughout this book. My approach throughout might be called "deconstructive" (though a good bit of this work questions deconstruction as an institutional category), but I emphasize from the start that it is *not* a matter of distilling a determinate/determining logic out of Derrida's texts and applying it to a horizon of other philosophical and literary texts. Rather, it is a matter of marking and negotiating paths through specific texts and institutions while simultaneously attempting to open them up to something other; in short, it is a matter of double reading.[21]

21. I regret that I was unable to consult Michael Bérubé's recently published *Marginal Forces/Cultural Centers* when composing this chapter. His analysis of the institution does much to inflect and enhance my own. See especially pp. 18–61.

2 / The Discipline
of Deconstruction

Today, how can we not speak of the University?
—JACQUES DERRIDA
"The Principle of Reason:
The University in the Eyes of Its Pupils"

Deconstruction, it seems, is dead in literature departments to-day. There is still plenty of discourse being produced concerning deconstruction, but deconstruction's heyday has clearly passed. Precious few critics would identify themselves any longer as "deconstructionists." The term no longer dominates Modern Language Association conference panels. Indeed, Barbara Johnson delivered in 1992 at the School of Criticism and Theory an address titled "The Wake of Deconstruction," in which she explored, among other things, its untimely passing. Perhaps most decisively, the death knell is sounded in a *Justice League Europe* comic book, where we read the following characterization of deconstruction: "Quite the academic fad in France and America, it was. Becoming *passé* now, I understand" (Jones et al. 10). Deconstruction's death is usually attributed either to suicide, that deconstruction fell back into the dead-end formalism it was supposed to remedy, or to murder at the hands of the new historicists, whose calls for rehistoricizing and re-contextualizing the study of literature have successfully challenged the supposed self-canceling textualism of the deconstructionists. Consider the following (for the time being, anonymous) assessments—the first, representative of the "suicide" theory; the second, of the "murder" theory:

Deconstructive criticism, which, however important, is but an off-spring of New Criticism, . . . has done little more than apply what it takes to be a method for reading literary texts to the unprob-lematized horizon of its discipline.

By neglecting the pragmatic and historical context of the utterance of what is dramatized in such a manner as to cancel it out, the criticism in question reveals its origins in Romantic (as well as, in a certain interpretation, Idealist) philosophy. It is a suprahistorical criticism that pretends to speak from a position free of ideology—that is, from an absolute point of view.

Critics of deconstruction will agree, I think, that these quotations well sum up the critiques that brought its short, happy life in Amer-ican literature departments to an end.

The first quotation represents the critique usually associated with, for lack of a better word, "skeptical" detractors of deconstruction—those who hold that although deconstructive reading claims to be something radically new, it is actually just another version of new criticism's traditional methodology of close reading, cloaked in a theoretical vocabulary and reapplied to a series of texts in order to yield "new" readings.[1] These detractors point to the way in which deconstructive readers of literary texts hunt for self-canceling binary oppositions in the same (essentially unproblematic) way the new critics hunted for themes and ironies. In addition, according to this line of reasoning, the end result of both readings is the same: a new-critical reading totalizes the text by offering an all-inclusive meaning or interpretation, whereas a deconstructive reading totalizes the text in exactly the opposite way—by simply denying meaning or inter-pretation by showing how oppositions in the text cancel themselves out. For the skeptic, deconstruction in literature departments com-mitted suicide after it realized it was unable to break away from the tradition it wished to supersede.

The second quotation reflects the critique of deconstructive criti-cism generally advanced by those concerned about its political di-

1. See, for example, Tompkins's "Reader in History": "What is most striking about reader-response criticism and its close relative, deconstructive criticism, is their failure to break out of the mold into which critical writing was cast by the formalist identification of criticism with explication. Interpretation reigns supreme both in teaching and in publication just as it did when the New Criticism was in its heyday in the 1940s and 1950s" (224–25).

mension—or rather, its lack of political dimension. Deconstructive readings are faulted, in this line of reasoning, primarily for "neglecting the pragmatic and historical context" of literature and the production of literature, thereby performing a "suprahistorical criticism that pretends to speak from a position free of ideology." Additionally, and perhaps more damning, those concerned with the political dimension of literature studies point to the political despair inevitably fostered by deconstructionist notions of simple textual self-cancellation, which, they assert, foster passive acceptance as the political result of a reactionary and nihilistic textual undecidability.[2] For Marxist, feminist, or (new) historical literary critics, deconstruction was murdered by a reorientation in literature departments toward the political and social dimensions of literary texts.

In any case, the quotations with which I began are certainly representative of compelling critiques of the practice of deconstructive criticism from two distinct points of view, the "skeptical" and the "political," at odds with deconstruction. It is indeed odd, then, that both these critiques are cited from an apology for deconstruction, Rodolphe Gasché's The Tain of the Mirror (255 and 139). Gasché vehemently critiques a certain kind of deconstructive practice, but, unlike most of deconstruction's critics within literature departments, Gasché attacks and subverts this practice of deconstructive literary criticism in defense of deconstruction, in the name of "deconstruction, properly speaking" (135)—in defense of Derrida's thought against those who (ab)use it by turning it into an unproblematic, nihilistic method for reading literary texts.

There are, then, different readings of the role or value of deconstruction at work for Gasché and for the skeptical or political critics of deconstruction I characterized earlier; yet somehow both Gasché—a defender of deconstruction—and the skeptical and political critics of deconstruction can come to the same general conclusions about the inadequacy of deconstructive literary criticism as it was and currently is practiced in America, especially by the "Yale school"

2. See, for example, Eagleton's assessment in Literary Theory: deconstruction "frees you at a stroke from having to assume a position on an important issue, since what you say of such things will be no more than a passing product of the signifier and so in no sense to be taken as 'true' or 'serious.' . . . Since it commits you to affirming nothing, it is as injurious as blank ammunition" (145).

and its followers. Gasché, rather than dismissing deconstruction out of hand, as the skeptics and political critics often do, argues that Derrida's thought has been grossly misrepresented by his American disciples, that there has never been a properly deconstructive criticism in America, *and that there is nothing inherent in Derrida's work which makes it applicable in any simple way to literary criticism.*[3] For Gasché, Derrida is, like many before him, a philosopher who has an interest in literature, but Gasché argues that this interest in no way makes Derrida's thought readily or easily available to be taken up for use in literary criticism. He writes, against deconstructive criticism, that "to quarry from Derrida's writings is not automatically to become deconstructive" (2). In fact, in his opinion, "the importance of Derrida's thinking for the discipline of literary criticism is not immediately evident" (*Tain of the Mirror* 255).

If Gasché is correct—and I believe that, for the most part, he is— the question for those of us interested in deconstruction and literature then becomes what, if anything, can be made of, written of, thought of, the relation between the body of texts we call Derrida's philosophy and the body of texts we call literature? If we agree that, for the most part, what passed as "deconstruction" in literature departments in the 1970s and beyond had little to do with Derrida's thought, perhaps deconstruction needs to be reexamined. In short, it seems to me that now that the wave of deconstruction as a *method for interpreting texts* has crested, perhaps we can reexamine deconstruction as a *philosophy*, a way of thinking that is overtly interested in the literature and institutions of the postmodern world, or, more precisely, a way of thinking that is interested in the process by which borders (the borders that separate literature and philosophy, texts and institutions, thinking and action) are assigned. I must stress that I am not interested here in aligning myself for or against those who see postmodern thought as valid solely in relation to postmodern cultural artifacts and texts; but, at the same time, I would like to question the value of critical projects that aim at simply rereading the tradition from another (in this case, deconstructive) point of view. Or, perhaps phrased more precisely, I would like to question a certain reading of deconstruction which would allow it a properly

3. Gasché made this point as early as 1979, in his "Deconstruction as Criticism."

critical disciplinary project or a kind of worldview. In this chapter, I examine the institutional rise of American deconstruction and its reading of Derrida, and then point out where this dominant reading—the reading upon which the skeptical and political critiques of deconstruction are based—fails to account for the complexities of Derrida's work. I conclude with a brief discussion of the problem of Derrida's own odd inscription within these institutional debates, a disciplinary question inseparable from the more recognizable systematic or theoretical ones.

Indeed, the very question of the application of a methodology broaches inescapably institutional concerns, concerns to which deconstruction can and does speak. As Derrida writes in "Conflict of Faculties":

> Precisely because it is never concerned only with signified content, deconstruction should not be separable from this politico-institutional problematic. . . . Deconstruction is neither a methodological reform that should reassure the organization in place nor a flourish of irresponsible and irresponsible-making destruction, whose most certain effect would be to leave everything as it is and to consolidate the most immobile forces within the university. (In Culler, *On Deconstruction* 156)

Deconstruction, despite Derrida's protests, has been and remains thematized within the North American academy precisely as "irresponsible and irresponsible-making destruction," and as a critical movement that "leave[s] everything as it is . . . within the university." Even when deconstruction is treated well, it is often credited with bringing about little more than what Derrida calls a "methodological reform" within literary criticism.

A key problem surrounding the reception of deconstruction in America is its thematization as a master term, something Derrida warns against:

> The word "deconstruction" like all other words acquires its value only from its inscription in a chain of possible substitutions, in what is too blithely called a "context." For me, for what I have tried and still try to write, the word only has an interest within a

certain context where it replaces and lets itself be determined by such other words as "écriture," "trace," "supplément," "hymen," "pharmakon," "margin," [etc.]...." ("Letter to a Japanese Friend" 7)

I will try to respect the complexity within what may seem to be the monolithic category "deconstructive criticism"—a necessary move, given the double bind I find myself in as someone who could quite easily be called a "deconstructive critic." There are, of course, many deconstructions: the "rhetorical" deconstruction of Paul de Man is different from the "pedagogical" deconstruction of Gregory Ulmer, which in turn is different from the "political" deconstruction of Michael Ryan, the "postcolonial" deconstruction of Gayatri Spivak, the "philosophical" deconstruction of Gasché, or the "feminist" deconstruction of Barbara Johnson, and these differences must be attended to. I should make it clear, then, that most of my comments concerning "deconstructive literary criticism in America" will be directed toward the rhetorical or tropological brand of Yale school deconstruction, perhaps most clearly represented by de Man and J. Hillis Miller. I turn my attention here because it is this rhetorical mode that has offered the greatest possibility to thematize deconstruction as a critical method—as a discursive tool for producing readings, and thereby for bolstering the work of a discipline.

The Commodification of Deconstruction in America

Deconstruction in America has a well-known genealogy; it was, so the story goes, imported from France and received enthusiastically by many scholars in North American literature departments, many following the lead of the Yale critics. Deconstruction helped to bring "theory" to the foreground in the study of literature in America. Soon, theory classes in English graduate departments were a must, and a wave of deconstruction "handbooks" was produced to introduce the profession—especially graduate students—to its complexities. (Derrida's own writings were and still are, for the most part, scrupulously avoided in introductory courses because of their complexity and difficulty—or so the story goes.) Deconstruction was, to put it bluntly, commodified for an American market, simplified and watered down for use in how-to books, which gave (and continue to give) an entire generation of literature students a suspiciously de Manian overview of what was supposedly Derrida's work. For example, the following quotations are taken from two of the leading handbooks used to represent deconstruction in theory seminars—the first from Jonathan Culler's *On Deconstruction* and the second from Christopher Norris's *Deconstruction: Theory and Practice*:[4]

> In undoing the oppositions on which it relies and between which it urges the reader to choose, the text places the reader in an impossible situation that cannot end in triumph but only in an outcome already deemed inappropriate: an unwarranted choice or a failure to choose. (81)[5]

> To deconstruct a text in Nietzschean-Derridean terms is to arrive at a limit point or deadlocked *aporia* of meaning which offers no hold for Marxist-historical understanding. The textual 'ideology' uncovered by Derrida's readings is a kind of aboriginal swerve into metaphor and figurative detour which language embraces. (80)

If we compare these handbook accounts of deconstruction with the characterizations of the skeptical and political critiques with which I began, I think we can see the critiques vindicated. Culler characterizes deconstruction as an essentially formalist reading *method* that emphasizes a predetermined fall into meaninglessness resulting from the self-cancellation of oppositions in any text.[6] Norris

---

4. The title of Norris's book, with its dependence on the metaphysical distinction between *theoria* and *praxis*—the very distinction on which philosophy first configures itself—suggests that Norris has seriously underestimated the stakes of Derrida's project. "Différance," Derrida writes, is "a system that no longer tolerates the opposition of activity and passivity" (*Margins of Philosophy* 16).

5. To be fair, this quotation from Culler comes in the context of his reading of de Man, but my argument here will be that Culler effectively conflates de Man's project with Derrida's. He writes, for example, that deconstruction, of whatever kind, "emerges from the writings of Derrida and de Man" (228).

6. This reading is so institutionally canonized, in fact, that it has made it onto the GRE Literature in English Test. Sample questions 31 and 32 in the 1989–91 GRE Literature in English test booklet concern a passage comparing the new critics' "prior knowledge that all literature is paradoxical" to "the deconstructionists' foreknowledge that all texts are allegories of their own unreadability" (16). This is a point well taken, as I am arguing here;

concerns himself with the political implications of the "deadlocked *aporia* of meaning" that results from the deconstructive act by insisting that it has *no* political implications, that the ideology uncovered by (and, presumably, championed in) Derrida's readings is indeed that we are trapped in a prison-house of metaphoric language.[7]

Neither view reflects Derrida's own writings. Time and time again Derrida warns of the metaphysical and political danger of simply neutralizing oppositions in the name of deconstruction. Derrida emphasizes that deconstruction involves a *double* reading, a neutralization *and a reinscription*. He writes:

> Deconstruction cannot limit itself or proceed immediately to a neutralization: it must, by means of a double gesture, a double science, a double writing, practice an *overturning* of the classical opposition *and* a general *displacement* of the system. It is only on this condition that deconstruction will provide itself the means with which to *intervene* in the field of oppositions that it criticizes, which is also a field of non-discursive forces. (*Margins of Philosophy* 329)

For Derrida, contra many of his followers and critics, deconstruction is not merely a move toward neutralization. Derrida's thought does not move toward an end constituted by a "deadlocked *aporia* of meaning" leading to "an impossible situation which cannot end in triumph." Rather, this deadlock, this undecidability, this unreadability is only the first gesture in a double reading. It is the "overturning" gesture, which shows the untenability of the "classical opposition," the fact that the (present) privileged term in the opposition can structure itself only with reference to the (absent) non-

---

however, the GRE's question concerns the proper names of the founders of these literary critical movements. The answer: "Cleanth Brooks and Jacques Derrida."

7. Norris's later work, it should be noted, takes up a critique very much like the one that I am following here. Indeed, his 1991 Afterword to the second edition of *Deconstruction: Theory and Practice* criticizes "the vulgar-deconstructionist view that 'all concepts come down to metaphors in the end' " (143). However, Norris is equally suspicious of his own earlier reading of Derrida on metaphor, admitting that it grew out of "a false—or very partial—reading of Derrida's arguments in 'White Mythology' and elsewhere. For it is precisely his point in that essay that one has said nothing of interest on the topics of metaphor, writing, and philosophy if one takes it as read (whether on Nietzsche's or Derrida's authority) that all concepts are a species of disguised metaphor" (151).

privileged term, leaving nonpresence as a structuring principle of presence and calling into question the privilege of the master term over the subservient term. This overturning gesture is indeed first-level deconstruction, but it leaves the crucial operation of Derrida's thought unperformed: the wholesale displacement of the systematics of binary opposition and the reinscription of the opposition within a larger field—a "textual" field that can account for nonpresence as other than lack of presence. It is this second move of a double reading in which "deconstruction will provide itself the means with which to *intervene* in the field of oppositions that it criticizes." For Derrida, deconstruction can intervene only by displacing a mode of thinking that leads precisely to these deadlocks, by negotiating its way through *specific* textual impasses and demonstrating that these impasses arise due to a radical alterity within the supposedly monologic categories of traditional thinking.[8] So, Derrida, in the end, actually *agrees* with the skeptical and political critics of deconstruction as literary criticism: deconstruction will not be able to intervene in the field of oppositions it criticizes until it goes beyond neutralization—that is, unless it makes this second move of double reading, a general displacement of that system whose logic leads it inexorably to these neutralizations, these pure negations.

Deconstructive literary criticism, as it is summed up by Culler and Norris and practiced in America, has yet to acknowledge the importance of this displacement in Derrida's thought. Derrida writes:

> Deconstruction involves an indispensable phase of *reversal* [i.e., first-level deconstruction]. To remain content with reversal is of course to operate within the immanence of the system to be destroyed. But to sit back . . . and take an attitude of neutralizing indifference with respect to the classical oppositions would be to give free rein to the existing forces that effectively and historically dominate the field. It would be, for not having seized the

8. See Derrida's *Positions:* "To 'deconstruct' philosophy, thus, would be to think—in the most faithful, interior way—the structured genealogy of philosophy's concepts, but at the same time to determine—from a certain exterior that is unqualifiable or unnameable by philosophy—what this history has been able to dissimulate or forbid, making itself into a history by means of this somewhere motivated repression" (6).

means to *intervene,* to confirm the established equilibrium. (*Dissemination* 6)

If deconstruction as literary criticism limits itself to neutralization, to first-level deconstruction, Derrida here agrees that it is then politically impotent and even reactionary. Simple "neutralizing indifference" gives "free rein to the existing forces that effectively and historically dominate the field," leaving the field of oppositions—a field that Derrida emphasizes is made up of both discursive and nondiscursive forces—itself undisrupted. To fail to make the second move of double reading would be simply "to confirm the established equilibrium." This confirmation, in Derrida's own words, is the unfortunate legacy of deconstructive literary criticism.

Of course, deconstructive critics often do discuss doubling and reinscription. For example, Culler's *On Deconstruction* argues for the centrality of deconstructive "reinscription" or "displacement" and against a reading of deconstruction as mere destruction; as he writes, "an opposition that is deconstructed is not destroyed or abandoned but reinscribed" (133). In fact, he *begins* his discussion of Derrida proper with the quotation that I cite from *Margins of Philosophy* (329). Culler likewise discusses the "double, aporetic logic" (109) of deconstruction, wherein the first movement levels an opposition, and the second movement reinscribes or displaces this opposition. For example, he writes that "affirmations of equality will not disrupt the hierarchy. Only if it includes an inversion or reversal does a deconstruction have the chance of dislocating the hierarchical structure" (166). So at first blush it would seem that Culler and I read Derrida similarly—and, in some respects, we do; however, Culler's notion of the displacement or reinscription of a deconstructed opposition—which he would want to locate as the second of two deconstructive moves—can be shown to be part of what I have called a first-level movement of neutralization.

In short, it seems that for Culler, the reversal or inversion of an opposition *is* its displacement. For example, about the "program" of deconstruction, he writes, "There is no program already established, Derrida says, because attempts *to reverse and thus displace* major hierarchical oppositions of Western thought open possibilities of change that are incalculable" (158, my emphasis). According to

Culler, it is reversal—in and of itself—that causes displacement. As a concrete example of the displacement caused by such "deconstructive reversals" (161), he cites the power of Freud's discourse, a power that "is linked to the ability of its *hierarchical reversals to transform thought and behavior.* . . . Indeed, Freudian theory is an excellent example of the way in which an apparently specialized or perverse investigation may *transform a whole domain by inverting and displacing the oppositions* that made its concerns marginal" (159, my emphasis). While for Derrida it is deconstructively essential that there be a disruption—a reversal or inversion—of traditional metaphysical oppositions, such a dialectical inversion is a first-level deconstructive maneuver that, in the end, adds up to a neutralization of the opposition. In other words, the leveling of an opposition will not, in and of itself, "transform a whole domain" of thinking. In fact, reversal tends to leave such a field intact; it rearranges the terms rather than examining the structure of the opposition itself. According to Derrida, there needs to be an other reading after the inversion or reversal of terms—a reading that can account for such chiasmic reversal as other than a failure or a lack of plenitude.

Perhaps, though, a displacing movement can be located in what Culler calls the "reinscription" of an opposition. According to Culler, reinscribing an opposition is accomplished by "reinstating it with a reversal that gives it a different status and impact" (150). As an example of what he calls deconstruction's "double movement" (150), he offers the following: "The distinction between the literal and the figurative, essential to discussions of the functioning of language, works differently when the deconstructive reversal identifies literal language as figures whose figurality has been forgotten" (150). Here again it seems fairly clear that for Culler reinscription or displacement is a matter of reversal: the "reinscription" of this opposition amounts to the recognition that all positive claims are doomed to failure; any claim for literal truth is bound to fall short because of its inherent figurality.

The reason deconstructive criticism has read the second move of the double gesture this way can, I think, be traced to the Yale school's influential (mis)reading of Derrida's notion of "undecidability," the notion that the majority of deconstruction's critics attack most stringently. The skeptic sees undecidability as the simple opposite of decidability, which makes undecidability quite decidable. The political critic sees undecidability as an assertion of the futility of political action, a notion that cannot help but bolster the social status quo. Deconstructive criticism, as Gasché has shown, often mistakes the inability to decide brought about by oppositions canceling themselves out—what de Man, the deconstructive critic par excellence, calls "unreadability"—for Derrida's notion of undecidability; they are, however, not the same. According to de Man, "A text . . . can literally be called 'unreadable' in that it leads to a set of assertions that radically exclude each other" (*Allegories of Reading* 245). This statement would, of course, hold for Derrida also, but only as a first-level deconstruction. Textual assertions canceling each other out are, for Derrida, a sign that a certain totalizing way of reading is experiencing its closure, a sign that this way of reading (thinking) must be radically displaced, that its grounds must be rethought carefully and the opposition must be reinscribed in a system that respects separation and stands on a discontinuous, withdrawing ground. Insofar as double reading attends to undecidability as other than *lack* of decidability, this double reading is, then, strangely *necessary* if reading is to continue—if reading is not simply to be stifled always and everywhere.

The second movement of the double reading is, generally speaking, the intervention of an outside or excluded term within the very constitution of wholeness; however, this intervention of the second movement—for better or worse—cannot be generalized as a method, for it always arises from and within a specific situation, in terms of a specific choice. According to Derrida, "There is no such thing as a deconstructive *enterprise*—the idea of *project* is incompatible with deconstruction. Deconstruction is a situation" ("On Colleges and Philosophy" 222). A radically singular situation, of course, demands a radically singular intervention rather than the application of a predetermined or prescriptive critical methodology. Derrida's myriad "methodological" terms (supplément, pharmakon, shibboleth, spirit) are taken from—rather than applied to—other texts. They are, in other words, specific terms, which have arisen within particular situations and with respect to particular decisions; they are undecidable in specific contexts, and gesture toward a way of reading that is not generalizable. For Derrida, there is no undecidability in general (see *Limited Inc.* 148–49). In fact, he has had considerable trouble defending or explaining certain words that seem to have a more general conceptual or methodological applicability—words such as "différance" or, more disastrous, "text." These words have been and are taken as generalizable tools useful in producing readings from a number of differing contexts—and, in the process, they have fostered the notion that undecidability-as-impasse is the inexorable and final upshot of Derridean deconstruction.

For Derrida, undecidability—the neutralization of oppositions within a generalizing system—entails a distinctly ethical imperative to rethink decision carefully and problematically.[9] For de Man, on the other hand, the upshot of this self-cancellation is that texts "compel us to choose while destroying the foundations of any choice" (*Allegories of Reading* 245). These formulations may seem similar, but the undecidability fostered by unreadability turns out to be the end, the telos, of deconstruction for de Man,[10] just as, for de Man, deconstruction is the negative movement that founds or constitutes the text.[11] And this genesis-to-revelation movement of de Manian deconstruction is tailor-made for a critical or institutional project. Note, for example, de Man's comments about deconstructive reading—reading that inexorably leads to "indetermination": "We seem to end up in a mood of negative assurance that is highly productive of critical discourse" (*Allegories of Reading* 16). Highly productive indeed. Since deconstruction in a de Manian sense can be said both to constitute the text (as a system of rhetorical or thematic patterns) and likewise to predict the text's productive end (its assured indetermination), it seems to be the ultimate critical discourse to which literature can and should be submitted. For de Man, deconstruction is a generalizable method applicable to any text; it will yield similarly indeterminate results in any (con)text. In fact, he baldly makes this

---

9. As Bernasconi has pointed out, there is no ethics without undecidability. See his "Deconstruction and the Possibility of Ethics" (especially 135). See also Derrida very clearly making this point in his afterword to *Limited Inc.*
10. See "Shelley Disfigured," in which de Man characterizes criticism as a "system of recuperation that repeats itself regardless of the exposure of its fallacy" (68–69).
11. See de Man's "Semiology and Rhetoric": "The deconstruction is not something that we have added to the text but it constituted the text in the first place" (*Allegories of Reading* 17). For an excellent discussion of de Man and Derrida on this point, see Harvey's article "The *Différance* between Derrida and de Man."

claim when discussing the response of Proust's texts to the critical project of deconstructive reading:

> The whole of literature would respond in similar fashion, although the techniques and patterns would have to vary considerably, of course, from author to author. But there is absolutely no reason why analyses of the kind here suggested for Proust would not be applicable, with proper modifications of technique, to Milton or to Dante or to Hölderlin. *This in fact will be the task of literary criticism in the coming years.* (*Allegories of Reading* 16–17, my emphasis)

Here we see deconstructive reading opening itself onto or into a wide-ranging critical project—into the discipline of deconstruction. Here the discipline of deconstructive reading's patience and rigor inexorably slips into another meaning of the word discipline: a regulated and easily transmittable form or branch of knowledge, a critical project sure of its abilities, requiring only "proper modifications of technique" as it confidently moves from one disciplinary object to another until it covers "the whole of literature." For de Man, deconstruction is the critical project par excellence, the determination (as indetermination) that no text can escape. Of course, to reiterate a point that myriad critics have argued, this determining of the whole of literature as simply unreadable makes it possible to thematize deconstruction as a "new new criticism,"[12] a criticism that reveals the meaning of literature as and in its unreadability. This de Manian unreadability, in turn, allows the reader "to see that failure lies in the nature of things" (*Blindness and Insight* 18).

Such is, however, not the case for Derrida, who touches on the question of unreadability in his treatment of Maurice Blanchot's *L'arrêt de mort*:

> If reading means making accessible a meaning that can be transmitted as such, in its own unequivocal, translatable identity, then

12. In fact, de Man has no trouble thematizing his project in this way: "I don't have a bad conscience when I'm being told that, to the extent that it is didactic, my work is academic or even, as it is used as a supreme insult, it is just more New Criticism. I can live with that very easily, because I think that only what is, in a sense, classically didactic, can be really and effectively subversive" ("Interview with Paul de Man" 306).

this title is unreadable. But this unreadability does not arrest reading, does not leave it paralyzed in the face of an opaque surface:
*rather, it starts reading and writing and translation moving again. The
unreadable is not the opposite of the readable, but rather the ridge that
also gives it momentum, movement, sets it in motion.* ("Living On—
Border Lines" 116, my emphasis)

For Derrida, the unreadable or the undecidable is not the revelation
of a "failure [that] lies in the nature of things"; rather, for Derrida,
the unreadable is where deconstruction becomes most *enabling,* most
aware of the need to displace the system that leads to such an
impasse. For Derrida, undecidability is a condition of possibility for
reading; the very impossibility of totalizing reading, of self-identical
meaning, makes it possible for reading to be set in motion in other
ways. De Man and many other deconstructionist literary critics do
not, for the most part, see undecidability this way. For them, the
impossibility of reading is the telos of deconstruction, what deconstructive readings seek to reveal.[13]

Likewise, it is here that we most clearly see the difference between
Culler's and de Man's understanding of deconstruction's double
logic and Derrida's: for Culler and de Man, the second or "reinscribing" movement of a deconstruction is this movement or moment of paralyzation—a reinscription of the deconstructed concept
back into a discourse, as a marker to recall its always and everywhere
failure to escape from the figurality of language. This is perhaps most
clear when Culler metaphorizes the "double procedure of deconstruction" (*On Deconstruction* 149) as sawing off the branch upon
which the critic is standing: "If 'sawing off the branch on which one
is sitting' seems foolhardy to men of common sense, it is not so for
Nietzsche, Freud, Heidegger, and Derrida; for they suspect that if
they fall there is no 'ground' to hit and that the most clear-sighted
act may be a certain reckless sawing" (149). Although this is a description of deconstructive effects rather than a definitive charac-

13. The notion that indecision is the telos of deconstruction is consistently attributed to
Derrida as well as to deconstructive criticism. See Arac, *Critical Genealogies:* "De Man and
Derrida scrupulously, brilliantly, pointed out others' errors and incidentally suggested
whole new dimensions of the texts they read. There they stopped, Derrida with a question
and beyond that an impasse, de Man with a paradox that rescued him from arrogance"
(100).

terization, I think the metaphor chosen here describes nicely the neutralizing upshot of deconstruction as inversion: the first movement of deconstruction walks out on a limb (risks the reversal or inversion of an opposition), and the second movement reinscribes the opposition as a marker of the failure (or chiasmic reversal) of such a binary economy of meaning—it saws the limb off.

Even if one were to see Culler's double reading as having the same movement as Derrida's—a restricted economy opening onto a general one, a writing opening onto archi-writing—Culler's de Manian thematization of that "other" economy as one of constant failure would radically separate the project of deconstructive criticism from Derrida's. As Culler writes, for Derrida "proto- or archi-writing displaces the ordinary distinction between speech and writing" (174)— in other words, the "restricted" distinction between speech and writing is based on a prior "general" economy of meaning, an economy of archi-writing or différance. This is a point well taken, but Culler's understanding of this other economy is quite different from Derrida's. As Culler writes about Derrida's famous discussion of speech and writing in Rousseau:

> Writing can be compensatory, a supplement to speech, only because speech is already marked by the qualities generally predicated of writing: absence and misunderstanding. . . . Derrida's discussion of "this dangerous supplement" in Rousseau describes this structure in a variety of domains: Rousseau's various external supplements are called in to supplement precisely because *there is always a lack* in what is supplemented, *an originary lack.* (103, my emphasis)

In Culler's reading, supplementation is made possible and necessary because of a general economy of failure or lack that grounds all others: the "absence and misunderstanding" characteristic of this general economy cannot be purged in any particular restricted economy. Revealing this absence or misunderstanding as a kind of ontological anti-ground is then the work of deconstructive criticism. As Culler writes, "Rousseau's texts, like many others, teach that presence is always deferred, that supplementation is possible only because of an *originary lack*" (105, my emphasis). Of course, once this "lack" is seen to be "originary," the door is wide open for the deconstructive critic to show this différance-as-lack at work always and everywhere—in Rousseau and "many others"; criticism is here reinvested with a well-defined deconstructive job to do. Instead of revealing the meaning of texts, the deconstructive critic reveals the failure of that meaning; for Culler, deconstructive criticism's double movement first shows or demonstrates this failure (as the neutralization—reversal or inversion—of oppositions) and then reinscribes the failed opposition back into the system, as a marker of the originary lack or absence for which it stands. And, of course, such a double movement remains totalizing.

This move toward totalization in deconstructive literary criticism is not particularly surprising, however, because literary criticism, as such, has *always* depended on a notion of decidability, of totalizing readability—even if the totality is thematized as absence, as *un*readability. It has always been considered necessary to isolate a text and then produce "the" reading of it. Decidability, it seems, is a notion central to any literary criticism—even deconstructive literary criticism. For example, Miller writes in "The Critic as Host" (which was written for the famous "deconstructive manifesto" *Deconstruction and Criticism*):

> "Deconstruction," which is analytic criticism as such, encounters always, if it is carried far enough, some mode of oscillation. In this oscillation two genuine insights into literature in general and into a given text in particular inhibit, subvert, and undercut one another. This inhibition makes it impossible for either insight to function as a firm resting place, the end point of analysis. . . . "[U]ndecidability" names the experience of a ceaseless dissatisfied movement in the relation of the critic to the text.
>
> The ultimate justification for this mode of criticism, as of any conceivable mode, is that it works. (252)

Here we see Miller giving an account of deconstruction similar to de Man's: deconstruction is a method that, if taken far enough, reveals the self-cancellation of binary oppositions in a text. What this movement finally affirms is the text's fall into a ceaseless undecidability predetermined by its—for the most part unconscious—

self-subversion through its employment of figural language. This account is, by now, familiar ground, but what is particularly interesting to me here is Miller's "justification" of deconstructive criticism, "as of *any conceivable mode* [of criticism], is that it *works.*" Miller here indulges a contradiction: criticism must be "undecidable" as deconstruction, but, *at the same time*, it must "work" as literary criticism—it must decide for/in/about the text.

The paradigms of literary criticism do indeed "work"; they throw themselves into a dialectical process that *defines* work as movement toward decidability, toward meaning, work that shows itself in literary criticism as the production of an interpretation of a text, a polished reading, a decision about the meaning of a text.[14] As Miller writes, " 'Deconstruction' is neither nihilism nor metaphysics but simply interpretation as such, the untangling of the inherence of metaphysics in nihilism and of nihilism in metaphysics by way of the close reading of texts" ("Critic as Host" 230). For Miller, deconstruction is "simply interpretation as such"; it is part and parcel of the "untangling" *work* of traditional criticism. In short, deconstructive criticism here is explicitly tied to decidability, the work of—what works in—traditional literary criticism. The recognition of an interpretative undecidability is, then, the "work" of deconstructive criticism, what it reveals in its readings as a transhistorical principle.[15]

Derridean deconstruction, though, always problematizes this decidability, although not in any simple, dialectical way; hence, a relation between Derridean deconstruction and literary criticism is not readily apparent—that is, a relation other than one in which literary criticism is a discipline to be deconstructed. As Derrida puts it, "Deconstruction is not a critical operation. The critical is its object;

14. Fish aptly summarizes this type of literary critical work when he writes, "Theories always work and they will always produce exactly the results they predict. . . . Indeed, the trick would be to find a theory that *didn't* work" (*Is There a Text in This Class?* 68). I contend that Derridean deconstruction is precisely such a "theory"—one that, *unlike* deconstructive criticism, doesn't (allow) work.

15. According to Miller, for example, texts deconstruct themselves, uniformly and without reference to or differentiation among historical circumstances: "Logocentric metaphysics deconstitutes itself, according to a regular law which can be demonstrated in the self-subversion of all the great texts of Western metaphysics from Plato onward" ("Critic as Host" 228). Likewise for de Man, who actually mentions this point as the principal difference between Derrida and himself: "I would hold to the statement that 'the text deconstructs itself, is self-deconstructive' rather than being deconstructed by a philosophical intervention" ("Interview with Paul de Man" 307).

the deconstruction always bears, at one moment or another, on the confidence invested in the critical or critico-theoretical process, that is to say, in the act of decision, in the ultimate possibility of the decidable" ("Ja, ou le faux bond" 103; trans. and cited in Culler, *On Deconstruction* 247).[16] Derrida here argues that criticism, the dialectical movement of affirmation, negation, and synthesis on the way to a totalized realization of truth, is the object of deconstruction, that-which-is-to-be-deconstructed. This notion of knowledge as critique can be read in the movement of the history of philosophy, with the great system-builders criticizing those before them and replacing the old systems with new and improved systems on the way to or in the name of synthesis, identity, and the realization of truth. But this movement of critique is *also* the movement of literary criticism, insofar as literary criticism is tied to a search for the meaning of texts, to the decidability of texts, to synthesis, to "*transcendent* reading, in that search for the signified" (*Of Grammatology* 160). As Derrida writes in "The Double Session," "The critical desire—which is also the philosophical desire—can only, as such, attempt to regain . . . lost mastery" (in *Dissemination* 230).[17]

Arguing for the transhistorical principle of the undecidability of texts is deconstructive criticism's move to regain this lost mastery, to reempower literary criticism. In fact, reempowering literary criticism is overtly mentioned by Geoffrey Hartman as one of the "shared set of problems" facing those writing in *Deconstruction and Criticism:*

These problems center on two issues that affect literary criticism today. One is the situation of criticism itself, what kind of maturer function it may claim—a function beyond the obviously academic

16. Culler, rather bafflingly, lets this quotation from Derrida stand virtually without comment—in a section *titled* "Deconstructive Criticism." He does, however, gloss Derrida's quotation with the following from de Man: " 'A deconstruction,' writes de Man, '*always has for its target to reveal the existence of hidden articulations and fragmentations within assumedly monadic totalities*' " (*On Deconstruction* 247, my emphasis). When he uses de Man to gloss Derrida here, Culler sums up two of my arguments in a nutshell: (1) de Man "always" wishes to *reveal* a certain undecidability as the *end* of his project; and (2) the project of deconstructive criticism is consistently conflated with Derrida's—here in Culler's book, as it is in a great deal of secondary literature.

17. Cf. earlier in "The Double Session," in which Derrida argues that his undecidables "mark the spots of what can never be mastered, sublated, or dialectized" (in *Dissemination* 221).

or pedagogical. While teaching, criticizing, and presenting the great texts of our culture are essential tasks, to insist on the importance of literature should not entail assigning to literary criticism only a service function. Criticism is part of the world of letters, and has its own mixed philosophical and literary, reflective and figural strength. (vii)

Hartman here seems to begin with an interesting notion of a possible "function beyond the obviously academic or pedagogical" for criticism, but ends up simply wanting to have criticism recognized for its "figural strength," the strength it gains from its recognition of and use of a privileged figural language, within "the world of letters." Again, this sort of account leaves the door open for deconstruction to be read as a traditional—or even traditional*ist*[18]—method of thematized reading, one that assigns and removes mastery from texts by the single criterion of their employment of figurative language. Indeed, Hartman's worries about criticism's rising above a "service function" rather overtly suggest this critical will-to-mastery. But it seems to me that if there is to be a relation between deconstruction and literary criticism, if deconstruction is to be "useful" at all to literary criticism, if there is a "lesson to be learned" from deconstruction, it is that deconstructive literary criticism must face up to the questions posed by Derridean deconstruction: it must do something other than attempt to reassert mastery over texts.

Undecidability and Structure

Yale deconstructive criticism has from its inception in America been characterized by its proponents as a sort of criticism that does something other than provide such totalized readings. As I argue above, it fails because it finds the same rock-bottom simple undecidability in all texts. For the deconstructionist critic, undecidability is a function of and is grounded in the irreducibly rich signification

18. For example, Hartman's notion that "teaching, criticizing, and presenting the great texts of our culture are essential tasks" is debatable on many fronts: who is the "we" implied by "our culture"; to *whom* are these tasks "essential"; what are (the stakes of assigning the status of) "great texts"? In the end, it seems that all of this quite clearly reinforces a notion of criticism as simply and "obviously academic and pedagogical."

of literary language. Hartman writes that all deconstructors are interested in "figurative language, its excesses over any assigned
meaning" (*Deconstruction and Criticism* vii). The undecidability of a
text is the product of the figural, metaphoric language always at
play within the text's attempted constitution of scientific, objectified
truth. As Miller puts it, "Deconstruction is an investigation of what
is implied by this inherence in one another of figure, concept, and
narrative" ("Critic as Host" 223). In other words, because figurative
language, which is irreducibly rich in significance or signification,
is part of the constitution of the notions of concept and narrative,
these notions cannot be made univocally significant. For Miller, the
"concept" literature and the specific text's "narrative" remain undecidable because of the inherence of "figure" (figurative language)
within their makeup. Thus the ground of deconstructive literary
criticism's notion of undecidability is specifically the undecidability
of figurative language.[19]

This realization of the figural or metaphoric nature of all language
is generally taken to be something that deconstructive criticism has
lifted right out of Derrida. As Norris writes about Derrida's work,
"Deconstruction finds its rock-bottom sense [in] the irreducibility of
metaphor, the *différance* at play within the very constitution of 'literal'
meaning" (*Deconstruction* 66). Here Norris characterizes a turn to the
irreducible richness of metaphorical or figurative language (against
the univocality of literal language, against philosophy) as the thrust
of Derrida's work, especially in his famous text on metaphor, "White
Mythology." This, again, is not the case. Derrida writes, against
those who take "White Mythology" to be a text about the privilege
of metaphor over metonymy, "The whole of 'White Mythology'
constantly puts into question the current and currently philosophical
interpretation of metaphor as a transfer from the sensible to the
intelligible, as well as the privilege accorded this trope in the deconstruction of metaphysical rhetoric" ("*Retrait* of Metaphor" 13).
For Derrida, metaphor is not a trope that can have an unproble-

19. In "Search for Grounds in Literary Study," Miller states that a double emphasis on
the tropological and narrative (taken together, figural) nature of language in a story is both
"the underlying *logos* or *Grund* and at the same time [that which] interrupts or deconstructs
that story—this double emphasis tends to break down generic distinctions and to recognize,
for example, the fundamental role of tropes in novels" (34).

matically privileged place in the *disruption* or deconstruction of meta-physical rhetoric because it is part and parcel of this rhetoric, a ground-concept of metaphysics. He writes in "White Mythology": "Above all, the movement of metaphorization (origin and then era-sure of the metaphor, transition from the proper sensory meaning to the proper spiritual meaning by means of the detour of figures) is nothing other than the movement of idealization. . . . Each time that a rhetoric defines a metaphor, not only is *a* philosophy implied, but also a conceptual network in which philosophy *itself* has been constituted" (in *Margins of Philosophy* 226, 230). For Derrida, a turn to metaphor, an affirmation of figural or metaphoric language, is a metaphysical move. The concept of metaphor—the sensible standing in for the intelligible by means of tropes—*is* the movement of meta-physics, of idealization, so it could hardly function quite so un-problematically as the ground for a concept of undecidability that could disrupt this movement.

Undecidability, for Derrida, is not solely concerned with or brought about by the semantic, metaphorical richness of figural lan-guage.[20] He writes, in his discussion of the undecidability of hymen in Mallarmé, " 'Undecidability' is not caused here by some enigmatic equivocality, some inexhaustible ambivalence of a word in a 'natural' language" (*Dissemination* 220). Although Derrida is certainly inter-ested in metaphoricity and figuration, for him it is not the richness of figural language that brings about undecidability; rather, the rich-ness of figural language is symptomatic of the *structure* of the field

20. This assertion, of course, needs to be qualified a bit, because for Derrida too the tropological aspects of literary writing have a certain privilege; they gesture toward or allow access to an other. As he writes, "It is quite possible that literary writing in the modern period is more than one example among others, rather a privileged guiding thread for access to the general structure of textuality" (*Acts of Literature* 71). Nevertheless, as I argue above, the difference between Derrida and a de Manian deconstructive criticism is what happens *after* the recognition of this "privileged guiding thread" of textual undecidability. For Derrida, this "privilege" is momentary—the first of two gestures. The upshot of this undecidability is the ethical gesture toward alterity, the necessary structuring position of difference within sameness. I would argue that this is not de Man's reading of undecid-ability. As Bennington writes, about the undecidable " 'aberration' [de Man] regularly produces as reading machine": "De Man's readings generate ethical preoccupations that they cannot dominate: they do this not through any lack of rigor, but because of their rigor" ("Aberrations" 220). It seems clear that de Man's texts "generate" certain "ethical preoccupations," but it is equally clear that de Man does not, on the whole, attempt to follow them up, although it is precisely these preoccupations that Derrida takes up in his readings of de Man.

itself—a field that engenders undecidability as a symptom of the *closure* of a certain totalizing way of thinking, of the need for the *displacement* of such a system.[21] In his own words, "If totalization no longer has any meaning, it is not because the infiniteness of a field cannot be covered by a finite glance or a finite discourse, *but because the nature of the field . . . excludes totalization"* (*Writing and Difference* 289, my emphasis). For Derrida, it is the nature or structure of the field—of systematicity or metaphoricity in general—rather than some sort of inherent ambiguity in a certain tropic use of figural language that is the ground of undecidability. According to Derrida, the nature of the field, which, he emphasizes, is made up of both discursive and nondiscursive forces, inscribes difference within the heart of identity.

Where Derrida locates the ground of undecidability can best be explained, I think, in terms of his interest in Saussurean linguistics, wherein the systematicity of language is accounted for solely in terms of "differences *without positive terms"* (Saussure, *Course in General Linguistics,* 120). For Derrida, undecidability is a consequence of the functioning of the general system, a system that is grounded in difference rather than identity, a system that cannot purge the difference, the nonpresence, which is part of its very structure. As Gasché writes, "[For Derrida,] since concepts are produced within a discursive network of differences, they not only are what they are by virtue of other concepts, but they also, in a fundamental way, inscribe that Otherness within themselves" (*Tain of the Mirror* 128, my emphasis). Undecidability is brought about because of this irreducible otherness inscribed in each concept; the necessary inclusion of alterity within this systematicity forces the concept to constitute itself in/by relation to a chain of other terms. One term cannot function as a master term and rule the system from without because the term is configured in and functions within a system always already in place. There is no pure, positive term constituted (from) without a system.

The upshot of all this for deconstructive criticism's reading of undecidability, then, is that for Derrida this undecidability cannot

---

21. This discussion is very much indebted to Gasché's discussion of structure and systematicity in *Tain of the Mirror,* especially 143–47.

be a "positive" consequence of the richness or ambiguity of figural language for the same reason that a signified cannot be a "positive" consequence of a signifier for Saussure: systematicity excludes the possibility[22] of a positive master term ruling within a field. Hence, the inability to totalize—the undecidability—that Derrida speaks of is not the "positive" consequence of a certain sort of tropic language use; rather, it is conditioned by the nature of the system: it is due to the always already fact of systematicity at work in the very constitution of supposedly pure, "origin-al" concepts, concepts that wish to rule the chain and assure its decidability, concepts such as deconstructive criticism's transcategorial, transhistorical notion of undecidability. In short, a systematic rather than figural or rhetorical notion of undecidability separates Derrida from deconstructive criticism.

Derrida's Inscription

Derrida's work has been conflated with a kind of de Manian deconstructive criticism. I wish to make a distinction between Derrida's work and this criticism. Yet I am faced with an odd problem: Derrida himself makes no such rigid distinction. He is, in fact, quite generous in his readings of critics such as de Man and Culler. His work on de Man is well known,[23] and he refers to Culler's *On Deconstruction* as "fundamental" (*Memoires* 88n). How, one might ask, am I to account for this? Certainly one way to answer such a question might be to reiterate that Derrida's readings do not *criticize* anyone—insisting again that deconstruction is not a *critical* operation. Having said that, however, I find it interesting that Derrida has recently involved himself in certain selective—and recognizably "critical"— polemics: he has, for example, quite effectively and polemically defended his work in the pages of *Critical Inquiry*.[24]

22. As a kind of ground, systematicity also engenders this possibility, making Derrida's notion of ground quasi-transcendental, giving simultaneously conditions of possibility and impossibility. Cf. Derrida, *Dissemination*, 166–68, and *Limited Inc.*, 127–31, as well as throughout *Glas*.

23. See, for example, his *Memoires*, "Psyche," and "Like the Sound of the Sea Deep within a Shell," the last being his response to de Man's wartime writings.

24. See "But, beyond . . . ," Derrida's response to a critique of his article "Racism's Last

In order to get a handle on Derrida's own inscription within these institutional debates, I would like to look briefly at a lesser known, though just as vehement, Derridean polemic, his response to one of Jürgen Habermas's lectures in *The Philosophical Discourse of Modernity*. Derrida argues, in a long footnote to the collection *Limited Inc.*, that Habermas has not based his critique on a reading of Derrida's texts, but has rather taken a caricature of deconstruction found in Culler's *On Deconstruction*.[25] More specifically, Derrida accuses Habermas of proceeding "without citing me, then, a single time, and abusing citations of Jonathan Culler at points where, it being a question of relations between a generality and its 'cases,' the latter is occasionally obliged to rigidify my arguments out of pedagogical considerations" (157n). The instance that Derrida brings up here clearly names an institutional network of mis- or non-reading: Habermas avoids an actual engagement with Derrida's work when he takes Culler's book to stand in for Derrida's texts. Rather, Habermas takes on a "rigidif[ied]" representation of Derrida from Culler, and proceeds to criticize it. The polemic is fairly clear, and one can understand Derrida's frustration at being criticized without having been read. The difficult thing to understand in this critical exchange, however, is that Derrida's polemical force is brought to bear solely on Habermas; Culler escapes unharmed. Since Derrida has (quite understandably) chosen to adopt a critical vocabulary here, one might wonder how or why Culler escapes similar criticism, insofar as Habermas's reading of Derrida is wholly based on or reproduces Culler's.

This question becomes even more baffling if we look at the specific readings that Derrida takes issue with in Habermas's text. Derrida writes:

Although *I am not cited a single time,* although not one of my texts is even indicated as a reference in a chapter of twenty-five pages

---

Word," and "Biodegradables," his response to several critiques of "Like the Sound of the Sea Deep within a Shell."

25. And this does, in fact, seem to be the case in Habermas's second lecture on Derrida, "Excursus on Leveling the Genre Distinction between Literature and Philosophy." Habermas argues that since Derrida's work does not proceed by means of traditional arguments, "it is expedient to take a closer look at his disciples in literary criticism within the Anglo-Saxon climate" (193).

that claims to be a long critique of my work, phrases such as the following can be found: "Derrida is particularly interested in standing the primacy of logic over rhetoric, canonized since Aristotle, on its head"; " . . . the deconstructionist can deal with the works of philosophy as works of literature . . ."; " . . . in his business of deconstruction, Derrida does not proceed analytically. . . . Instead [he] proceeds by a critique of style . . ."

That is false. I say *false* as opposed to *true*, and I defy Habermas to prove the presence in my work of that "primacy of rhetoric" which he attributes to me. (156–57n)

I would likewise defy Habermas to find a "primacy of rhetoric" or a reduction of philosophy to literature in Derrida's texts; however, I admit with alacrity that it *is* fairly easy to find each of these things operative in the work of deconstructive critics, especially in the texts of de Man, whose work quite clearly privileges rhetoric over logic and likewise argues that the distinction between literature and philosophy is delusive.[26] In the end, then, it seems that Derrida is criticizing Habermas for reducing him to or confusing him with de Man—a reading that is, as I note above, clearly authorized by Culler. The question remains, however, why Derrida was reluctant to criticize de Man or Culler?

The answer is, I suspect, a complicated one—and one that I may not be in the best position to provide. It is tempting to dismiss Derrida's apparent inconsistency as an instance of cronyism, but although there certainly are personal considerations at work here— friendships and reputations to be respected—these reasons are not, I think, wholly or exclusively the issue. The more complex reasons

26. Each of Habermas's characterizations of Derrida's work can be applied to de Man. Habermas asserts that "Derrida is particularly interested in standing the primacy of logic over rhetoric, canonized since Aristotle, on its head." De Man writes, "Rhetoric radically suspends logic and opens up vertiginous possibilities of referential aberration" (*Allegories of Reading* 10). Habermas continues: "The deconstructionist can deal with the works of philosophy as works of literature." Gasché makes this point quite clearly in "In-difference to Philosophy," in which he quotes de Man: "The critical deconstruction that leads to the discovery of the literary, rhetorical nature of the philosophical claim to truth is genuine enough and cannot be refuted: literature turns out to be the main topic of philosophy, and the model for the kind of truth to which it aspires" (*Allegories of Reading* 115). Habermas finally charges, "In his business of deconstruction, Derrida does not proceed analytically. . . . Instead [he] proceeds by a critique of style." This last strikes me as weak, no matter whom it might be leveled against (as if stylistics were not itself an exacting analytical enterprise), but I suppose one could take de Man's analyses to be concerned with "style."

are institutional in nature and concern the networks of institutional dissemination (publishing, organizing and promoting conferences, teaching, and hiring) that inevitably and unfortunately pit one theory against another. Those still associated with or sympathetic to deconstruction inevitably share an institutionally produced defensive posture, a posture heightened by the de Man scandal and the continued pounding that deconstruction takes in the popular press, even after its demise. Deconstruction was under siege throughout its "reign" in literature departments, and this siege mentality may explain Derrida's loyalty to de Man and Culler, who share a kind of broad affiliation with Derrida in these pitched institutional battles. It is important, however, to recall that the rhetorical deconstruction associated with critics such as de Man and Culler remains one deconstruction among many. Despite having what at times seems like Derrida's imprimatur, the methods of rhetorical deconstructive criticism cannot be conflated with his work.

In no way am I calling for Derrida to issue a sort of deconstructive papal bull. Nor do I suggest that Derrida somehow controls the myriad institutional combinations and permutations undertaken in the name of deconstruction. Tracing these networks shows quite the opposite, actually; and, as Derrida has shown quite clearly, the subject's inscription of an authorizing signature cannot and does not stop the play of substitutions and appropriations.[27] Derrida himself is inscribed in the various institutional networks of reading that this book attempts to describe—and is likewise subject to the play of these networks. But, having said that, I still think it is important to distinguish among deconstructions, not, however, in order to save a deconstructive orthodoxy, but rather to recall the specificity that is at the heart of Derrida's itinerary, and to pose a question to that still-dominant thematization of deconstruction which reduces it to a method for producing readings. When deconstruction becomes a method, its specificity is lost; the singularity of deconstruction and its concern with alterity becomes smoothed out into an all-encompassing, easily reproducible disciplinary project, a project to which Derrida's texts pose an essential question. From the "start" (or perhaps "in the end"), the question of deconstruction will have

27. See, for example, his essay "Signature, Event, Context," in *Margins of Philosophy*.

been a question of the discipline of deconstruction—it will have been an institutional as well as a systematic question.[28] At this juncture, I find it useful to discuss Foucault and the problem of institutionalization—because his work on institutionalization can be brought to bear on deconstruction, and the institutionalization of his work mirrors and comments on the commodification of Derrida's.

28. See, for an example of Derrida's work on institutional questions, his "Principle of Reason: The University in the Eyes of Its Pupils." Likewise, Derrida's work with the International College of Philosophy and the *Groupe de recherches sur l'enseignement philosophique* in France is becoming more well known in North America. See, for general accounts, Derrida's "Sendoffs" and the interview "On Colleges and Philosophy," as well as Fynsk's overview "A Decelebration of Philosophy"; at this writing, two volumes of Derrida's work on institutions are being prepared in English.

3 / Exteriority and Appropriation: Foucault, Derrida, and the Discipline of Literary Criticism

Discursive practices are not purely and simply ways of producing discourse. They are embodied in technical processes, in institutions, in patterns for general behavior, in forms for transmission and diffusion, and in pedagogical forms which, at once, impose and maintain them.
—MICHEL FOUCAULT
Language, Counter-Memory, Practice

If one were to plot schematically the rise and fall of theories in literature departments, one could rather easily tie the rise of Michel Foucault's genealogical discourse to the fall of Derrida's deconstruction. In fact, Foucault's thought first comes on the American literary critical scene thematized as a socially and institutionally engaged alternative to what many politically oriented critics saw as the paralyzing textualism of Derrida and his disciples at Yale. Edward Said gives us a representative account of the debate in *The World, the Text, and the Critic:* "Derrida is concerned only with reading a text, and . . . a text is nothing more than what is in it for the reader. For if the text is important to Derrida because its real situation is literally a textual element with no ground in actuality . . . then for Foucault the text is important because it inhabits an element of power with a decisive claim on actuality. . . . Derrida's criticism moves us *into* the text, Foucault's *in* and *out*" (183). Thus Foucault is brought to bear on deconstruction in order to reorient literary criticism to the real world, to the "actuality" of "power" in discourse and history outside the text as well as inside it. In fact, a whole school of criticism has sprouted up around Foucault's texts, "new historicism," which takes from a reading of Foucault its ground notion that "discourse is like everything else in our society: the object of a struggle for power" (Harari, *Textual Strategies*, 43).

I take issue with the terms of this debate, specifically with the notion that Foucault is somehow a champion of historical *praxis* over Derrida's purely textual *theoria*. I do so not in order to expose mis- readings of either Foucault or Derrida in the service of a better understanding of their relationship to literary criticism, but, rather, in order to say some things about the discipline of literary criticism itself. In other words, I am interested less in exposing supposed "misreadings" of either thinker's work within this second-hand de- bate than I am in examining the institutional and disciplinary im- peratives that make these misreadings possible. In fact, I contend that a certain economy of misreading may even be *necessary* if literary criticism is to "use" either Foucault or Derrida at all.

And attempt to *use* them it does. The discipline of literary criticism is hungry for new paradigms. The theory explosion of the 1970s brought with it an entire "theory industry" within and around lit- erature departments. The backbone of this industry is the theoretical guidebook: there are evaluative studies such as Said's, Terry Eag- leton's *Literary Theory: An Introduction,* much of Jonathan Culler's early work, or Frank Lentricchia's *After the New Criticism;* and there are essay collections, such as Donald Keesey's *Contexts for Criticism,* Josué Harari's *Textual Strategies: Perspectives in Poststructuralist Crit- icism,* or H. Aram Veeser's *New Historicism.* Books such as these are a major source of "theory" for many literary critics, and they present to the profession various methods or strategies for reading texts and producing critical analyses.[1] As Harari writes in his hugely successful collection *Textual Strategies,* "Method has become a strategy" (72), and for him, the future of literary criticism is to be a struggle among these critical strategies, these truth-strategies: "I have presented the various critical struggles at play among contemporary theorists. It remains to inscribe these strategies in a more global framework, to

1. These types of books are, of course, especially prevalent in—and, I hasten to add, important for—introductory courses in graduate curricula, where the traditional "Bibli- ography and Methods" course is quickly metamorphosing into a theory course.

put them in the ring of criticism as it were, and to determine how the rounds are to be scored" (68–69). Harari here invokes a perhaps all-too-familiar picture of the literature department, indeed of "pluralistic" society on the whole, as engaged in a violent struggle for the truth, for truth as strategic victory, for truth as appropriation.[2] Such a conception, unfortunately, seems to replicate rather than displace the violent will-to-truth that is in question in many of the theoretical discussions he presents. Also, Harari's notion of truth as critical struggle recuperates thinking such as Foucault's or Derrida's within an institution rather problematically; it names and preserves the interior, protected space of the university as the nexus of discourse's truth, the "ring" in which various truth strategies will be tested and a winner declared.

The notion of a "ring of criticism" is particularly apt here because the space of interiority suggested by the image of a ring is precisely what literary criticism has to secure for itself in order to isolate its object and perform its work. If a truth about a text is to be revealed and preserved in criticism, then there must be a protected interior space where this truth can rest: the structure of the work, the biography of the author and its relation to his or her other works, the relation of the work to its historical circumstances, and so on. But any such notion of interiority—a place protected from the play of a larger network where meaning can rest unmolested—is precisely one of the issues in question in many of these "critical strategies," such as Foucault's or Derrida's.[3] For example, in "What Is an Author?" an essay anthologized (I am tempted to say canonized) in

---

2. In fact, Harari gleefully celebrates criticism as violent appropriation: "All criticism *is* strategic. To the question: how should the critic approach knowledge? I know of only one answer: *strategically*. The power and productivity, the gains and losses, the advances and retrenchments of criticism are inscribed in this term: strategy, reminding us of its obsolete— obsolete?—definition: 'A violent and bloody act.' In the game of knowledge, method has become a strategy: the 'violent and bloody' agent by which criticism *executes* the work and in so doing, paradoxically, canonizes it" (*Textual Strategies* 72).

3. Foucault and Derrida do, of course, perform "readings" of texts, philosophical and literary, but their readings differ from the majority of literary critical thematizations by having a certain exterior or reflexive moment. Crudely put, there is the genealogical moment in Foucault, where the will to truth puts itself in question; and for Derrida, there is the second move of the double reading, which is a displacement and reinscription of the opposition uncovered in the first reading. Literary criticism attempts to reproduce these reflexive moments, but generally preserves an interiority of meaning by valorizing the *reflexivity itself* as the crux of all readings, the meaning of all texts.

Harari's collection, Foucault calls for a writing about literature that is not based on the accepted interior unities of the author or the book; rather, he speaks of the possibility of a topology of discourse based on statements, on positivities that "cannot be constructed solely from the grammatical features, formal structures, and objects of discourse" (157). Statements cannot be expected, as Harari hopes, to stay in one place and fight it out in the ring of criticism because, as Gilles Deleuze notes, "Each statement is itself a multiplicity, not a structure or a system" (*Foucault* 6).

It is precisely here, with the *exteriority* of the statement, that Foucault poses his most dangerous question to literary criticism; he writes in *The Archaeology of Knowledge:* "Language, in its appearance as a mode of being, is the statement [*l'énoncé*]: as such, it belongs to a description that is neither transcendental nor anthropological" (113/148). He goes on to explain this:

> The analysis of statements treats them in the systematic form of exteriority. Usually, the historical description of things said is shot through with [*tout entière traversée par*] the opposition of interior and exterior; and wholly directed by [*tout entière commandée par*] a desire to move from the exterior—which may be no more than contingency or mere material necessity, a visible body or uncertain translation—towards the essential nucleus of interiority. (120–21/158–59)

This formulation of the "historical description of things said" also holds, I think, for the literary critical description of things said: literary criticism moves from the exterior (the other, the untranslatable, the unthematized) to the interior (the same, the translation, the theme). Foucault challenges the possibility of such a totalizing impulse in the human sciences and outlines a thinking whose task is "to describe a group of statements not with reference to the interiority of an intention, a thought, or a subject, but in accordance with the dispersion of an exteriority" (125/164).

Notions such as dispersion and exteriority pose serious problems for literary criticism, whose traditional field enables it to explain what is *inside* a text by putting to work certain notions from *outside* a text, from a constructed place of critical privilege such as the author, reader, structure, or historical circumstances of the text. Paradoxically then, in the literary critical model, "outside" the text does *not* indicate an exteriority that would disperse the text's meanings, but rather—and perhaps more perniciously—an *interiority* that would protect and preserve them. In other words, for criticism, the "outside" of the text is simply another name for an interior space that maintains its purity by avoiding the play of the textual network. For example, in "What Is an Author?" Foucault takes up the problem of the relation of the text to the author, "the manner in which the text points to this 'figure' that, at least in appearance, is outside it and antecedes it" (141), and argues that the author is one such privileged space of interiority that is outside the text: "[The author] is a certain functional principle by which, in our culture, one limits, excludes, and chooses; in short, by which one impedes the free circulation, the free manipulation, the free composition, decomposition, and recomposition of fiction" (159). Foucault here points out that criticism employs the notion of the author to preserve a space of meaning, an interiority that can arrest the exterior hazards of signification. But it is problematic—if not impossible—to locate and maintain such spaces of interiority because, as Foucault notes, "the margins of a book are never clear-cut: beyond the title, the first lines, and the last full stop, beyond its internal configuration and its autonomous form, it is caught up in a system of references [*un système de renvois*] to other books, other texts, other sentences: it is a node within a network" (*Archaeology of Knowledge* 23/34, translation slightly modified). For Foucault, the book exists in an exterior network of statements where the interiority of totality is always dispersed; hence, there is no protected interior space within this network that could rule the entire network. Likewise, there is no place above or below the surface of discourse—no "outside," no pure interior space beyond the reach of the exterior network's effects—that could explain discourse, that could force discourse to render up a secret truth. This dispersal he calls the flattening of discourse: no instance of discourse can claim to rule from outside the flat surface; no instance of discourse can explain or ground the entire chain or preserve an instance of determinate meaning within the network. He writes, "There is no sub-text [*Il n'y a pas de texte d'en dessous*]. And therefore

no plethora. The enunciative domain is identical with its own surface" (119/157).

Consider literary criticism's recent romancing of Foucault at the
expense of Derrida. Raman Selden writes in his *Reader's Guide to
Literary Theory:* "Like other post-structuralists, Foucault regards discourse as a central human activity, but not as a universal, 'general
text,' a vast sea of signification" (98). This summary seems to be the
party line on the huge difference between Foucault's thought and
Derrida's: Foucault is interested in active power and history, Derrida
in passive thought and textuality.[4] But I recommend stepping back
and reading Derrida and Foucault together at the point where they
seem farthest apart, at that "place" in Derrida's text which a whole
host of his critics (including Foucault) point to as the metaphysical
Achilles' heel of deconstruction: Derrida's notion of "general text,"
which Selden glosses as a totalizing "universal" that denies the
world and history in favor of a "vast sea of signification."[5]

As I argue in Chapter 2, with his notion of general text Derrida
is not attempting to cast the text and the world in what Foucault
calls "the gray light of neutralization" ("What Is an Author?" 145),
but rather to complicate notions of exterior and interior—not attempting "to extend the reassuring notion of the text to a whole
extra-textual realm and to transform the world into a library by doing
away with all boundaries, all framework, all sharp edges," but rather

---

4. Foucault is, of course, more than partially responsible for this thematization of his
thought vis-à-vis Derrida's, but I am not considering in this book his rather vitriolic—and,
it seems to me, unfair—response to Derrida in "My Body, This Paper, This Fire." This
may seem like an outrageous avoidance on my part, but I justify it on two counts: First,
Foucault's text consists almost entirely of a point-by-point refutation of Derrida's reading
of Descartes on the dreamer and the madman, something which does not directly concern
me here (The essay's infamous remarks concerning the metaphysical and pedagogical
danger of "there is nothing outside the text" are dealt with below). Second, Foucault himself
later criticizes *Historie de la folie,* as I also outline later, for its naive notions of the metaphysical "experience" of madness—a criticism which, to a great extent, actually *agrees with*
Derrida's: "Everything [in *Historie de la folie*] transpires as if Foucault *knew* what 'madness'
means. Everything transpires as if, in a continuous and underlying way, an assured and
rigorous precomprehension of the concept of madness, or at least of its normal definition,
were possible and acquired" (Derrida, "Cogito," 41). Geoff Bennington's "Cogito Incognito," the brief but insightful introduction to his translation of Foucault's essay, is an
excellent discussion of the conflict.

5. The secondary sources for such a reading of Derrida are too numerous to mention—
it has become critical commonplace; so, instead, let me cite a book concerning Derrida and
criticism that *doesn't* contain such a reading of general text: Gasché's *Tain of the Mirror.*

"to work out the theoretical and practical system of these margins, these borders, once more, from the ground up" ("Living On—Border Lines" 84). Derrida's notion of text, then, seems to have at least this much in common with Foucault's notion of the exteriority of a network of statements: both posit a discursive field or network in which no term is absolutely privileged;[6] and both share what Foucault calls a "limit-attitude" ("What Is Enlightenment?" 45), an interest in reworking thought's borders.

But it is at this limit that the dominant literary critical–political reading of Foucault triumphs over that of Derrida. Foucault is held to be interested in "reference and reality," with the "world of institutions and action" (Arac, "To Regress" 250, 243),[7] whereas Derrida is taken as reinscribing everything within the rigid limit of the prison-house of language. Again, I think this is an inadequate reading of both thinkers. Derrida sums up the relation between text and limit or context as follows: "I set down here as an axiom and as that which is to be proved, that the reconstitution cannot be finished. This is my starting point: no meaning can be determined out of context, but no context permits saturation. What I am referring to here is not richness of substance, semantic fertility, but rather structure: the structure of the remnant or of iteration" ("Living On—Border Lines" 81). Foucault writes, "A statement always has borders [marges] peopled by other statements. These borders are not what is usually meant by 'context'—real or verbal—that is, all the situational or linguistic elements, taken together, that motivate a formulation and determine its meaning. They are distinct from such a 'context' precisely in so far as they make it possible" (Archaeology of Knowledge 97–98/128–29). Here again it seems that we see Foucault and Derrida in general agreement against traditional and critical

6. In fact, one could gloss Derrida on the undecidability of text by quoting Foucault on the network of statements: "There is no statement in general, no free, independent statement; but a statement always belongs to a series or a whole, always plays a role among other statements, deriving support from them and distinguishing itself from them: it is always part of a network of statements" (Archaeology of Knowledge 99/130).

7. Arac's "To Regress from the Rigor of Shelley," a review of Harari's Textual Strategies and Bloom's Deconstruction and Criticism, champions the essays in the Harari collection that have an overt historical or political agenda, but does not question the institutional imperatives that might give rise to such collections. He writes, building on an image from Shelley: "The 1970s have experienced critical fermentation, following the notable effervescence that began the decade" (242).

notions of context: one cannot appeal to (historical or extratextual) context to rein in the significations of a statement or a text; a space of interior privilege cannot be maintained outside the text. In fact, both Derrida and Foucault seem to agree that context cannot rule text—a place of interiority cannot be maintained in an exterior field— precisely because context is not really "outside" the text at all. Quite the contrary: both text and context are engendered or made possible in the same field, under the same conditions. For Foucault this field is the "flat" network of statements; for Derrida it is the "structure of the remnant or of iteration."[8] Both notions serve to make it impossible for literary criticism to preserve a space of interiority by which it could construct a critical system—a saturated critical context above, below, or outside the text—to reveal and protect meaning.

This denial of interiority seems to be precisely why many literary critics simply *have* to read Derrida as the last in a transcendentalist philosophical line and Foucault as the last in a materialist historicist line, Derrida as the founder of a "textual" deconstructive criticism and Foucault as the founder of a "worldly" new historicism. Such readings are necessary if literary criticism is to continue as an autonomous discipline, because if literary criticism accepts a notion of exteriority, it not only has to face the problem of doing something other than revealing meanings in texts, it has the much more pervasive problem of actually isolating its object, of separating text from extra-text. Hence we see the institutional imperative for literary critics to read Derrida's famous phrase "il n'y a pas de hors-texte" as "there is nothing outside of the text": if everything can be found within texts or textuality, and critics read texts for a living, then obviously the place or role of criticism is secured. Yet if one translates this phrase as "there is no extra-text [literally, out-text]," it brings out a much different reading: a network of exteriority (here named "text") is given, has no determinable origin or telos, and within it no one term or discourse can claim privilege over another. In other words, no space can be protected from the play of the network. Obviously, the latter reading is positively disastrous for literary crit-

8. Cf. Porter's "History and Literature," in which she tries similarly to read Derrida and Foucault together: "To say that there is nothing outside the text because there is no transcendental signified is precisely to cancel depth in order to foreground a signifying process which operates in and constitutes a horizonless plane" (266).

icism. The former interpretation, however, consolidates and reassures criticism in a continued central role. As I argue in Chapter 2, it allows critics to produce a deconstructive methodology and apply it to the whole of their field, which reveals that, indeed, there is nothing outside the determinate text if one applies to it a deconstructive methodology from this ultra-privileged site of the outside. This tendency in "deconstruction" to construct methodologies is the object of one of Foucault's central critiques of Derrida's thought. Foucault argues that certain notions of the intransitivity of literature, extracted from the work of Barthes and Blanchot, "are quickly taken up in the interior of an institution . . . : the institution of the university" (*Foucault Live* 114). But, as we have seen, only a certain (rather suspect) reading of Derrida's thought can supply such institutional imperatives. Moreover, as is becoming clear in the movement or methodology called new historicism, Foucault's thought is no less prone to hypostatization.

One might profitably object here that Foucault's work has no essential relation to new historicism—as Gasché argues concerning Derrida and deconstructive criticism—but there is no denying the *perceived* influence of Foucault's work on new historicism, both in the texts of new historicists and critics of new historicism alike. Foucault's perceived link to new historicism is so strong that, for example, Frank Lentricchia's essay in *The New Historicism*, "Foucault's Legacy: A New Historicism?" does not quote *one word of Foucault;* granted, the original printing of Lentricchia's essay places it after his long and involved discussion of Foucault in *Ariel and the Police,* but when Lentricchia turns specifically to discuss new historicism, he mentions Foucault throughout in the same breath as Stephen Greenblatt, reinforcing the widespread belief that new historicism is simply a translation of Foucault—that because "Foucault's key obsessions and terms shape Greenblatt's argument" (242n), the relation between Foucault's texts and new historicism is an unproblematic one.[9] This claim, in fact, could be said to comprise the "dom-

---

9. It should be noted that Greenblatt is scarcely responsible for such a reading. In fact, Greenblatt stubbornly refuses to offer a methodologization of Foucault. He cites Foucault quite sparsely, only twice in *Shakespearean Negotiations,* and refuses to offer a ready-made method for his own project, defining cultural poetics rather open-endedly as the "study

inant" reading of new historicism: it supposedly takes directly from Foucault its ground notion, its "key obsession," a discontinuous power that moves through everything. For example, Carolyn Porter reads Greenblatt's assertion that "theatricality . . . is not set over against power but is one of power's essential modes" as a translation of Foucault's claim that power "induces pleasure, forms knowledge, produces discourse" ("History and Literature" 262). In a crowning irony, one can now find Foucault being referred to as a practitioner of Berkeley new historicism,[10] just as Derrida was or is thought of as a Yale critic.

Insofar as Foucault (infamously) criticizes Derrida's thinking as "a historically well-determined little pedagogy" ("My Body" 27), all of this institutional attention creates something of a problem for him, though it seems fairly easy to locate the beginning of a Foucauldian response to his own methodization: power produces, an institutional discipline produces, and it consistently needs new processes by which to produce new objects of study or new thematizations; in short, a discipline such as literary criticism *needs* determinate—and determin*ing*—methodologies. New historicism, then, takes Foucault's exterior notions of power and discontinuity in historical analysis and turns them into usable, interior, ontological notions: new historicism often analyzes texts by studying the slippery relations of power in texts and in history. This historicism is "new" in that it takes into account the discontinuity of history, but it can quickly become "old" again when it takes up a notion of discontinuity as a simple, declarable discontinuity: studies are produced that tell us that although we used to think history was continuous, it was in fact *dis*continuous. For example, in *Habits of Thought in the English Renaissance* (volume 13 of Greenblatt's New Historicism series), Debora K. Shuger takes up "the new historicist critique of traditional formulations of Renaissance thought" (1): She writes:

---

of the collective making of distinct cultural practices and inquiry into the relations among these practices" (5). Likewise, Greenblatt stresses the institutional focus of cultural poetics. See, for example, "Shakespeare and the Exorcists" in *Shakespearean Negotiations*.

10. See Lehan's "Theoretical Limits of the New Historicism," in which, citing Hayden White, he attacks "the logic of new historicism, at least as practiced by Foucault" (540). Lehan goes on to name Foucault's thinking the dominant component of "a theory that has now fashionably emerged as the representation school" (540).

Investigation of these habits of thought in the dominant culture of the English Renaissance yields surprising results. Despite their general agreement on doctrinal matters, the figures studied present an unexpected and sometimes drastic ideological pluralism. *Instead of a monologic world picture, one uncovers complex and divergent assumptions.* . . . The [Renaissance] impulse to define and distinguish . . . results from a *prior sense of confusion and lack of demarcation.* (9–10, my emphases)

For Shuger, new historicism uncovers the "complex and divergent assumptions" that underlie a supposedly or traditionally "monologic world picture." In fact, she seems to argue that behind any modern historical or intellectual order(ing) there is "a prior sense of confusion and lack of demarcation." She concludes her introduction with what seems to be an apt formulation of the new historicist critique: "Renaissance works noticeably lack a systematic coherence, *their discontinuities instead exposing the struggle for meaning that fissures the last premodern generation*" (16, my emphasis).

If this is the case, then the place or value of Foucault in new historicism is his discovery or *exposure* of the disorder that lies under or behind the supposed order of history, his discovery that behind what seems to be a historical continuity, one can always and everywhere find or uncover discontinuity. Yet we have already seen Foucault's skepticism concerning this language of depth and the "exposing" of hidden origins (whether origins of order or disorder). Moreover, such a reading of Foucault also allows the easy methodological institutionalization that he criticizes Derrida for promoting. Such a reading of Foucault finds discontinuity behind every continuity and allows for the exposure of this discontinuity as/in the end of a discipline or method. Foucault responds to such a fetishizing of discontinuity: "My problem was not at all to say, '*Voilà*, long live discontinuity, we are in the discontinuous and a good thing too,' but to pose the question, 'How is it that at certain moments and in certain orders of knowledge, there are these sudden take-offs, these hastenings of evolution, these transformations which fail to correspond to the calm, continuist image that is normally accredited?' " (*Power/Knowledge* 112). For Foucault, it is not a matter of offering a choppy, discontinuist image of history to combat the "normally accredited" image of calm continuity, but rather a matter of attending to the disruptions themselves. Discontinuity, as a declarable historical or philosophical principle, can and does lead back to a totalizing image or picture of the historical "orders of knowledge" and is part and parcel of a very continuous institutional and methodological project. As Foucault writes about historical discourse at the end of the eighteenth century: "The regular historians were revealing continuities, while the historians of ideas were liberating discontinuities. *But I believe that they are two symmetrical and inverse effects of the same methodological renewal of history in general*" (*Foucault Live* 47, my emphasis).

The methodological problematic that Foucault outlines here, no doubt, doubles my own: I do not wish simply or primarily to offer a "symmetrical and inverse picture" of Foucault and Derrida in order to say, "*Voilà*, literary criticism misreads Foucault and Derrida, and here is the correct way to read them," but to try to ask how or why it is, in some sense, *inevitable* that they will be misread by a discipline, to ask if there is a mechanism in either thinker's text for explaining this appropriation (perhaps also complicating it), and to locate difference(s) through this operation. As I state above, I am less interested in "exposing" poor readings and misappropriations (though here and there I obviously adopt a critical or polemical tone) than I am in tracing the institutional and systematic imperatives of these appropriations. The question at hand becomes, then, can Foucault and/or Derrida provide a rationale for their own appropriation by the discipline of literary criticism—can their thinking of the reflexive moment of exteriority explain its own, for lack of a better word, re-interiorization within an institution or a method, within "new historicism" or "deconstructive criticism"?[11] Perhaps tracing possible answers to this question will help bring out important differences that, so far at least, I have been at great pains to collapse.

As I have argued, Foucault's explanation for his own appropriation revolves around the problematics of power and how instances

11. I find interesting Spivak's provocative comments on her position in the new historicism/deconstruction debate: she writes, citing Derrida, that "the conflict between New Historicism and deconstruction can now be narrowed down to a turf battle between Berkeley and Irvine, Berkeley and Los Angeles. . . . At any rate, since I see the *new* historicism as a sort of media hype mounted against deconstruction, I find it hard to position myself in its regard" ("New Historicism" 280).

of power tend to move the exterior toward the interior. Even institutional studies that liberate in some way also create a new object
or topic for discourse or study, a new subject(ification). Foucault
puts it quite succinctly in "La folie, l'absence d'oeuvre," an appendix
to the second edition of *Historie de la folie:* "[Someday,] everything
that we experience today in the form of a limit or as foreign or
insupportable, will have taken on the serene characteristics of what
is positive. And what for us today designates this Exterior risks one
day designating us" (in Carroll, *Paraesthetics,* 76). Later in his career,
Foucault criticizes *Madness and Civilization* for its naive notions of
power (*Power/Knowledge* 118–19) and of "experience" (*Archaeology of
Knowledge* 16/27, in which the translation renders *expérience* as "experiment"),[12] but this "early" quotation seems to be consistent with
"late" Foucauldian interest in "a form of power which makes individuals subjects . . . a form of power which subjugates and makes
subject to" ("Subject and Power" 212). Every liberation (of a cause,
a discourse, a group, especially of an "individual" such as the madman liberated from his madness) can and will transform into a type
of subjugation by defining a subject and subsequently by allowing
conditions to emerge for later (re)definitions, (re)designations of that
subject.[13] The exterior does not remain exterior; it "risks one day
designating us." Through this formulation, Foucault names the logic
by which his thought is brought into an institution. He offers no
"counter-formulation" precisely because he does not want to play
into the hands of this logic by designating alternative conditions of
possibility; his texts do not attempt to theorize or "ground" an outside precisely as a buffer against a totalizing logic that would then
subsume or sublate it. He refuses to play the game on the Hegelian
terms of transcendental/dialectical philosophy.

Indeed, Hegel is the thinker who poses the greatest question to
thinking in our postmodern epoch (insofar as he is the thinker of
the completion or totalization of the modern): how does one think
against a Hegelian system that is fueled by negation, that diffuses

12. See Carroll's excellent discussion of this problem in *Paraesthetics,* 53–67. He also drew
my attention to the mistranslation (195n).
13. Cf. Deleuze, *Foucault:* "From *Madness and Civilization* on, Foucault analyzed the discourse of the 'philanthropist' who freed madmen from their chains, without concealing
the more effective set of chains to which he destined them" (54).

contradiction or opposition by consuming it as merely a higher form of the system's own truth? As Derrida summarizes Hegelian sublation in an essay on Bataille, "The Hegelian *Aufhebung* is produced entirely from within discourse, from within the system or the work of signification. A determination is negated and conserved in another determination which reveals the truth of the former" (*Writing and Difference* 275). All critical discourse, then, risks playing directly into Hegel's hand, "risks agreeing to the reasonableness of reason, of philosophy, of Hegel, who is always right, as soon as one opens one's mouth in order to articulate meaning" (263). For Foucault, this question of Hegel is perhaps the most important question for postmodern thought:

> Truly to escape Hegel involves an exact appreciation of the price we have to pay to detach ourselves from him. It assumes that we are aware of [*suppose de savoir*] the extent to which Hegel, insidiously perhaps, is close to us; it implies a knowledge, in that which permits us to think against Hegel, of that which remains Hegelian. We have to determine the extent to which our anti-Hegelianism is possibly one of his tricks directed against us, at the end of which he stands, motionless, waiting for us. (*Discourse on Language* 235/ 74–75)

Here Foucault takes up the question that Hegel poses to contemporary thought: how to think against a structure that anticipates or negates such thinking, that in fact thrives on determinate negation? And it is precisely because of his suspicion of Hegelian sublation that it is difficult to read Foucault as ideology critique—as Habermas, for example, would like to read him.[14] Ideology critique depends on a moment of liberation through reason, on the demystification of ideology in order to unmask knowledge. As Louis Althusser writes, ideology critique moves in the service of "*scientific* knowledge, against all the mystifications of *ideological* 'knowledge.' Against the merely moral denunciation of myths and lies, for their rational and

14. Habermas's first lecture on Foucault in *The Philosophical Discourse of Modernity* is titled "An Unmasking of the Human Sciences: Foucault," and although he clearly sympathizes with the "critical" side of Foucauldian analyses, he cannot agree with Foucault's genealogical analyses insofar as they deny the moment of "liberating" knowledge that ideology critique seeks.

rigorous criticism" (*Lenin and Philosophy* 11). But, for Foucault, "criticism"—as an attempt to stake out a more excellent reason or ground—guarantees that the winner has already been declared, and that it is Hegel in a unanimous decision; the dialectic continues undisrupted, and reason is reassured. Foucault writes, " 'Dialectic' is a way of evading the always open and hazardous reality of conflict by reducing it to a Hegelian skeleton" (*Power/Knowledge* 114–15).

The overarching criticism of Foucault's work in literary critical circles revolves around his refusal to acknowledge a moment of liberation through reason. For example, Said, although sympathetic to components of Foucault's work, refuses to accept the notion that there is no space or end of liberation in criticism, or that a discipline such as literary criticism necessarily creates a kind of subjugation as it studies phenomena. As he puts it, "Criticism must think of itself as life-enhancing and constitutively opposed to every form of tyranny, domination, and abuse; its social goals are *noncoercive knowledge produced in the interests of human freedom*" (*World* 29, my emphasis). These certainly are reassuring sentiments, but for Foucault reassurance is precisely the problem here: Said's "belief in noncoercive human community" (*World* 247) is a claim for the self-evidence of the critical project and ultimately a justification that cannot be examined or questioned, just as the ideological justifications for the political powers Said would wish to demystify ultimately protect themselves from examination. Likewise, it seems that the most traditional critic could see his or her project in Said's formulation: "noncoercive knowledge" seems precisely a translation of "disinterested knowledge," and as such serves to protect the institutional interests of criticism all the more strongly.[15] For Foucault, there is no simple liberation through knowledge; for him, "Knowledge is not made for understanding; it is made for cutting" ("Nietzsche, Genealogy, History" 88). The "knowledge" produced by the human sciences cannot move away from its origins as and in a kind of violence, and literary criticism (in both its institutional

15. See Bové's insightful discussion of Said and Foucault in chapter 5 of *Intellectuals in Power*, in which he writes: "My objection . . . to Said's position is that it leaves this regime [the regime of truth] unchanged insofar as it validates the traditional role played by the leading intellectual who, above all, will not call into question his or her own interests in exploiting the ability to imagine and promote 'alternatives' continually in order to maintain or achieve authority and identity in society" (234).

and its systematic functions) is implicated in the movement of liberation through the subjugation of knowing: a discipline makes a new object to be studied out of the liberation itself, thereby reasserting reason's control. Liberation is confronted at its end by the smiling figure of Hegel, who has been there all along.

Of course, this line of reasoning is not terribly persuasive to Said, who finds "a disturbing circularity" in "Foucault's theory of power" (*World* 246). As an example of Foucault's evasive circularity, Said cites a debate between Noam Chomsky and Foucault concerning their willingness to support a hypothetical "oppressed proletariat if as a class it made justice the goal of its struggle" (246). Chomsky answers with a resounding yes, and outlines a two-pronged task for political criticism: "to imagine a future society that conforms to the exigencies of human nature as best we understand them . . . [and] to analyze the nature of power and oppression in our present societies." Foucault's response to the question, however, is not quite so positive; he has little trouble with the second of Chomsky's tasks, but hesitates to embrace quite so enthusiastically concepts such as "human nature" and "justice." He responds, "The idea of justice in itself is an idea which in effect has been invented and put to work in different societies as an instrument of a certain political and economic power or as a weapon against that power" (246). For Foucault, concepts like "justice" and "human nature" are more often than not used to *oppress* and *control* marginal groups, and certainly much of his work in *Discipline and Punish* would bear that conclusion out. Because of that fact, a revolution merely in the name of these metaphysical concepts cannot be depended upon quite so blithely to produce a revolutionary society. Chances are it will reproduce the orders that it seeks to overturn. Foucault states this quite succinctly elsewhere: "I think that to imagine another system is to extend our participation in the present system" (*Counter-Memory* 230).

For Said, this hyperskepticism is the unsurpassable weakness and ultimate tautology of Foucault's thought. Said writes, about the upshot of the Foucault/Chomsky debate: "This is a perfect instance of Foucault's unwillingness to take seriously his own ideas about resistances to power. . . . Resistance cannot equally be an adversarial alternative to power and a dependent function of it, except in some metaphysical, ultimately trivial sense. Even if the distinction is hard to draw, there is a distinction to be made" (*World* 246).[16] Here Said argues that if disparate or even contradictory instances of power have a common origin, it necessarily follows that all cultural struggle is reduced to "some metaphysical, ultimately trivial" level. If the power of liberation has a common origin with or in the power of oppression, then, in Thomas McCarthy's words, "Power becomes all too like the night in which all cows are black" (*Ideals and Illusions* 54).[17] Unable to make crucial distinctions, robbed of a methodology, and unable to imagine a better future, a Foucauldian discourse is (according to its detractors) thereby necessarily reduced to silence and stagnation.

Still, it seems fairly clear that Foucault is neither stagnant nor silent. The absence of a determinate methodology in his work and his denial of liberation within a discourse—so frustrating and ultimately paralyzing to some—have certainly not curtailed his production of important studies that have had wide-ranging consequences for many disciplines: studies of the madhouse, the prison, the clinic, sexuality. But, one might profitably ask, why does Foucault produce studies if they do not lead to the Enlightenment goals of heightened understanding or liberating knowledge? Why go on? He discusses his "projects":

> The analyses I intend to undertake fall into two groups. On the one hand, the "critical" group which sets the reversal-principle to work. I shall attempt to distinguish forms of exclusion, limitation and appropriation. . . . I shall try to show how they are formed, in answer to which needs, how they are modified and displaced, which constraints they have effectively exercised, to what extent they have been worked on. On the other hand, the "genealogical"

16. Cf. Merod's *Political Responsibility of the Critic*, on this very debate: "Chomsky stresses 'the normal creativity of everyday life' which prompts the emergence of language, culture, and both individual and societal practices that cannot be thought of as regulatory or repressive in any systematic way, but rather as life-giving and constructive, genuinely experimental" (168). Foucault would be rather suspicious of the claim that there is nothing "repressive" about "everyday life"—not to mention his suspicion of the metaphysics buried in Chomsky's concept of the "normal" and the idea of individualist "creativity."

17. McCarthy's cows, it seems, do a lot of traveling at night; as he writes, "Derrida's deconstructionism" likewise leads us "into the night in which all cows are black" ("Politics of the Ineffable" 156). I discuss McCarthy in greater detail in the conclusion.

group, which brings the other three principles [chance, discontinuity, and materiality] into play: how series of discourse are
formed, through, in spite of, or with the aid of these systems of
constraint: what were the specific forms for each, and what were
their conditions of appearance, growth, and variation. (*Discourse
on Language* 231–32/61–62)

Foucault's answer is necessarily double and entails thinking necessarily both inside and outside a system that is to be interrogated.
For Foucault, like Derrida, analysis begins with an indispensable
"critical" or polemical phase of reversal, a phase that attempts "to
distinguish forms of exclusion, limitation and appropriation." But,
and this is the crucial point (as it is with Derrida), Foucault's *analysis
does not stop here* with an overturning; if it did, it could not truly
escape Hegel, but would rather be doomed to repeat the exclusions
it uncovered. The overturning or uncovering itself must be examined, but in a manner that brings a sort of indeterminacy to bear on
the overturning, on its emergence among various possibilities,
chances, and discontinuities. Contra many of his critics, Foucault
certainly does recognize a kind of "progress" in or through disciplines and the human sciences,[18] but it is necessarily a progress that
leads to other (admittedly, often more humane or palatable) forms
of exclusion and subjugation, *not* to a space of unproblematic, reassuring freedom. The progress of knowledge is itself a Hegelian
ruse. For Foucault, it is only if one takes into account a certain
exteriority in the conditions of emergence for a discourse—thereby
refusing an alternative, determinate ground or higher knowledge—
that one has the chance of denying Hegel his otherwise predetermined victory. In short, one must refuse to play the game of knowledge on Hegel's terms.

This is perhaps the major point of conflict between Foucault and
Derrida: Derrida, rather than refusing to play on Hegel's terms,

---

18. Cf. Rorty's critique in "Foucault/Dewey/Nietzsche," in which he writes: "We liberals
in the USA wish that Foucault could have managed, just once, what . . . he always resisted:
'some positive evaluation of the liberal state.' . . . You would never guess, from Foucault's
account of the changes in European social institutions during the last three hundred years,
that during that period suffering had decreased considerably, nor that people's chances of
choosing their own styles of life increased considerably" (3). I think we should be very
suspicious of this notion of progress as increasing lifestyle choices for Western "liberals."

attempts to beat Hegel at his own game. He tries to disrupt transcendental/dialectical philosophy by theorizing *its* conditions of possibility—which must, he argues, be impure or partially nontranscendental. Thus a Derridean reading of how his ideas have been appropriated by literary criticism could be as follows: transcendental or critical discourse will, to be sure, expel the otherness within it—the dialectic will totalize, will bring becoming into being—but an otherness will still remain. He writes:

> There is no choosing here: each time a discourse *contra* the transcendental is held, a matrix—the (con)striction itself—constrains the discourse to place the nontranscendental, the outside of the transcendental field, the excluded, in a structuring position. The matrix in question constitutes the excluded as transcendental of the transcendental, as imitation transcendental, transcendental contra-band. The contra-band is *not yet* dialectical contradiction. To be sure, the contra-band necessarily becomes that, but its not-yet is not-yet the teleological anticipation, which results in it never becoming dialectical contradiction. The contra-band *remains* something other than what, necessarily, it is to become.
>
> Such would be the (nondialectical) law of the (dialectical) stricture, of the bond, of the ligature, of the garrote, of the *desmos* in general when it comes to clench tightly in order to make be. Lock of the dialectical. (*Glas* 244a)

Derrida offers a logic of his own appropriation that is at once very similar to Foucault's and at the same time radically different. Derrida's text can explain its interiorization in terms of the violence of dialectical thinking, that is, in terms of the violence of the dialectical stricture "when it comes to clench tightly in order to make be"; in terms of the need within dialectical thinking (which is also critical thinking) for definition and synthesis; and in terms of critical thinking's necessary interiorizing of an outside in order to cover up the structuring (literally *transcendental*) position of an outside within that thinking. Derrida attempts to disrupt this movement of making be by thinking the "transcendental of the transcendental," the structuring principle that the transcendental itself cannot think—if it is to do the work of a traditional transcendental.

And here Derrida and Foucault most radically part company. For Foucault, Derrida's "transcendentalist" emphasis is simply unacceptable, too prone to become a new orthodoxy. For all the similar effects and attributes of a Foucauldian network of statements and Derridean general text, the overriding difference is that "for statements it is not a condition of possibility but a law of coexistence" (*Archaeology of Knowledge* 116/153).[19] For Foucault, Derrida's involvement with a transcendental vocabulary allows the possibility that a transcendental space of interiority "can be purified in the problematic of a trace, which, prior to all speech, is the opening of inscription and the difference of deferred time [*écart du temps différé*]; it is always the historico-transcendental theme that is reinvested" (*Archaeology of Knowledge* 121/159, translation modified). Such a potential for reification, according to Foucault, plays into the hands of institutional, status-quo thinking. But it seems that, in the wake of Hegel, these are the risks of thinking itself—the risks of thinking or speaking at all.[20] Foucault's disruptive materialist discourse is no less difficult to take up for institutional use than Derrida's disruptive transcendental discourse. And Derrida, for his part, is acutely aware of the institutionalization of undecidability or unreadability as a method in American literary criticism; Derrida writes his essay in *Deconstruction and Criticism* with this caveat concerning Blanchot's *L'Arrêt de mort:*

> The readability of unreadability is as improbable as an *arrêt de mort.* No law of (normal) reading can guarantee its *legitimacy.* By normal reading I mean every reading that insures knowledge transmittable in its own language, in a language, in a school or academy, knowledge constructed and insured in institutional constructions, in accordance with *laws* made so as to resist (precisely because they are weaker) the ambiguous threats with which the *arrêt de mort* troubles so many conceptual oppositions, boundaries, borders. The *arrêt de mort* brings about the *arrêt* of the law. ("Living On— Border Lines" 171)

19. See Dreyfus and Rabinow, who make much of this distinction in their *Michel Foucault*, 52–58.
20. Cf. Derrida's "Principle of Reason," 17–20.

This *arrêt*, this interruption, this gap, this falling out of (the dialectical movement of) work, lives on and remains un-institutionalizable, untranslatable, impossible to legitimize, precisely because it disrupts the laws by which it could be institutionalized, defined, or legitimated. Even after its seeming sublation, for Derrida the *arrêt* remains.

And perhaps it is here that Derrida and Foucault can be thought together again. They both attempt to bring about and attend to a certain absence of work, an *arrêt*, a break, a fissure, a discontinuity of/at/on/in the otherwise smooth, confident flow of dialectical thinking. Whether this break is located at a transcendental or at an emergent level seems, to me anyway, not as important as the insistence on the break or hesitation itself, the moment of exteriority that poses a very difficult question for critical thinking—including literary critical thinking: can this hesitation, this otherness, be attended to "critically," that is thematically or in a revelatory discourse, in a discourse that attempts to uncover a determinate truth? Or does it require thinking differently? Perhaps Foucault puts the question most succinctly—the question that both he and Derrida, in different ways, pose to the critics:

> There are times in life when the question of knowing if one can think differently than one thinks, and perceive differently than one sees, is absolutely necessary if one is to go on looking and reflecting at all. . . . [W]hat is philosophy today—philosophical activity, I mean—if it is not the critical work that thought brings to bear on itself? In what does it consist, if not in the endeavor to know how and to what extent it might be possible to think differently, instead of legitimating what is already known? (*Use of Pleasure* 8–9)

But how, one might ask, does one think differently, especially if one cannot simply escape a certain thinking of the same? What exactly does "postmodern" mean in the context of this questioning? How can it be thematized? What do the necessarily "double" analyses of the postmodern look like, and what do they accomplish? And (at long last) how does this thinking differently pertain specifically to literature?

Perhaps we also need to ask why such questions become pressing at a particular historical space or time we call postmodern. Why, in other words, do these questions and problems arise "now"? Perhaps, as much postmodern discourse suggests, we are indeed at the end of something—the end of the subject, the end of art, the end of history—but what does or can "end" mean in this displaced postmodern context? In the following chapters, I will attempt to take up these topics—to perform, for lack of another word, "positive" analyses of postmodern thought and literature.

4 / Theorizing the Postmodern: At the End of Metaphysics

> Criticism, if it is called upon to enter into explication and
> exchange with literary writing, some day will not have to
> wait for this resistance first to be organized into a "philos-
> ophy" which would govern some methodology of aesthet-
> ics whose principles criticism would receive. . . . But this
> enterprise is hopeless if one muses on the fact that literary
> criticism has already been determined, knowingly or not,
> voluntarily or not, as the philosophy of literature.
>
> —JACQUES DERRIDA
> *Writing and Difference*

Theorizing the postmodern has become a full-time profession
for a cross-disciplinary army of thinkers. Generally speaking, defining the postmodern is a vexing problem that has led to widely vary-
ing critical positions on the matter; however, the one thing that
various postmodernisms and postmodernists seem to have in common is their assertion that there is no stable, knowable, transcendental ground of "truth." From there, agreement ends, though at
the risk of being reductive, I venture to say that thematizations of
the postmodern among literary critics tend to fall into two camps:
those who define postmodernism as a *stylistic* or *systematic* phenomenon and those who define it as a *historical* phenomenon. Both kinds
of definition have proven problematic. If postmodernism is a stylistic
phenomenon (defined by a system of features such as playfulness,
open-endedness, discontinuity, self-conscious reflection on the production of literature, excess, reader participation, etc.),[1] then why

1. See, for example, Lodge, *Modes of Modern Writing*, which discusses "the formal principles underlying postmodernist writing" (228–45), among them contradiction, permuta-

isn't, for example, *Tristram Shandy* postmodern? *Tale of a Tub?* Chaucer? Ovid? Why not Milton, for that matter?[2] Defining the postmodern as a stylistic phenomenon tends to rob it of any historical significance or specificity. In fact, at its strongest, this notion tends to reduce the complex play of the history of literature to the transhistorical battle of postmodernism and its other by turning postmodernism into a kind of *Geist* that animates the whole of literary history.[3]

Historical characterizations of postmodernism seem to offer an escape from the totalizing or generalizing problems inherent in a more descriptive or systematic theory, but such characterizations often end up trapped in a kind of historical determinism that is a version of the transcendental truth postmodernism wants to question. If postmodernism is primarily a paralogistic reaction to a monologic modernism,[4] or is inexorably brought about by determining societal factors (such as the emergence of "late capitalism"),[5] then how can it escape having its truth given by a kind of lock-step, determining Hegelian historicism, in which the truth of postmodernism is secured and guaranteed through the work of dialectical opposition and sublation?

The vexing problem—made all the more difficult both by the complexity of the issue and the sheer volume of critical material on the subject—becomes, then, where to situate oneself in this impasse between system and history. Rather than take sides in this complex argument, I would like to step back and investigate the terms of the opposition itself. In general, my question is, what is the status or

tion, discontinuity, randomness, excess. See also Hassan's *Postmodern Turn*, 91–92, in which he offers a conveniently dialectical list of the features of modernism and postmodernism.

2. For just such a treatment of Milton—and an impressive one at that—see Rapaport's *Milton and the Postmodern*. I find his reading of Milton compelling, but I wonder whether it doesn't fall into the de Manian problematic I discuss in Chapter 2, in which all literature becomes fodder for a method or discipline. Rapaport writes (or admits?) that in composing the book he "was interested in attempting to use Milton as a test case for a poststructuralist reading" (xiii).

3. This is especially true in the work of Hassan; in *The Postmodern Turn* he writes, "There is enhancement of life in certain anarchies of the spirit, in humor and play, in love released and freedom of the imagination to overreach itself, in a cosmic consciousness of variousness as of unity. I recognize these as the values intended by Postmodern art, and see the latter as closer, not only in time, but even more in tenor, to the transformation of hope itself" (45).

4. See Lyotard's *Postmodern Condition*.

5. See Jameson's "Postmodernism, or The Cultural Logic of Late Capitalism."

force of the opposition between history and system in a postmodern context? To anticipate a bit, I contend that an engagement between the postmodern and literary criticism must go "through" the discourse of philosophy; specifically, it must go "through" the "problem" of philosophy's closure or end because, as Derrida notes, "literary criticism has already been determined, knowingly or not, voluntarily or not, as the philosophy of literature" (*Writing and Difference* 28). Any criticism presupposes a theory, and literary theory is first and foremost a philosophy of literature. Because literary criticism and theory are bound to philosophy, it seems necessary to examine or reevaluate criticism and theory in (to use an incredibly ironic term) the "light" of philosophy's closure. Such an examination is, it seems, doubly pressing in relation to the postmodern, insofar as the closure of philosophy and the concomitant withdrawal of a stable ground for critical thinking are precisely what give rise to the question of the postmodern. But rather than try to construct a historical or systematic narrative leading up to postmodernism's withdrawal of truth, I will attempt briefly to outline the genealogy of this withdrawal—to trace a path back to this "event."

One need look no further than Nietzsche. With his (in)famous "God is dead," a Madman announces the withdrawal of transcendental ground with a kind of terrifying simplicity. One is tempted to say that this announcement, and the *ethos* that surrounds it, ushers in the era of "ends" that is so familiar to the postmodern: the end of metaphysics, the end of religion, the end of history. Although this proclamation certainly does not *instigate* or *cause* these various "ends"—the Madman's remark, remember, is already directed at "those who did not believe in God" (*Gay Science* 181)—one could argue that it certainly does name or mark the "logic" of these ends: metaphysics, religion, and history terminate with the death of God precisely because each of them, whether they are conceived of as disciplines, belief systems, or both, had lived on the promise of meaning in an end or telos; each organized itself around the guarantee of meaning beyond or beside the physical realm, a guarantee inscribed in the very word *meta*physics. So, if metaphysics is first philosophy, the discipline or belief system that can secure the ground for all others, it is clearly terminated if first principles are deemed to be "dead": arbitrary, fictional, merely invented, impossible to ground as transcendental. One can certainly recuperate these principles or mourn their loss. What else characterized the literary period known as "modernism," and what else continues to animate many critiques of the postmodern?[6] After the death of God, it is no longer possible simply to assert the self-evidence of ground. A stable ground must be *recuperated* or argued, which attests to the impact of what Nietzsche's thought names: thinking can no longer be self-grounded in reason, subjectivity, method, history, God. As Schürmann writes, with the "death" of God, "The schema of reference to an *arche* then reveals itself to be the product of a certain type of thinking, of an ensemble of philosophical rules that have their genesis, their period of glory, and that today perhaps are experiencing their decline" (*Heidegger on Being and Acting* 5). When reason has to ground itself as reason—when this category can no longer be taken for granted or a ground for it secured—a certain kind of thinking begins to draw to a close: when speculation must ask about the value of speculation (as when Warhol's Brillo box poses the question, "Why is this not art?"),[7] a category—indeed, an entire system of thinking through which one constructs categories and defines the world—begins to draw to a close. But, as Schürmann reminds us, this closure is not simply a matter for thought, but rather systematic and historical: "This hypothesis functions doubly (even though the opposition between system and history will eventually fall victim to that same hypothesis): it is a *systematic* closure, inasmuch as the norms for action 'proceed from' the corresponding first philosophies; and it is a *historical* closure, since deconstructionist discourse can arise only from the boundary of the era over which it is exercised" (*Heidegger on Being and Acting* 4). At the closure, then, thinking runs up against a systematic and historical limit within itself: when metaphysical thinking shows itself to be "historical," when thinking as reference to stable ground can be thematized as a *kind or type* of thinking rather than as thinking itself, it also runs up against certain debilitating "systematic" consequences. In other words, the *historical*

---

6. The dominant critique of postmodernism, in whatever form, is that it does not attend to such a metaphysical or historical "real." See, for example, Graff, who writes that the upshot of Derrida's work—and postmodernism in general—is "the absence of any reality or meaning in life to which effort might be directed" (*Literature against Itself* 62).

7. Cf. Charles Bernstein's discussion of Arthur Danto's reading of Warhol in *A Poetics* (170–74).

closure of metaphysics is itself systematic, and vice versa: the cause-and-effect categories by which one could name the prior or proper origin are rendered problematic by the inability to secure a ground outside the closure by which it could be judged in a summary fashion, or upon which a narrative historical account of it could be rendered. The peculiar and pernicious problem in all this, however, is that the notion of ground and the concepts of philosophical thinking cannot simply be abandoned. As Philippe Lacoue-Labarthe puts it, "We are still living on philosophical ground and we cannot just go and live somewhere else" (*Heidegger, Art, and Politics* 3).

Metaphysical thinking, then, finds itself at an impasse at the closure, the death of God, the loss of a stable ground—an impasse we have already begun to examine in terms of the nihilist reversals to which it inevitably leads. Truth shows itself to be a lie; critical thinking can neither be affirmed nor denied; anti-professionalism shows itself to be professionalism; and so on. In the face of this impasse, the recuperation of a kind of metaphysical ground is certainly possible (at least discursively); however, such a recuperation is not necessarily desirable in a postmodern epoch because, from its "end," metaphysical thinking also shows itself to have been grounded in a kind of violent exclusion that must efface its other and eliminate difference to preserve its purity. So, in the nihilist reversals that signal the closure of metaphysical thinking, we see a kind of cruel joke played out: nihilism, rather than helping to displace the privilege of the same, protects it all the more greedily, bringing, with its reversals, literally more of the same. From its "end," then, as Heidegger notes, the history of this thinking shows itself—in the triumph of will to power and the age of technology—to be precisely the history of this nihilism: nihilism as metaphysics' final and most glorious moment in the control and elimination of its other. And, in the most chilling of reversals, the legacy of this thinking reveals itself (often brutally) in twentieth-century history. Lacoue-Labarthe summarizes the legacy left to our age of technology: "There is a kind of 'lethal' essence of technology, which means that its 'everything is possible' does in fact end up introducing, that is to say *bringing about*, if not the impossible, then at least the unthinkable (Extermination or genetic manipulation—and the latter is still on the agenda today)" (*Heidegger, Art, and Politics* 69). The "unthinkable"

former, extermination, has indeed been brought about—in the holocaust; and Lacoue-Labarthe argues that the holocaust is "a phenomenon which follows *essentially* no logic (political, economic, social,
military, etc.) other than a spiritual [metaphysical] one, degraded
as it may be, and therefore a historical one. In the Auschwitz apocalypse, it was nothing less than the West, in its essence, that revealed
itself" (35).[8]

For Lacoue-Labarthe the holocaust is both a horrifyingly "logical"
extension of metaphysical logic and an absolutely unique event (an
event that shatters any possibility of "explanation," any attempt to
account for it within a larger, ultimately reassuring narrative).[9] In
fact, Lacoue-Labarthe argues that the holocaust cannot be explained
in terms of any narrative that makes the Jews remotely "sacrificial"—
as having died to bring about some greater revelation; even "holocaust" is the wrong word: it "was a pure and simple *elimination.*
Without trace or residue. And if it is true that the age is that of the
accomplishment of nihilism, then it is at Auschwitz that that accomplishment took place in its purest formless form. God in fact died
at Auschwitz" (*Heidegger, Art, and Politics* 37). For Lacoue-Labarthe,
the completion of metaphysics in the death of God can be "read"
in the holocaust: a wholly bankrupt way of thinking and acting burns
itself up in attempting to exterminate its other, but leaves no possibility for a Phoenix-type rising from the ashes. The "formless form"
of the holocaust is nonetheless quite concrete; it is an irreducible

---

8. To many critics of the postmodern, this seems an outrageous claim. For example,
Huyssen writes, "Auschwitz, after all, did *not* result from too much enlightened reason—
even though it was organized as a perfectly rationalized death factory—but from a violent anti-
enlightenment and anti-modernity effect, which *exploited modernity ruthlessly for its own
purposes*" (*After the Great Divide* 203, last two emphases mine). For Huyssen (citing Habermas), the Enlightenment, as the strictly benign or progressive movement of reason, is
"exploited" by the evil of Nazism in the holocaust; this formulation, of course, allows
reason to emerge safe, having banished terror once more by explaining it away. It seems
astonishing, however, that reason can emerge unscathed from the "perfectly *rationalized*
death factory" that was Auschwitz. Huyssen is forced to refer to a pure, benign intention
to salvage reason here, and in the process ironically offers what he accuses the postmoderns
of supplying, "too limited an account of modernity" (203).

9. Insofar as the holocaust can be spoken of as a "unique event," this does not imply
that it is somehow more horrific than the Stalinist purges or the Cambodian genocide—
that the violence against the Jews was so much more violent that it remains unique. Rather,
the status of genocide as an "event" suggests that no comparison is possible, no simple
accounting can be rendered that would allow us to say that one genocide was "worse" or
"better" than another.

event in that it cannot be reassuringly reduced to a logic that can be said to have brought it about. It remains simply too horrific to be adequately explained or—in a philosophical phrase with a chilling body-count resonance—"accounted for." I do not mean by this that there are no historical and systematic reasons or precedents for the holocaust; a long historical tradition of anti-Semitism and its theoretical defenses certainly cannot be simply ignored. Nevertheless, the holocaust remains an event that a rationalist history cannot explain within its own logic, insofar as that logic is itself implicated in the event.[10] As Lacoue-Labarthe writes, "And this event, we must admit, is historical in the strongest sense, i.e. in the sense that it does not simply arise from history, but itself makes history, cuts into history and opens up another history, or else unmakes all history" (*Heidegger, Art, and Politics* 5). As an irreducible "event," the holocaust shatters any possibility of accounting for it in what is traditionally called historical terms. Rather, this event "opens up another history, or else unmakes all history"; this event, in unmaking history and the systematic thinking upon which it depends, perhaps opens up another history, the history of that which or those who would disrupt the purity of meaning upon which history depends. As Derrida writes, "The very concept of history has lived only upon the possibility of meaning, upon the past, present, or promised presence of meaning and of truth. Outside this system, it is impossible to resort to the concept of history without reinscribing it elsewhere, according to some specific systematic strategy" (*Dissemination* 184). Given the realization of the exclusionary violence of a will-to-wholeness, the postmodern project can be neither properly "historical" nor "systematic." It perhaps becomes a matter, as Derrida suggests here, of constructing a logic that "works" without

10. Lacoue-Labarthe gives two reasons for the essential irreducibility of the "event" of the holocaust's genocide: First, Jews posed no threat to the Nazis, had no revolutionary social cohesion, "were not in 1933 agents of social dissension (except of course in phantasy)" (36). Second, the means used in the slaughter of the Jews were not of an essentially police or punitive nature. Although police tactics were indispensable in rounding the Jews up, there were no confessions to be forced or guilt to be feigned. "None of the 'machines' invented to extract confessions or remorse or to mount the edifying spectacle of terror, was of any use. The Jews were treated in the same way as industrial waste of the proliferation of parasites is 'treated.' . . . As Kafka had long since understood, the 'final solution' consisted in taking literally the centuries-old metaphors of insult and contempt—*vermin, filth*—and providing oneself with the technological means for such an effective literalization" (36–37).

working in the Hegelian sense of coming to an *Aufhebung* of whole-ness. Rather, it becomes a matter of reinscribing "the possibility of meaning" as other than "the past, present, or promised presence of meaning and of truth." This reinscription is, I have suggested, a *necessary* project at the closure of metaphysics, insofar as ignoring this closure leads inexorably to nihilistic impasses. Traditional think-ing, then, must always fail to "work" because it cannot account for a founding moment of otherness, and it is this "moment" that must be taken into account "according to some specific strategy" that is not merely a reinscription of a transcategorial or transhistorical sys-tem. As Foucault phrases the problematic, "We must elaborate—outside philosophies of time and subject—a theory of discontinuous systematisation" (*Discourse on Language* 231/60).

Derrida and the Postmodern

Despite the problems we have raised concerning the concept of history, despite the furor raised by many of his critics over his lack of attention to history,[11] it seems to me that Derrida is careful to *historicize* his thought precisely in order to avoid its being taken as a transcategorial and transhistorical system. He historicizes it as postmodern and situates it at the historico/systematic closure of metaphysics. He does this—often quite subtly—in virtually all of his texts. Take, for example, the passage from *Writing and Difference* I quoted earlier, this time with a different emphasis: "*If totalization no longer has any meaning,* it is not because the infiniteness of a field cannot be covered by a finite glance or a finite discourse, but because the nature of the field . . . excludes totalization" (289). Note, here, the first part of the sentence, in which Derrida addresses some issues that he is often criticized for neglecting: first, totalization has had meaning, was possible to think given certain societal and historical circumstances, which no longer exist at the closure of metaphysics. Also, totalization may still have meaning (he writes "*if* totalization no longer has any meaning"), but any meaning it has is radically

11. For such a criticism of Derrida as ahistorical, see Said's readings in *The World, the Text, and the Critic*, especially chapter 9.

altered by a contemporary—dare I say "postmodern"—notion of the conditions of possibility (and impossibility) for any kind of totalization. Derrida sets out to historicize—and we have, I hope, managed to complicate this word—his thought most overtly in "No Apocalypse, Not Now," his essay on nuclear society, on living after the holocaust under the shadow of the bomb. He writes of the (im)possibility of nuclear holocaust:

> The hypothesis of this total destruction watches over deconstruction, it guides its footsteps; it becomes possible to recognize, in the light, so to speak, of that hypothesis, of that fantasy, or phantasm, the characteristic structures and historicity of the discourses, strategies, texts, or institutions to be deconstructed. *That is why deconstruction, at least what is being advanced today in its name, belongs to the nuclear age. And to the age of literature.* (27, my emphasis)

The possibility of apocalypse without revelation is what makes it possible for deconstruction to take notice of both systematic and historical accounts of the contemporary situation. It allows deconstruction to account for "the characteristic *structures and historicity* of the discourses, strategies, texts, or institutions to be deconstructed." How so? Derrida writes, "As you know, Apocalypse means Revelation, of Truth, *Un-veiling*" ("No Apocalypse, Not Now" 24); but, of course, at the closure or end of metaphysics, there is no determinate "revelation" of truth, but only its withdrawal—not truth but impasse. Again, the "structure" of metaphysics shows itself to have a (debilitating) historicity. Likewise, the historical situation of nuclear society is infused by the structure of a nuclear logic of apocalypse with no revelation—the impossible possibility of a horrifying telos without an accompanying revelation of the meaning of history. Given these historical and systematic conditions, the stakes of a writing, the stakes of truth, the stakes of living at the closure, in a nuclear logic, are irreducibly *different:* these stakes are not reducible to a thinking of the *same,* to a thinking based on the assumption of wholeness in a beginning or an end, to a thought based on revelation of truth or meaning, to a thinking that can confidently answer the metaphysical question "What is it?"

But what are we to make of Derrida's claim for this apocalyptic age as the age of literature, and his claim that deconstruction belongs to this age? There is certainly a temptation to gloss this comment as an example of Derrida's reduction of philosophy (the literal) to literature (the figural): deconstruction shows us the figural basis of any literal truth claim, and hence ushers in the age of literature, when everything can be read literarily. I try to complicate such a reading of Derrida in Chapter 2 with respect to the question of metaphor, but Derrida's concept of "literature" likewise does not allow itself to be so easily taken up. As Gasché puts it, "If it were possible to draw one major proposition from Derrida's statements on literature, it would certainly not be that everything is literature, but on the contrary that 'there is no—or hardly any, ever so little— literature' " (*Tain of the Mirror* 256, quoting *Dissemination* 223). Gasché rather forcefully shows that Derrida is certainly *not* attempting to reduce everything to literature; however, having said that, we are still left with the problem of understanding Derrida's inverse—and seemingly perverse—claim that there is a radical scarcity of literature, even in this, the "age of literature." Gasché glosses Derrida's comment as follows: "With the exception of certain rare examples, literary writing has subjugated itself to the constraints of the concept and to the ethos of philosophy. . . . There has hardly ever been any literature, if literature is supposed to mean something other than philosophy" (256). According to Derrida's notion of literature's scarcity, there is "ever so little" literature because what we call literature has existed, at least since the Greeks thematized it as mimesis, merely within the horizion of philosophy; literature has, for the most part, moved solely within philosophy's apocalyptic structure of revelation.[12]

In Derrida's sense, however, literature is that ever-so-small body of texts that is in some way enabled by the relation between thought and this postmodern notion of apocalypse without revelation and end without summary. And deconstruction belongs to this age, adopts its peculiar kind of postmodern apocalyptic tone, the tone

12. Cf. Derrida's summary of the onto-theological notion of apocalypse: "Truth itself is the end, the destination, and that truth unveils itself is the advent of the end. Truth is the end and the instance of the last judgment. The structure of the truth here would be apocalyptic. And that is why there would not be any truth of the apocalypse that is not the truth of the truth" ("Of an Apocalyptic Tone" 24).

that recognizes, in Derrida's words, "the apocalyptic structure of language, of writing, of the experience of presence, in other words of the text or of the mark in general: *that is, of the divisible dispatch for which there is no self-presentation nor assured destination*" ("Of an Apocalyptic Tone" 28). Thinking has, up until the nuclear age of its closure, proceeded for the most part under the impression that it could reveal truth, that it could totalize, that it could assure its destination. Even the skeptical tradition works under the auspices of revealing the truth that there is no knowable truth. The postmodern epoch, however, is conditioned by this apocalyptic structure "of the text or of the mark in general," a structure that frustrates the arrival of truth, the structure of what Derrida elsewhere calls "general text."

This notion of the general text is the most criticized and misunderstood component of Derrida's thought. It is often read as Derrida's attempt to turn the world into a text, and in the process effectively to diffuse the real, historical problems of political and social existence by treating them as mere textual conundrums.[13] Such is, as I argue in Chapters 2 and 3, simply not the case. For Derrida, general text is *not* the text, the book, but rather a realm of mediation, something of a phenomenological life-world, the "given" network or chain that makes discourse—in the broad sense of the word as a place where things are mediated—possible but at the same time makes it impossible for this discourse to arrive at any ontologically determinable destination, any merely singular telos. With his notion of general text, Derrida works out the consequences of "the apocalyptic structure of language," in which nothing outside the differential network, the general text, can guarantee meaning or arrest the chain of referrals. There is, in this sense, no extra-text, no term that can rule, organize, or regulate the system from without the

13. This is a very popular misconception, and one that came to a head in the pages of *Critical Inquiry* in 1986. Derrida was taken to task for stepping out of his hermetically sealed textual world to write about apartheid. He replied: "*Text*, as I use the word, is not the book. No more than writing or trace, it is not limited to the *paper* which you cover with your graphism. It is precisely for strategic reasons . . . that I found it necessary to recast the context of text by generalizing it almost without any limit. . . . That is why there is nothing 'beyond the text.' That's why South Africa and *apartheid* are, like you and me, part of this general text, which is not to say that it can be read the way one reads a book. That's why the text is always a field of forces: heterogeneous, differential, open, and so on. . . . That's why I do not go '*beyond* the text,' in this *new* sense of the word text, by fighting and calling for a fight against *apartheid*" ("But, beyond . . ." 167–68).

system, precisely because the supposed master term must constitute itself *within* this network of referrals by referring always to something other than itself.[14] There is no simple outside or beyond the closure.

It is crucial here to note that general text is, despite the flood of claims to the contrary, a historical formulation. "There is no extra-text," the infamous phrase by which Derrida supposedly kills history, *is itself an irreducibly historical formulation*, situated at the historical site of the closure. In other words, Derrida's is a postmodern thought, conditioned by a world that lives after Auschwitz, after Hiroshima, always under the shadow of an apocalypse without revelation. In fact, for Derrida, the postmodern world is conditioned not so much by living, but by "LIVING ON, the very progression that belongs, without belonging, to the progression of life and death. Living on is not the opposite of living, just as it is not identical with living. The relationship is different, different from being identical, from the difference of distinctions—undecided" ("Living On—Border Lines" 135). Here we see most clearly the "worldly" aspect of Derrida's thought; it is concerned not simply with texts and their internal workings, but it grows out of a *postmodern* consciousness: a consciousness of being a survivor, a consciousness of living on rather than simply living or dying, of living on in the undecided— of not closing off possibility (difference) merely for the sake of actuality (sameness). Living on in the postmodern is living beyond (which is to say *between*, as there is no simple beyond) the oppositions or hierarchies that have allowed and validated the horrors of the twentieth century.[15]

Living on in the between, in the undecided, at the limits, disrupting the will to sameness or truth (as mentioned, disrupting the metaphysical question "What is it?"), is "characteristic" of writing the postmodern. As Julia Kristeva writes:

Postmodernism is that literature which writes itself with the more or less conscious intention of expanding the signifiable and thus

14. For the latest instance of Derrida discussing—or should I say defending?—general text, see his afterword to *Limited Inc.* (136–37, 148).

15. As McKenna writes, "The question of the postmodern in its most far-reaching implications, which are nonetheless the most concrete, is the question of survival, of living on after the dead. A postmodern consciousness is indissociable, for demonstrable, concrete reasons bearing on the recent past as they affect the possibility of a future, from the consciousness of being a survivor, of living on" ("Postmodernism" 229).

human realm. With this in mind, I should call this practice of writing an "experience of limits," to use Georges Bataille's formulation: limits of language as a communicative system, limits of the subjective and naturally the sexual identity, limits of sociality. ... Never before in the history of humanity has this exploration of the limits of meaning taken place in such an unprotected manner, and by this I mean without religious, mystical, or any other justification. ("Postmodernism?" 137, 141)

This questioning of the will-to-truth through an examination of the limits of truth is "characteristic" of postmodern writing and reading, in which this interruptive questioning is done, as Kristeva notes, in an unprecedented, "unprotected manner," without a traditional ontological justification. Here, however, we should be careful of a kind of privileging historicism slipping in the back door. There are, of course, earlier writers who deal with the "problem" of end without revelation (Cervantes, Mallarmé, Joyce, Sterne, Kafka, Woolf, Chaucer) as well as contemporary writers (even writers referred to as "postmodern")[16] who do not. But this postmodern questioning of limits, including the notion of general text, which Derrida explicitly ties to the question of limits, is, in a certain way, impossible to think outside a "postmodern" culture. I do not mean by this that certain structures of remark and supplementarity cannot be found at work in texts written previous to the nuclear age, but rather that it is nuclear logic that allows us to think these structures, to read their "work," and its suppression, in a tradition.[17]

16. Take, for example, the group of American poets known as "the postmoderns"—a broad term used to refer to the Beats, the San Francisco Renaissance, the Projectivists, the New York School, and the Confessional poets—whose aesthetics are summed up by Altieri: "Postmodern poets have been seeking to uncover the ways man and nature are unified, so that value can be seen as the result of immanent processes in which man is as much object as he is agent of creativity" ("From Symbolist Thought to Immanence" 608). The revelation of meaning is taken here "directly from experience, in fact from the fundamental experiences of human life like eating and making love, and does not require a mediating mythology" (635).

17. As Derrida writes concerning the seemingly ignored, disruptive work of writing in a tradition, "It is a peculiarity of our epoch that, at the moment when the phoneticization of writing—the historical origin and structural possibility of philosophy as of science, the condition of the *epistémè*—begins to lay hold on world culture, science, in its advancements, can no longer be satisfied with it. *This inadequation had always already begun to make its presence felt. But today something lets it appear as such,* allows it a kind of takeover without our being able to translate this novelty into clear-cut notions of mutation, explication, accumulation, revolution, or tradition. These values belong no doubt to the system whose dislocation is

This reevaluation of the stakes of the assignment of limits and this quasi-ethical imperative to expand the realm of the signifiable—which grows, according to Kristeva, out of an experience of limits brought about by undecidability of the postmodern writing/reading of texts—is finally, I think, where deconstruction can be put into a relation with writing that we would call literary, that is if this distinction between thinking and writing even holds at this point in the discussion. The undecidability or unthematizability of texts—brought about by the societal and textual structure of the postmodern field in which they exist—represents, in a certain way, the limits from which discourse becomes possible in a postmodern context. These limits have dire consequences for the totalizing impulse of the discourse of literary criticism, based as it is on the discourse of philosophy. As Gasché explains it, "If, *in the last resort*, the unthematizable because undecidable agencies of modern literary texts—agencies that are not of the order of image or concept, content or form, but that are textual structures—radically subvert the possibility of literary hermeneutics, it is because they represent the limits from which understanding and knowing become possible" (*Tain of the Mirror* 267). It is in the exploration of these limits from which understanding and knowing become possible in a postmodern context that I see a possible relation between deconstruction and postmodern literary texts. Here "postmodern" names a *situation* rather than a text or a reading; in fact, it names the specificity of the hesitation or negotiation between text (in all its complex Derridean associations) and reading at the space of metaphysical closure, where both the possibility and the ends of reading and writing are radically unsure. Still, I will continue to use the word "postmodern" to refer to contemporary literary writing that explores these limits and possibilities of writing and thinking the postmodern situation. However, I must stress again that it is highly problematic to "define" this writing in terms of its features or historicity; the disruptions or transgressions of postmodern literary texts are necessarily *written* or performed as part and parcel of the reading and writing process, or else they fall back into such a descriptive category or theory.

---

today presented as such, they described the styles of an historical movement which was meaningful—like the concept of history itself—only within a logocentric epoch" (*Of Grammatology* 4, my emphasis).

It is here, at or from the place called the closure of metaphysics, that a relation between deconstruction and literature, as, crudely, a postmodern thinking and a postmodern writing, could begin to be thought, and it is around this set of concerns that I examine the postmodern in subsequent chapters. To find, however, some kind of specificity for these notions of postmodern thinking and writing requires discussing the "problem" of representation in postmodern literature. I call representation in postmodern writing a "problem" because any disruptions it would perform or bring about must, in some way, go "through" representation—must be represented— even as representation experiences its closure.

Representation and Postmodernism

Writing about representation and postmodern literature is difficult from the very beginning. There is a certain way in which I can write about nothing *but* representation, because a structure governed by a privilege of representation is what makes it possible for me to say anything at all. Foucault thematizes this difficulty:

> The human sciences, when dealing with what is representation (in either conscious or unconscious form), *find themselves treating as their object what is in fact their condition of possibility.* They are always animated, therefore, by a sort of transcendental mobility. . . . They proceed from that which is given to representation to that which renders representation possible, but which is still representation. (*Order of Things* 364, my emphasis)

There is, then, no way I can place my two concerns in a simple relation and discuss one vis-à-vis the other. An essay accurately titled "The Problems of Representation in Postmodern Literature" cannot be written because there is no "place" outside representation from which to speak about it or about whatever "postmodern literature" might turn out to be. Simply to assume such an outside "place" would be to treat as the object of my discourse that which, in fact, constitutes the very conditions of possibility for discourse in general: a representative metaphysical structure characteristic of the epoch of modern subjectivity that sets up parameters for what can be said and the ways in which it can be said. The only way to begin speaking about this system, then, is from within. The only way to deconstruct the system is by thinking its ground—*its* conditions of possibility—carefully and problematically. These parameters do not constitute a prime directive, but rather a recognition of what Derrida calls "a necessary dependency of all destructive discourses: they must inhabit the structures they demolish" (*Writing and Difference* 194).

Discussions of representation, then, are rendered highly problematic by their "necessary dependency" on the structure of representation itself. Much discussion of postmodern thought and literature revolves around what theorists perceive to be postmodernism's critique and/or outright rejection of representation. Many such readings presuppose, in fact, that postmodern texts are in a rather simple oppositional relation with representation, i.e. postmodernism *against* representation.[18] It seems to me that the question is much more complicated than that. As Derrida writes in his essay "Sending: On Representation":

> Today there is a great deal of thought against representation. In a more or less articulated or rigorous way, this judgment is easily arrived at: representation is bad. And this without being able to assign, in the final analysis, the place and necessity of that evaluation. . . . And yet, whatever the strength and the obscurity of this dominant current, the authority of representation constrains us, imposing itself on our thought through a whole dense, enigmatic, and heavily stratified history. It programs us and precedes us and warns us too severely for us to make a mere object of it, a representation, an object of representation confronting us, before us like a theme. It is even difficult to pose a systematic and his-

---

18. See, for example, Rorty's *Philosophy and the Mirror of Nature:* "Wittgenstein, Heidegger, and Dewey are in agreement that the notion of knowledge as accurate representation, made possible by special mental processes, and intelligible through a general theory of representation, needs to be abandoned" (6). Cf. *After the Great Divide*, in which Huyssen characterizes postmodernism as a brand of decadent modernism "confident in its rejection of representation and reality" (209). For an excellent discussion of representation and postmodernism, see Arac's introduction to *Postmodernism and Politics,* in which he addresses the reception of Derrida's work in the United States, especially the mistaken notion that his work is essentially epistemological and that it is characterized by a "rejection of representation" (xxiv). I must also credit Arac for drawing my attention to the opening quotation from Foucault.

torical question on the topic (a question of the type: "What is the system and history of representation?") now that our concepts of system and history are essentially marked by the structure and the closure of representation. (304)

If we take our cue from Derrida, in order to discuss representation in a postmodern context, we need first to work out "the place and necessity" of representation "now that our concepts of system and history are essentially marked by the structure and the closure of representation." To paraphrase, we need to think about what it might mean to come to the limits of the structure of representation (the limits of modern subjectivity). Approaching the place or space of this "end," we begin to recognize aporias, gaps, fissures at its limits, while still inhabiting a discursive world made possible by the traces of this structure. In tracing this movement, I draw on Heidegger's reading of the rise of representational thinking in modern philosophy and Derrida's reading of this concept's "fall" in postmodern thought. This fall brings about the closure of representation and in some sense makes possible an investigation of modern philosophy's ground, as it affects both philosophy and literature after subjectivity. In broaching the question of the literary, I will pay particular attention to Ronald Sukenick's *Endless Short Story*.

Already there are any number of problems, not the least of which is keeping this analysis from simply replicating the dialectical movement of critique, which is the mainspring of representation. Likewise, we need here to confront the slippage created by employing the sense of the words "modern" and "postmodern" across two different disciplines in which they carry different significations: in short, "modernism" in literary studies designates a movement among early twentieth-century artists, a literary period running from the beginning of the century to the second world war, whereas "modernism" in philosophy designates the philosophies of the subject, a period in the history of Western philosophy running from Descartes to Hegel. These two senses of the word "modern" have little in common, and there is little to be gained from drawing a conception of postmodernism out of a relation between them. I want to suggest here, however, that postmodernism in literature and the arts must confront postmodernism in philosophy; in other words, the postmodern in any disciplinary or periodized form must confront the "problem" of thinking after representation.

But, having said that, I discover that I have created more problems than I have solved: the disciplinary periodizing (modern/postmodern) and genre distinctions (literature/philosophy) that my argument takes for granted are rendered problematic by the closure of representation. Hence, my argument has both to trace the closure of representation and to recognize that the analysis itself is subject to this very closure and the slippage it engenders. Thinking/Writing the postmodern must account, in some way, for its own status as an other discourse—a discourse both inside and outside the problematics of representation. As Derrida puts it:

> This other discourse doubtless takes into account the conditions of . . . classical and binary logic, but it no longer depends entirely upon it. If the proponents of binary opposition think that the "ideal purity" to which they are obliged to appeal reveals itself to be "illusory," . . . then they are obliged to account for this fact. They must transform concepts, construct a different "logic," a different "general theory," perhaps even a discourse that, more powerful than this logic, will be able to account for it and reinscribe its possibility. (*Limited Inc.* 117)

It is this different logic that thinking/writing the postmodern calls for—a double logic that can think representation, end, and ground along a different way, a way that Heidegger and Derrida call, among other names, sending.

In his essay "The Age of the World Picture,"[19] Heidegger ties the rise of representational thinking to the rise of modern philosophy and its notion of the subject or Cartesian *cogito*. For Heidegger, thinking in this subjectivist mode literally becomes re-presenting: everything that presents itself must be referred or re-presented to the normativity of the human subject. He writes, "To re-present

19. The original title, "Die Zeit des Weltbildes," has been translated as "The Age of the World View." "World Picture" seems better than "World View" for at least two reasons: first, *Bild* is clearly "picture," not "view"; and, second, "world view" confuses this analysis of the rise of the subject with Heidegger's much earlier analysis of *Weltanschauung* philosophy in the introduction to *Basic Problems of Phenomenology*. Throughout, I will render *Bild* as "picture."

here [in the modern period] means to bring what is present before one [*Vorhandene*] as something confronting oneself, to relate it to oneself, the person representing it, and to force it back into this relation to oneself as the normative area" (351/84). This notion of re-presenting is impossible without modern philosophy's notion of the subject as that which must filter all things confronting it through its subjectivity, in turn forming the basis or ground for "this relation to oneself as the normative area."[20] For Heidegger, this privilege of the subject leads to a humanistic notion of the world as a totalizing subjectivist world picture with "man" as the absolute mean or measure for all things; in the epoch of re-presentational thinking, "man fights for the position in which he can be that existent which sets the standard for all existence and forms the directive for it" ("Age of the World Picture" 353/87).

But what happens to this ground of subjectivist re-presentation when "man," as that which would serve as the measure for all other things and the ground for all determinations, shows itself to be a problematic category—to paraphrase Foucault, a modern invention that is fast approaching its end?[21] When "man" approaches its end, the time of philosophical modernism—and its dominant modes of thinking—also approaches an end. And this end carries with it the end of an absolute privilege of re-presentation as well as the end of metaphysics, because, as Heidegger notes in "The End of Philosophy and the Task of Thinking," "Metaphysics thinks beings as being in the manner of representational thinking" (374/62). But here the analysis moves much too quickly, without asking what it might mean to come to the end of philosophy, or the end of metaphysics, or the end of representation. In Heidegger, this notion of end cannot be read in the traditional, metaphysical manner as a simple limit. He

20. Cf. Derrida's reading of Heidegger's notion here: "It is only the rendering available of the human subject that makes representation happen, and this rendering available is exactly that which constitutes the subject as subject. *The subject is what can or believes it can offer itself representations, disposing them and disposing of them*" ("Sending" 309, my emphasis).

21. Of course, representation itself plays a large role in this "death of man"; as Foucault notes, because "man" cannot be both that which represents and that which is represented, it must withdraw as a category. Cf. Derrida's "Sending": "The subject is no longer defined only in its essence as the place and the placing of its representations; it is also, as a subject and in its structure as *subjectum*, itself apprehended *as a representative*. Man, determined first and above all as a subject, as being-subject, finds himself interpreted throughout according to the structure of representation" (314).

writes, "We understand the end of something all too easily in the negative sense as a mere stopping, as the lack of continuation, perhaps even as decline and impotence" ("End of Philosophy" 374/62). For Heidegger, we cannot—without overtly and simplistically playing the game of metaphysics—understand the end of representative thinking (the end of philosophy) as a simple limit that stifles progress. Such thinking is still metaphysical and representational. But, and perhaps more important, neither can we thematize this end as the precondition to a simple breakthrough to where the ground of metaphysical thinking will no longer be problematic. The question of ground(s) is and will be crucial for (postmodern) thinking after subjectivity. The "end" of philosophy is not that "place" where the question of grounds can be abandoned and the tradition simply left behind or overcome. That is thinking "end as a simple limit or boundary." Heidegger sees the end of metaphysics as that place where these questions become most crucial, most problematic, and perhaps most enabling. He writes, "The end of philosophy is the place, that place in which the whole of philosophy's history is gathered in its most extreme possibility" (375/63). This characterization of end as radical possibility rather than simple limit calls for a rethinking of the tradition and the question of grounds.

There is, then, the task of *rethinking* modern philosophy's conception of representation rather than simply thematizing representation as "bad" and/or thinking that we can simply move beyond it; we must try to think its possibility as a condition of possibility. One could, in fact, argue that the crisis of postmodern politics and ethics rests in this problem of representation: how do we represent the other in institutions, or how do we rethink notions of normativity or legitimation without recourse to the subject or representation? We know that the modernist philosophical schema of representation cannot simply be criticized and replaced with another, equally problematic interpretative metatheory, for that would be to fall back into the metaphysical trap of representational, subjectivist, dialectical thinking. As Derrida puts it:

> We might say in another language that a criticism or a deconstruction of representation would remain feeble, vain, and irrelevant if it were to lead to some rehabilitation of immediacy, of original

simplicity, of presence without repetition or delegation, if it were to induce a criticism of calculable objectivity, of criticism, of science, of technique, or of political representation. The worst regressions can put themselves at the service of this antirepresentational prejudice. ("Sending" 311)

For Derrida, it is fruitless to "criticize" representation in any traditional way, because such a notion of "criticism" presupposes a displacement of representation and its replacement by another system on the way to a more objective or scientific understanding of truth.[22] A criticism based on an "antirepresentational prejudice" remains naive and, essentially, representational. If it attempts to recuperate another, simply nonrepresentational ground for interpretation, if it simply pushes representation to the margins and moves another notion to the center, it ends up simply recuperating a representational, metaphysical world view or hermeneutic in the name of an antirepresentational thinking.

Perhaps what we must do in a postmodern epoch is to think differently, to think the conditions of possibility for thinking and acting in a different way, to ask questions other than "how do we criticize this position or overcome this opposition"? As Derrida writes, all this "is difficult to conceive, as it is difficult to conceive anything at all beyond representation, but [it] commits us perhaps to thinking altogether differently" ("Sending" 326). Nevertheless, the question remains: how can we conceive of a relation to this ground, these conditions of possibility, that might make possible a "thinking altogether differently"?

In "Sending: On Representation," Derrida develops Heidegger's notion of the "sending" of being as a possible postmodern relation to philosophy's status as a ground for thinking, as a condition of possibility. Heidegger refines his notion of sending in the late lecture series "On Time and Being," in which he writes:

22. This is not, as many critics would have it, to say that deconstruction is an inherently status-quo thinking that merely stands impotent before oppositions or simply neutralizes them. As I argue throughout, criticism as the overturning or neutralizing of oppositions is a crucial part of deconstruction, but it does not constitute the "end" of a deconstructive analysis.

In the beginning of Western thinking, Being is thought, but not as the "It gives" [*Es gibt*] as such. The latter withdraws in favor of the gift which It gives. That gift is thought and conceptualized from then on exclusively as Being with regard to beings. *A giving which gives only its gift, but in the giving holds itself back and withdraws, such a giving we call a sending [das Schicken].* According to the meaning of giving which is to be thought in this way, Being—that which It gives—is what is sent. Each of its transformations remains destined [*geschickt*] in this manner. . . . *[T]o giving as sending there belongs keeping back—such that the denial of the present and the withholding of the present play within the giving of what has been and what will be.* (8,22/8,23; my emphasis)

For Heidegger, this peculiar sort of ground-as-sending both gives or sends itself (offers conditions of possibility) and holds itself back (withdraws). It is not a traditional, metaphysical notion of ground in that it does not offer the gift of presence in its sending; ground's withdrawal as it simultaneously offers conditions of possibility makes simple notions of presence impossible to uphold. In other words, if "to giving as sending there belongs keeping back," this necessitates taking into account the play of presence and absence—meaning and nonmeaning—within any supposed constitution of a pure state.

This notion of simultaneous withdrawing and offering from a shifting ground—which he names *Ereignis*—allows Heidegger to thematize the epochs of Being in an other-than-positivistic way. He writes, "To hold back is, in Greek, *epoche*. Hence we speak of epochs of the destiny of Being [*Epochen des Seinsgeschickes*]. Epoch does not here mean a span of time in occurrence, but rather the fundamental characteristic of sending, the actual holding-back of itself in favor of the discernibility of the gift" (9/9). For Derrida, Heidegger's notion of sending is a place to begin to think a postmodern (post-subjectivist) ground, a *quasi*-transcendental ground that is no longer a traditional, simply transcendental or immanent ground, but that nonetheless continues to function as that which gives a peculiar kind of universality through offering conditions of possibility. Gasché explains this notion:

The quasitranscendentals upon which philosophy's universality is grounded are no longer simply transcendentals, for they represent neither a priori structures of the subjective cognition of objects nor the structures of understanding of Being by the *Dasein*. The quasitranscendentals are, on the contrary, conditions of possibility and impossibility concerning the very conceptual difference between subject and object and even between *Dasein* and Being. (*Tain of the Mirror* 317)[23]

For Derrida, there is a certain sort of quasi-transcendentality in Heidegger's notion of sending—especially in ground's simultaneously giving and taking away conditions of possibility ("conditions of possibility and impossibility"), but Derrida maintains that Heidegger's notion remains haunted by the specter of teleological thinking in that sending is *destined [geschickt]* from ground to thinking in various epochs of Being.[24] Also, it seems suspect to Derrida that there could be a pure gift of time or Being, a giving prior to a system(aticity) that always already makes pure giving—giving without some kind of reciprocation, giving (from) without a system, "the actual holding back of itself in favor of the discernibility of the gift"—impossible.[25]

Given Derrida's reading, Heidegger's epochs of Being are destined or given from the ground of Being to arrive at certain points in the history of Being. To bolster this reading, Derrida turns to "The Age of the World Picture" and Heidegger's discussion of the vast difference between the Greeks' notion of truth as unconcealment or *aletheia* and the modern conception of truth as representation. Heidegger concludes that "in Greece the world cannot become a picture"; but he hastens to add that "the fact that for Plato the existent is determined as *eidos* (appearance, view) is the presupposition, coming far in advance [*die weit voraus geschickte*] and for a long time acting secretly and indirectly, for the eventual transformation of the world to a picture" (351/84). Derrida quickly picks up on this notion, arguing that such Heideggerian sendings and transformations are

23. Cf. Derrida, *Limited Inc.*, 127–29.
24. Cf. Heidegger's "On Time and Being": "What is historical in the history of Being is determined by what is sent forth in destining, *not by an indeterminately thought up occurrence [Das Geschichtliche der Geschichte des Seins bestimmt sich aus Geschickhaften eines Schickens*, nicht aus einem unbestimmt gemeinten Geschehen]" (8–9/8–9, my emphasis).
25. See Derrida, *Glas*, 242–44a.

"fated, predestined, *geschickte*, that is to say, literally sent, dispensed, assigned by a fate as a summary of history" ("Sending" 311). For Derrida, such a notion of sending presupposes that ground was, is, or could be present to itself, able to give the gift of presence but unwilling to do so, that, instead, it works "secretly and indirectly" to shape the history of being.

But, Derrida asks, what if this ground is always already divided, never present to itself, discontinuous, unable to gather itself and unable to send to a specific destination, unable to secure *the* narrative history of being?

> Wherever this being-together or with itself of the *envoi* of being divides itself, defies the *legein*, frustrates the destination of the *envoi*, is not the whole schema of Heidegger's reading challenged in principle, deconstructed from a historical point of view? If there has been representation, it is perhaps just because the *envoi* of being was originally menaced in its being-together, in its *Geschick*, by divisibility or dissension (what I would call dissemination). ("Sending" 322–23)

This quasi-transcendental ground that Derrida posits—a ground that itself is subject to dissemination and trace—calls for a different kind of thinking of ground: a ground "older" than any philosophical distinction, but one that in no way offers a pure origin or beginning point to validate the traditional work of these distinctions; a ground that could not assure the arrival of a sending, could not determine "positive," inexorable circumstances and thereby a ground that could not function metaphysically. Rather, in Derrida's notion of sending as *envoi*,

> The *envoi* is as it were pre-ontological, because it does not gather itself together or because it gathers itself only in dividing itself, in differentiating itself, because it is not original or originally a sending-from (the *envoi* of something-that-is or of a present which would precede it, still less of a subject, or of an object by and for a subject), because it is not single and does not begin with itself although nothing precedes it; and it issues forth only in already sending back; it issues forth only on the basis of the other, the other in itself without itself. Everything begins by referring back,

that is to say, does not begin . . . from the very start, every *renvoi*,
there is not a single *renvoi* but from then on, always, a multiplicity
of *renvois*, so many different traces referring back to other traces
and to traces of others. (324)

Such a notion of ground as discontinuous and never present to
itself—a radically plural ground which issues forth only by issuing
back to "itself"—necessitates that the *envoi* be at the same time "a
multiplicity of *renvois*," an unsheltered origin that cannot master
that which it engenders. This ground, which respects the unthematizability of the other and moves through the *entre* of *difference*
rather than the binary oppositions of *sameness*, may be a way to
conceive of the thinking differently about representation that the
postmodern calls for.

But perhaps Derrida has all-too-hastily denied Heidegger's *Ereignis* such a status as a withdrawing, postmodern ground. Derrida
often calls attention to Heidegger's claim that the essence of important terms in his thinking (technology, representation, *Ereignis*)
does not belong to those terms: so the essence of technology is
nothing technological,[26] the essence of representation is not a representation ("Sending" 314), and *Ereignis* (which makes the history
of Being as sending possible) is itself unhistorical. About this move
in the Heideggerian text, Derrida writes, "It is in any case by a
gesture of this type that Heidegger interrupts or disqualifies, in
different domains, specular reiteration or infinite regress [*renvoi à
l'infini*]" ("Sending" 314). Derrida argues that when Heidegger removes the "essence" of his terms from the field(s) they engender,
he shelters this grounding function—precisely protecting ground
from the play of the network and from the potential slippage of
dissemination and thereby guaranteeing the arrival of Being's sending. For Derrida, Heidegger's withdrawal of ground serves primarily
to protect ground's purity more rigorously.

Derrida's reading, though, can be complicated considerably by
closely examining Heidegger's notion of the "grounding" function
of *Ereignis*. In "On Time and Being," for example, Heidegger insists
that *Ereignis*, not Being, is the matter for thinking—that "Being,

26. On this point, see the brief exchange between Derrida and Geoff Bennington in
Derrida's "On Reading Heidegger," 175–76.

which lies in sending, is no longer what is to be thought explicitly."
He continues: "Thinking then stands in and before that which has
sent the various forms of epochal Being. This, however, what sends
as *Ereignis*, is itself unhistorical [*ungeschichtlich*], or more precisely
without destiny [*geschicklos*]. . . . With the entry into *Ereignis*, its own
way of concealment proper to it also arrives. *Ereignis* [appropriation]
is itself *Enteignis* [expropriation]" (41/44). Here we see Heidegger
performing the very move that Derrida thematizes as protective:
Heidegger seemingly removes *Ereignis* from the history of being that
it renders possible, thereby mystifying *Ereignis* by attempting to seal
it hermetically, beyond the reach of contamination. But what are we
to make of Heidegger's claim that the thinking of *Ereignis* "stands
in and before [*in und vor*] that which has sent the various forms of
epochal Being"? It would seem that *Ereignis* is already divided as a
ground, standing not simply before what it engenders (as an *a priori*
ground would) but both *in* and *before*—an already double(d) mark
at the origin. Also, Heidegger here refines the "unhistorical" essence
of *Ereignis* not as a transhistorical grounding function that fatalisti-
cally determines the field it makes possible, but as the ground of a
history that is itself without destiny—a *Geschick* that is, in and by
its "essence," *geschicklos*. Top this off with Heidegger's insistence
that the "concealment proper" to *Ereignis* is itself *Enteignis*—expropriation, dispersion, one could name it "dissemination"—and we
would seem to be a long way from the sheltered ground and the
assured sending and arrival of being that Derrida reads in Heidegger's texts. And, one could further ask, even if Derrida's deconstruction of Heidegger's grounding function is on the mark, what
is to be said about *différance*, which, it has been argued, is clearly
heterogeneous ("literally neither a word nor a concept" [*Margins of
Philosophy* 3]) to the field that it makes possible, and therefore precisely the sort of ground-beyond-question that Derrida accuses Heidegger of producing.[27] Derrida responds that *différance* is not an
essence or origin—that undecidability does not exist in general as a
sort of negative ground.[28] He argues that deconstruction is a situ-

27. See, for example, Boly's "Deconstruction as a General System": "*Différance* is a mys-
tified concept, an absolute, all-inclusive origin that is strategically, conveniently put beyond
analytical reach" (201).
28. See Derrida, "Différance," 26–27.

ation, not an essence.[29] The same argument, however, can be (and has been)[30] made in favor of Heidegger. And so on . . . in a sort of *renvoi à l'infini*.

I let citations stand in for arguments here not because, as Habermas would have it, postmodernists "[do] not belong to those philosophers who like to argue" (193),[31] but because an extended squabble over who is more "metaphysical" would ultimately prove unsatisfying and would remain (rather overtly) within the bounds of representation as critique. Rather, I step back and hesitate, pointing out that the critico-interpretative vertigo I outline here is part and parcel of the problem of thinking/writing the postmodern. The arrival of a message cannot be guaranteed. The economies of (mis)reading between and among Heidegger, Derrida, and their readers can be *accounted for* by the very "theory" under consideration here. This accounting for nonplenitude, nonarrival, and errancy in an other-than-negative way is part of the "project" of thinking/writing the postmodern. These texts are in-scribed within the network(s) they de-scribe, and must submit to its play.

Derrida likens the postmodern situation of nonarrival and dissemination to writing, receiving, thinking a postcard: "Its lack or excess of address prepares it to fall into all hands: a post card, an open letter in which the secret appears, but indecipherably. . . . What does a post card want to say to you? On what conditions is it possible?" ("17 November 1979," in *Post Card*). Derrida here poses the questions of end, sending, ground, and representation using the metaphor of a postcard: a representation (a "world picture," one might say) sent along its way with the distinct possibility of never reaching a specific destination, open to many readings along the way. Given its limited discursive space and the fact that unlike a letter its representations are open and inscribed directly on its surface, a postcard is also prone to many *mis*readings along the way, and this is what a think-

29. See Derrida, *Limited Inc.*, 115–17.

30. See Schürmann's *Heidegger on Being and Acting:* "In reading Heidegger from beginning to end . . . the practical implications of his thinking leap into view: the play of a flux of practice, without stabilization and presumably carried to the point of an incessant fluctuation in institutions, is an end in itself. The turn beyond metaphysics thus reveals the essence of praxis: exchange deprived of a principle" (18).

31. This charge is specifically leveled against Derrida. See his response to Habermas in a long footnote to *Limited Inc.*, 156–58, as well as my discussion of the debate in Chapter 2.

ing/writing of the postmodern attempts to account for: not only the possibility of plenitude, understanding, reading, but the simultaneous possibility, engendered by the same ground, by the same conditions of possibility, of nonplenitude, misunderstanding, misreading. And it is perhaps this ability to understand the problematics of the (non) arrival of the postcard that is the condition of possibility for postmodern writing and thinking; maybe it requires, as Derrida writes,

> Knowing how to play well with the *poste restante*. Knowing how not to be there and how to be strong for not being there right away. Knowing how not to deliver on command, how to wait and to make wait . . . to the point of dying without mastering anything of the final destination. The post is always *en reste*, and always *restante*. It always awaits the addressee [*destinataire*] who might always, *by chance*, not arrive. (*Post Card* 191/206)

Perhaps postmodern knowledge is "itself" this writing of the approach, the never-not-yet of the (im)possible (non)arrival of truth. A conception of end in this thinking differently about metaphysics and about literature—end as other than simple limit—allows us to thematize this approach without arrival of meaning, this *envoi*, as other than a lamentable situation. As Derrida writes, "This divisibility of the *envoi* has nothing negative about it, it is not a lack, it is altogether different from subject, from signifier" ("Sending" 324). We can thematize this *envoi* as a lamentable situation only from within an untenable metaphysical system that is experiencing its closure. And Derrida's *Post Card* not only thematizes but also enacts or performs this (im)possible (non)arrival of truth after the closure of representation: the text is written in short, cryptic, sometimes discontinuous sections that strain and finally crack traditional distinctions between letters and postcards, between philosophy and literature, between the discourse of truth and the discourse of fables.

But despite Derrida's insistence that a writing of the postcard shakes representation, it is important even—perhaps especially— here to hesitate, to point out that the "metaphor" of thinking/writing the postcard, if taken solely stylistically, as a mere metaphor or as the "form" of the postmodern, risks the arrival of a new representation, a new world picture centered around the cryptic ambiguity and catchy slogans of a postcard. One need only think of the myriad discourses (advertising and architecture, for example) that locate their notion of the "postmodern" in the short, ambiguous juxtaposition of unrelated images to see that this has already happened and to reiterate the inadequacy of reading the postmodern as a sheerly stylistic phenomenon (what Lacoue-Labarthe has called the "rag-bag" school of postmodernism).[32] Such misreadings and misappropriations are, of course, inevitable in any period, but postmodernists, in attempting to account for these misreadings, can also become aware of the cultural logic of (mis)appropriation that fuels them, and, to paraphrase an unlikely source, can understand how bad things happen to good ideas, and thereby remain aware of the *risks* of thinking/writing the postmodern. As Derrida writes:

> "Thought" risks in its turn (but I believe this risk is unavoidable— it is the risk of the future itself) being reappropriated by socio-political forces that could find it in their own interest in certain situations. Such a "thought" indeed cannot be produced outside of certain historical, techno-economic, politico-institutional and linguistic conditions. A strategic analysis that is to be as vigilant as possible must thus with its eyes wide open attempt to ward off such reappropriations. ("Principle of Reason" 17)

This problem of reappropriation—often criticized as something postmodernists celebrate—brings us back to the necessity of the double move: the necessity of both philosophical thematization (a thinking) as well as a kind of literary reflexivity (a writing) that can disrupt the reappropriation of dialectical sublation; a double move that can attempt to disrupt the reappropriation of the postmodern as a commodity, as a programmatic institutional scheme—in short, as a representation.

All of this is not, of course, to say that deconstruction or Heidegger's thinking is not commodifiable; aside from the more obvious academic commodifications, one need only note Bob Mackie's Spring 1990 advertising campaign with Bloomingdale's ("A new cool of

32. Lacoue-Labarthe's remark is cited in Gasché's "Postmodernism and Rationality" (534).

thought. A new philosophy of style. Deconstruct. Lighten up. It's a little more free") and the "Applied Heidegger" movement[33] to see that there is indeed a rampant appropriation mind-set at work in what is perhaps too blithely called late-capitalist society; however, it seems hasty to indict Derrida and Heidegger as cheerleaders for these appropriations, or to accuse them of being blissfully ignorant of the dangers of such reappropriation.[34] For all of their vast philosophical, political, and institutional differences, both Derrida and Heidegger insist on the double necessity of working from within the institutional constraints of a tradition even while trying to expose what that tradition has ignored or forgotten; both testify, in short, to the necessity of a kind of double gesture.

In fact, Derrida's only real "criticism," if one can call it that, of Heidegger in "Sending" concerns Heidegger's refusal to recognize this dual focus or account for the other headings that the history of being *might* have taken. As Derrida writes about Heidegger's attempt to tell the story of being, "As soon as there are *renvois*, and that is always already, something like representation no longer waits and we must arrange to tell this story differently, from *renvois* of *renvois* to *renvois* of *renvois*, in a destiny which is never certain of gathering itself up, of identifying itself, or of determining itself" (325). This postmodern call "to tell this story differently," to tell a story that does not move toward a transcendental signified, allows us to bring the question of literature onto the scene, as a challenge to the philosophical, representational mode of story telling. Though this challenge comes inexorably from within the horizon of philosophy, it testifies, perhaps, to an other destination, a neglected history.

This other emphasis returns us, though we have taken a roundabout course, to the question of the place of literature in a postmodern situation. Perhaps literature, what we call the literary, has always, from before the beginning, been that which poses the great-

---

33. See Gottlieb's "Heidegger for Fun and Profit."

34. Derrida has devoted several essays to this topic; and Heidegger's remarks about the university, capitalism, and the "gigantic" in "The Age of the World Picture," as well as his (in)famous "Rector's Address," show him to have been very much aware of the issues surrounding institutionalization, even though he never managed adequately to account for, apologize for, or explain his own inscription within the dominant institutions of Nazi Germany. For more on this question, see Derrida's *Of Spirit*, Lacoue-Labarthe's *Heidegger, Art and Politics*, and the essays collected in Brainard's "Heidegger and the Political."

est danger to representation: it might be called the "post" that has always haunted the "modern,"[35] the (im)possibility of representation which has haunted representation. Perhaps now, from the place we call the closure of representation, we can read this threat that literature poses. Literature has existed throughout the modern, subjectivist period (one could argue throughout its entire history) only in, by, and for philosophy, only within the problematics of a revelation of its *truth*. Literature exists in the subjectivist period primarily insofar as it *represents experience* as the edifying truth embedded in the fiction of the fable. But what happens after Nietzsche, when the discourse of truth shows itself to be a fable? Literature comes to be that which can, in some sense, mark the break, the interruption, the insufficiency of truth as representation, and the necessity to tell the story differently. Hence a certain privilege of literature, of writing, in coming to grips with a postmodern logic; but, as Lacoue-Labarthe warns, "If writing has this privilege . . . it is not because we are finally delivered from the world, from presence (and from representation)—as one now hastens to add rather quickly—by simply inverting (or even not inverting at all) metaphysical oppositions. Rather it is because writing is, above all, this reflection of experience where reflection (and hence experience) constantly undoes itself" ("Fable" 55–56). Postmodern writing (postmodern literature, postmodern text) then becomes the place (the site, the space) where the logic of the *renvois* (the logic of a writing that cannot control its own destination) moves and shows itself— as *thinking/writing*, that "reflection of experience where reflection (and hence experience) constantly undoes itself." It is not, as Lacoue-Labarthe maintains, a matter of inverting strategies—of scrapping the subjectivist category of representation—but rather of constantly undoing, of rethinking representation, end, and ground in writing: thinking/writing the postcard. So the literary seems a privileged place to ask the question of thinking/writing the postmodern, provided, however, that literature can somehow twist free[36] from before the law of of representation, which would give literature its form,

---

35. I steal this phrase from a conversation with John Protevi.

36. I lift this phrase from John Sallis, who allows it to resonate as "the slightest twist, setting one from that moment adrift from the logic of opposition, adrift in a certain oblique opposition to logic" (*Delimitations* 160).

its signifying transparency, its end. Literature can, perhaps, attempt
to twist free from representation by becoming end-less, by rejecting
the transcendental signified, by remaining a story without ends.

A text such as Ronald Sukenick's *Endless Short Story*, perhaps. In
the penultimate section of *The Endless Short Story*, "The End of the
Endless Short Story, Continued," Sukenick asks the question of
writing the postmodern, of writing the end-less, of writing a ten-
uously addressed postcard from the closure of representation: "The
end of one time is always the beginning of another kind of time,"
he writes; "And who knows what the mailman may bring?" (130).
Sukenick plays on notions of time and end in his text; his is a
continuing rather than a simple end, an "End, continued," an end
that, like the postcard, may or may not arrive. In fact, the text's final
endless story is titled "Post Card," and is characterized as

> a post card from THE ENDLESS SHORT STORY, THE ENDLESS SHORT
> STORY has a secret ambition it wants to write the Great Amer
> ican Postcard. These are some of the requirements for The
> Great American Postcard it has to have a Great Character.
> It has to have an All Encompassing Plot. It has to be Signific
> ant and easy to read. It should be Serious but not so seri
> ous as to make us feel bad. (130)[37]

The traditional criteria for the form of a representative narrative are
satirized here by Sukenick as the "requirements for the Great American Postcard": a totalizing, logical plot; a serious, significant (but
not too depressing) theme; and simple, consumable readability. Sukenick's text possesses precious few of these "requirements": it is
discontinuous, playful, and unreadable—if reading means the consumption of "an All Encompassing Plot." The fractured "form" of
Sukenick's text also doubles or performs the fracturing "content":
the fracturing of the text makes the call for the Great American
Postcard "to be Signific / ant and easy to read" a difficult one to
fulfill. In fact, because the Great American Postcard is itself a sending
from the already disseminated ground of Sukenick's text—"a post

---

37. This quotation, as well as the ones that follow, contain Sukenick's original line breaks
and spelling.

card from THE ENDLESS SHORT STORY," a postcard within a postcard—
the distinctions of form and content (origin and end, context and
text, philosophy and literature) are themselves subject to a fracturing. The "end," the revelation of meaning, the transcendental signified that representation has always dreamed of, is literally deformed here by Sukenick: the form of language as representation is
literally broken or cracked on the page in Sukenick's attempt to write/
think in an other way.

But Sukenick is not simply gushing abstract thoughts onto the
page in random order, which would be a romantic, subjectivist project indeed. Rather, his text both enacts and thematizes (in a double
movement) the destructuring of the language and tradition of representation—the conditions of possibility given to postmodern literature. Sukenick writes of the tradition as

> alphabet soup dissolving in the thick warm broth of humanism
> fish food again. For as Captain Postcard knows the target
> is always poetry. And the bullet is poetry. And the gun is
> poetry. Every poem destroys the language a little. Blows a
> hunk off the stale intractable block of it. Blows it to bit
> s so the fish can eat again and multiply in their many surpr
> ising species shapes and hues only to fall prey to bigger f
> ish or to fish that are smaller but more numerous and one ho
> pes more lively like dull unwieldy epistolary novels that break
> down into constituent postcards while tragic Captain Postcar
> d sails off his moment past to meet his fate in the bland de
> pths of cliche. What you hear is the sound of fish nibbling
> alphabets. It's three generations later and all of this has
> happened already. (131)

For Sukenick, the literature of the past gives conditions of possibility
to a postmodern literature, which must work within the framework
of the past insofar as it must use the same language and acknowledge
its tradition as representation. But Sukenick is here literally rethinking the tradition of subjective representation from the space of its
closure "three generations later." In Sukenick's text, this tradition
is to undergo not only a critique but a destructuring: "the target /
is always poetry. And the bullet is poetry. And the gun is / poetry";
each postmodern text "destroys the language a little. Blows a / hunk

off the stale intractable block of it. Blows it to bit / s." Postmodern text destroys the language of the past to allow others to feed on its innovations and further open up the system to the possibility of thinking differently. The language of representation is the only language we have, so the forms we take from the past (the "dull unwieldy epistolary novels") must "break down into constituent postcards." The monolith of writing as representation must be broken down "so the fish can eat again and multiply," so artists can produce new forms. Indeed, the question of form here is crucial for Sukenick. His text both uses and disrupts forms of language as representation, but it does so without offering a ready-made form with which to replace representation. In this way, his text is both inside and outside representation: it gives way to an endless rewriting/rethinking of form—an approach of form—and broaches the possibility of thinking differently, thinking end-lessly, thinking as writing, thinking/writing the postmodern.

This different thinking, an *other* thinking rather than *another* thinking, likewise calls for a different practice of literary criticism. Sukenick concludes his text with two literary critics fishing for the meaning of the Great American Postcard—for the end of *The Endless Short Story:*

> Two fishermen with elaborate gear stand o
> ver a pool and talk about it. They haul out fish one after
> another club them pull out their guts. When they're done the
> y string them up on their car and take a snapshot. And ther
> e it is. The Great American Postcard. They stutter off in the
> clumsy model T of analysis bringing home food for though
> t. Dear ESS. Went fishing today but all I caught was a pos
> tcard and it wasn't Serious. Didn't have no plot. No charac
> (132)

Here Sukenick suggests a certain practice of literary criticism: haul out the fish—the new texts fed on the bits of language blown off by the gun of postmodern writing—and "club them pull out their guts" for a meaning, a representation, a world picture, a snapshot. Such a practice allows the critics to "stutter off in the / clumsy model T of analysis bringing home food for though / t," to bring the food for thought to the classroom as a dead fish brought home in a model T of paradigmatic analysis. But what they will have caught is the "Great American Postcard"—a sending that, in the end, cannot be "hooked."

Or can it? A question remains: what have *I* caught here today? Indeed, am I myself caught in the wide-angle lens that takes the fishermen/critics' snapshot, next to any number of dead fish: Sukenick, Derrida, Heidegger? Have they become mounted and stuffed above these pages; has representation been waiting here, quietly at the end of this discussion, to reimpose its order? Perhaps, as there is no absolute escape from representation, no clean place or language—no untouched fishin' hole. But there remains also at this end an *other* notion of end, a hesitation rather than a resolution, a challenge to the fishing licence issued by representation, a sending that remains unapprehended: "Went fishing today but all I caught was a pos / tcard and it wasn't Serious. Didn't have no plot. No charac." End of story; end of a certain kind of story. Perhaps more precisely, end of a certain kind of writing; end of a certain kind of thinking; end of a certain notion of end(s).

5 / *Gravity's Rainbow* and the Postmodern Other

Alas, who is there
we can make use of? Not angels, not men;
and already the knowing brutes are aware
that we don't feel very securely at home
within our interpreted world.

    —RAINER MARIA RILKE
    Duino Elegies

Maybe the target nowadays is not to discover what we are,
but to refuse what we are.

    —MICHEL FOUCAULT
    "The Subject and Power"

There's no real decision here, neither lines of power nor cooperation. Decisions are never really *made*—at best they manage to emerge, from a chaos of peeves, whims, hallucinations and all-around assholery. This is less a fighting team than nest full of snits, blues, crotchets, and grudges, not a rare or fabled bird in the lot. Its survival seems, after all, only a mutter of blind fortune groping through the heavy marbling skies one Titanic-Night at a time. Which is why Slothrop now observes his coalition with hopes for success and hopes for disaster about equally high (and no, that *doesn't* cancel out to apathy—it makes a loud dissonance that dovetails inside you sharp as knives).

    —THOMAS PYNCHON
    Gravity's Rainbow

At this point, an urgent question reemerges: how does one proceed after the "end" of a notion of ends? How does or can one read the postmodern? How does one read—let alone write about or "criticize"—a text that is perhaps the postmodern text par excellence, *Gravity's Rainbow*, an encyclopedic, end-less text whose difficulty and resistance to interpretation are legendary, even within the criticism that would want to interpret it? How does a critic or discipline respond to a text that resists the paradigms of criticism, that always seems to elude being mastered, that puts aside the possibility of a determinate decision concerning its meaning? As I have suggested, one way to deal with such an impasse is "simply" to re-thematize the work of criticism, to allegorize reading or critical work as the revelation of its own impossibility, which is, by the way, the route taken by a certain kind of rhetorical deconstructive criticism. I find it strange that this route is largely untraveled in Pynchon criticism, though almost all readings of *Gravity's Rainbow* contain a caveat about the difficulty, impossibility, or undesirability of totalizing the text.[1] In fact, for the majority of Pynchon scholars, the way into a reading of *Gravity's Rainbow* is precisely through this difficulty, through the text's status somewhere *between* meaning and nonmeaning: *Gravity's Rainbow* is consistently thematized in terms of its richness (its vast size, complex use of sources, and highly complex narrative constructions and obfuscations), a richness that in turn offers to criticism multiple—perhaps infinite—interpretations.[2]

Paradoxically, however, such a critical maneuver can end up treating discontinuity or unthematizability as a continuous theme, which, once uncovered, reveals that *Gravity's Rainbow* is not *really* unthematizable at all. Its rich ambiguity becomes, rather, its overarching theme, and the novel becomes an allegory for the ambiguity of the world and of art. In the secondary literature, *Gravity's Rainbow* is consistently read as a text that affirms a sort of romantic, humanist freedom among myriad possibilities for being; the richness of the

1. See, as a general caveat, Bernard Duyfhuizen's "Taking Stock," a review essay of twenty-six years of Pynchon criticism. Duyfhuizen writes that "all future critics of Pynchon must remember the lessons of the past: his complex texts resist reduction, and patterns of meaning rarely extend beyond momentary, and sometimes illusory, conditions of being" (88). See also "Deconstructing *Gravity's Rainbow*," the special edition of *Pynchon Notes* that Duyfhuizen edited in 1984.

2. There is, in fact, an entire genre of Pynchon criticism that takes this "encyclopedic" route; see, in addition to Mendelson's seminal "Gravity's Encyclopedia," Tölölyan's "War as Background in *Gravity's Rainbow*," Weisenburger's "*Gravity's Rainbow*" *Companion* and "End of History?" Cowart's *Thomas Pynchon*, and Moore's *Style of Connectedness*.

text figures the freedom of the reader within the plurality of the world. I cite, almost at random: David Seed writes that its myriad patterns "raise multiple possibilities of arriving at knowledge. At the same time, since there is a continuity between characters' efforts to know and the readers', Pynchon raises different possible ways of interpreting his own novel" (*Fictional Labyrinths* 209). James Earl writes that we as readers "are all shocked . . . into a higher consciousness that can finally lead us to a transcendental freedom" ("Freedom and Knowledge" 249). Thomas Schaub argues that Pynchon's "writing succeeds in binding people together. . . . [His] fiction reminds us of what a true society would mean" (*Pynchon* 151–52). Molly Hite writes that "*Gravity's Rainbow* is another mammoth project of loving the people, loving even their preterition in its scatological profusion, avoiding a univocal standard of judgment, avoiding hierarchy. . . . It is instead a novel that affirms the nonsystematic, nontotalizing connections of a community based on making meanings" (*Ideas of Order* 156). Thomas Moore argues that "the reader of *Gravity's Rainbow* must learn to see the quasi-magical, part-hallucinatory web of interconnections, variously familiar, obscure, farfetched and hitherto unthought-of, among all these images, signs and omens" (*Style of Connectedness* 28). Lawrence Wolfley writes that for Pynchon "nothing really matters but individual freedom" ("Repression's Rainbow" 121). Christopher Ames argues that the Counterforce releases linguistic "possibilities that give hope and life to those outside" ("Power and the Obscene Word" 206). Even Kathryn Hume's study of myth in *Gravity's Rainbow* has a pluralist/humanist bent: "To our monomyth-shaped minds, openness, kindness, acceptance of preterition, and responsiveness to the Other Side seem terribly evanescent and fragile, but Pynchon organizes them into a structured model, so we can consider his proposition for its validity as a whole" (*Pynchon's Mythography* 139–40). And so on.[3]

My question concerning *Gravity's Rainbow* and the critical project

3. McHoul and Wills's *Writing Pynchon* is, in fact, the only major book that *doesn't* put forth such a humanist reading, and in fact has much to say about this reading's inadequacy to the complexities of *Gravity's Rainbow* (see 1–13). See also Kuberski's "Gravity's Angel" on humanist criticism of *Gravity's Rainbow*. Since completing this writing, I have also come across Michael Bérubé's excellent *Marginal Forces/Cultural Centers*, which is a thoroughgoing and rigorous reading of the institutional politics of Pynchon's work and work on Pynchon.

surrounding it, however, is what happens when criticism encounters a text that, far from offering the critic many possible interpretations, *radically resists any thematized reading whatsoever?* If, as I argue in the preceding chapter, the postmodern signals the end of a certain notion of ends, then an end-oriented discipline (if that is not a redundant formulation) that encounters an end-less writing must, in some way, domesticate this writing, put it to work in the service of a determinate end. Phrased in another—perhaps more combative— way, my question is what happens if one takes quite seriously criticism's ubiquitous claims about the nontotalizing (or nontotalizable) nature of *Gravity's Rainbow?* If one is to take these claims seriously, it seems to follow that this work is characterized not by a plurality of possible interpretative meanings but rather by a strange inability to interpret its meaning(s) at all.

Such a conclusion must, of course, be worked out, but I hasten to stress that I do not mean that *Gravity's Rainbow* is, à la Paul de Man, *simply* unreadable or without meaning. To clarify what might seem an obvious and inescapable inconsistency (the problem of my own reading of what I have called an unreadable text), I must make two points about my conception of reading or thematizing the postmodern: (1) of course *Gravity's Rainbow* can be read and thematized. What else characterizes the readings cited above and makes possible my own reading of it? And, (2) this thematization is a necessary and unavoidable step within a double gesture. The pull toward determinate meaning comes with any use of language; however, I want to suggest here that there is something other than thematization that is not simply the opposite of thematization, that *Gravity's Rainbow* poses a ground-question to criticism's pull toward determinate meaning through its disruptions of any *simply* thematized reading, through its disruptions of any attempt to assign it a comforting, consumable readability. In short, I will argue that *Gravity's Rainbow* produces neither the plurality of interpretations that most Pynchon critics argue for *nor* the reassuring unreadability that de Man practiced, but rather a fracturing unreadability coupled with the imperative to read differently. In other words, it produces an unreadability that is not simply the opposite of readability, but one that calls into question the field of opposition wherein the unreadable is simply opposed to the readable. Its unreadability *"doesn't* cancel out to apathy—it makes a loud dissonance that dovetails inside you sharp as knives" (*Gravity's Rainbow* 676).

Pynchon and Pluralism

It is well documented that Pynchon's books overtly discuss the status of thinking the "between," the middle ground between the exclusionary poles of binary thinking. Many critical discussions of Pynchon use his overt thematizations of the question of the between—in the final pages of *The Crying of Lot 49* and in the Pointsman/Mexico debate in *Gravity's Rainbow*—to ground a pluralist reading.[4] Hite sums up this pluralist reading in "Included Middles," the first chapter of *Ideas of Order in the Novels of Thomas Pynchon*, as follows: "There is an infinite 'middle' region between the hyperbolic extremes of an absolute, externally imposed . . . order and total chaos. . . . Pynchon's novels themselves are 'middles,' and they demonstrate how much significance can be included within a plurality of limited, contingent, overlapping systems that coexist and form relations with one another without achieving abstract intellectual closure" (16, 21). For Hite (as for the rest of the critics cited), Pynchon deals thematically with excluded middles in order to include them. He thematizes the "bad shit" (*Crying of Lot 49* 137) of excluded middles in the service of a pluralistic community of interpretations. Yet if this is the case, Pynchon's text has been placed in the rather sticky situation of valorizing or offering a vision of what is presumably the "good shit" of inclusive pluralism in dialectical contradiction to the "bad shit" of excluded middles. Including the middle by hypostatizing it as an inhabitable place populated by competing relational systems precisely allows this "middle" to be located and sublated by a dialectic; it allows dialectical thinking to achieve "abstract closure." *Gravity's Rainbow* seems to take this into account: pluralist criticism's notion of the between as a place to write your own solutions, as a place to be "included," is precisely the reading of the between given by Pointsman, one of the text's arch-villains, as he lusts after the minds of Kevin Spectro's *tabula rasa* shell-shocked

---

4. See *The Crying of Lot 49*, 136–37, and *Gravity's Rainbow*, 48–55.

victims, who are "egoless for one pulse of the Between . . . tablet erased, new writing about to begin" (50).[5] The logic of pluralism remains a logic of metaphysics and humanism. This pluralist "humanism," however, is something of a misnomer, insofar as pluralism is characterized not so much by a concern for the otherness of others, but by an obsession with manipulation and ends, with determinate meaning and rhetoric, persuasion, *use*. And Pointsman realizes the potential political economy of those in the between; he longs "to use their innocence, to write on them new words of himself, his own brown Realpolitik dreams" (50).

Up to this point, I have been (at least surreptitiously) advancing the argument that literary criticism is a kind of "human science": I have argued that literary criticism is, in many ways, a quasi-scientific discourse interested in producing ever-more methodologies in the hopes of better controlling and understanding its object, literature—just as Pointsman dreams of producing ever-more methodologies in the hopes of better controlling his human subjects. This argument can be developed here, I think, by looking at the question of "pluralism" in and around the text of *Gravity's Rainbow*, a text that rather overtly concerns itself with science and its workings,[6] and a text that has been given a thoroughly pluralist reading by literary criticism. But we need to pause here to ask if it is really fair to say that a pluralist brand of literary criticism is just another sort of human science, a determining discourse that constrains its object in the process of studying it. Isn't pluralism, as its proponents would argue, precisely an incredulous response to the iron-fisted, totalizing metanarratives of the sciences, a call to recognize and foreground the constructed nature of any interpretative claim, and hence a call to acknowledge the potential plurality of such claims?[7] Pluralism in this sense would seem precisely to invalidate the monologizing claims of the sciences—human or otherwise—and hence could be seen to be the "postmodern" discourse par excellence. As Brian McHale argues in "Telling Postmodernist Stories":

> To escape the general postmodernist incredulity toward metanarratives it is only necessary that we regard our *own* metanarrative

5. Throughout, ellipses are Pynchon's, except where enclosed in brackets.
6. See Friedman's "Science and Technology."
7. See, for example, Fish's "What Makes an Interpretation Acceptable?"

incredulously, in a certain sense, profferring it tentatively or pro-
visionally, as no more (but no less) than a strategically useful and
satisfying fiction. . . . I am recommending, in other words, that we
need not abandon metanarratives—which may, after all, do useful
work for us—so long as we "turn them down" from metanarratives
to "little narratives." (551)

This passage is, I think, a concise formulation of the pluralist logic
that underlies much criticism of *Gravity's Rainbow:* the myriad sections and various worldviews represented in the novel are consistently read as what McHale calls "little narratives," multiple
worldviews that can be and need to be adapted to fit various circumstances. As I argue above, this logic of pluralism could be said
to inform the dominant reading of the work as a text that offers
multiple readings, and in so doing, figures the freedom of the reader
to engender his or her own provisional, un-transcendental narratives—narratives that will avoid the totalizing violence and hege-
mony of binary, scientistic metanarratives.

But, again, it seems that the text of *Gravity's Rainbow* problematizes
such a humanist/pluralist reading precisely by implicating it in the
movement of a kind of violent, hegemonic scientism. For example,
Pointsman sums up the worldview of the master, Pavlov, in the
following way: "Pavlov believed that the ideal, the end we all struggle toward in science, is the true mechanistic explanation. He was
realistic enough not to expect it in this lifetime. Or in several lifetimes
more. But his hope was for a long chain of better and better ap-
proximations" (89).[8] Pavlov's scientific method, it seems, follows the
logic of a humanist pluralism, in which the totalizing *ends* of inquiry,
the "true mechanistic explanation" that Pavlov pragmatically knows
cannot be reached, are protected by what McHale calls "a strategically useful and satisfying fiction." In other words, what remains
unquestioned by this pluralism are the *ends* of inquiry, the unquestioned "useful work" that a discipline or method allows one to
perform.

Nevertheless, the ends of methodological or scientific inquiry

8. Compare this quotation with the MLA's 1981 *Introduction to Scholarship* on the present
and future of literary criticism: "Perhaps someday criticism *will* have become a science,
equipped with scrupulous (if not infallible) rules of procedure. Perhaps someday critics
will agree on most (if not all) of their principles. Everyone impatient with the current illogic
and anarchy of much of the field would welcome that day" (92).

often show themselves to be problematic rather than merely "useful and satisfying," and the technological world in which these ends remain unquestioned is one of the principal concerns of *Gravity's Rainbow*, in which a kind of pragmatico-pluralist humanism shows itself as the technological worldview par excellence, a world in which everything becomes available for use, to be taken up by a method and converted unproblematically to an end. As Ihab Hassan writes, quoting William James, the world of end-oriented thinking is the world of a pluralist/pragmatist thinking that "looks away from '*first things, principles, categories, supposed necessities*,' and looks toward '*last things, fruits, consequences, facts*,' and like a corridor in the great mansion of philosophy, it opens on many rooms" ("Making Sense" 453). In Hassan's words, pluralist thinking helps one breathe the fresh air of "many rooms" within "the great mansion of philosophy," opens thinking to the fresh air of many potential usages and many points of view, and allows this fresh air to invigorate the closed, stale air of the house of being; pragmatist thinking escapes totalization through its emphasis on multiple, provisional ends rather than on the inevitably metaphysical and unitary notion of grounds. Still, this naming of ends as simply provisional or pragmatic hardly shakes or opens up metaphysical thinking, as Hassan and many other pluralists seem to think it inexorably does.[9] The shift of emphasis from grounds to ends is *precisely* the movement of a technological, representational metaphysics—a metaphysics we see at work throughout *Gravity's Rainbow*, in the myriad forces that dog Slothrop, in the techno-representational world "where only destinations are important, [where] attention is to long-term statistics, not to individuals: and where the House always does, of course, keep turning a profit" (*Gravity's Rainbow* 209).

It is this profit, this end product, this *work*, that a technological worldview protects most greedily. It is also this end product that a pluralist humanism cannot live without. The economy of such a worldview dictates that ends must be determinable, that there be no reserve or excess, that inquiry proceed, as Lazslo Jamf's work

9. See, for an example of this faith in pragmatism's question to tradition, Hassan's reading of Rorty: "Pragmatism brackets Truth (capitalized), circumvents Metaphysics and Epistemology; it finds no universal 'ground' for discourse" ("Making Sense" 451).

does, "logically, dialectically" (250). In fact, it is the productive dialectic in which pluralism is grounded that carries most clearly this technological worldview.[10] For example, note how dialectics and the expenditure (or profit) of ends are related in the following passage, where Richard Rorty muses on what happens when the "the pragmatist hauls out his bag of tried-and-true dialectical gambits": "He proceeds to argue that there is no pragmatic difference . . . between 'it works because it's true' and 'it's true because it works.' . . . [The pragmatist] does not want to discuss necessary and sufficient conditions for a sentence being true, but precisely *whether* the practice which hopes to find a Philosophical way of isolating the essence of Truth has, in fact, paid off" (*Consequences of Pragmatism* xxix). For Rorty, the pragmatist's "dialectical gambit" will consistently have "paid off": in the metaphysican's game, Rorty offers the pawn of grounds in order to gain the favored strategic position of ends. For Rorty, "Truth" is a game for patsies insofar as it ignores the real business of thought: the payoff of work, of use, of return, the dialectical payoff that is the cornerstone of a well-functioning pragmatico-technological worldview.

I find it strange that this pragmatico-technological worldview in *Gravity's Rainbow* is most often analyzed by critics *not* in terms of its offering multiple pragmatic freedoms for individual decision, but in terms of the marriage of multinational corporations and government bureaucracies, wherein IG Farben's death-dealing arrangements with the Nazis come to prefigure the postwar order of multinational capitalism.[11] Herr Rathenau, "prophet and architect of the cartelized state" (*Gravity's Rainbow* 164), explains his corporate version of folk

10. The rise of technology is, perhaps, *the* concern of contemporary thought, for thinkers as disparate as Heidegger, Adorno, Foucault, and Bataille. Rebecca Comay nicely sums up the notion of technologization: "The progress of enlightenment brings new and seemingly irreversible forms of domination: the reification of experience and the introduction of the abstract measure of utility; the reduction of qualitative difference to the quantifiable identities of the market; the increasing centrality of productive labor as the determinant of thought and action; the expulsion of the mundane sacred and its replacement by an otherworldly deity; and, last but not least, the (Newtonian) determination of time as an inert continuum of exchangeable now-points" ("Gifts without Presents" 69).

11. See, for example, Mazurek, who argues that *Gravity's Rainbow* "describes the emergence of the permanent war economies of the United States and the USSR from the ashes of World War II, a world in which Lt. Slothrop, the middle-class everyman, is literally manipulated from cradle to grave by the multinational I.G. Farben" ("Courses and Canons" 156).

history and the future of multinational capitalism to financiers in pre-Hitler Germany:

"The persistence, then, of structures favoring death. Death converted into more death. Perfecting its reign, just as the buried coal grows denser, and overlaid with more strata—epoch on top of epoch, city on top of ruined city. This is the sign of Death the impersonator.

"These signs are real. They are also symptoms of a process. The process follows the same form, the same structure. To apprehend it you will follow the signs. All talk of cause and effect is secular history, and secular history is a diversionary tactic. Useful to you, gentlemen, but no longer to us here. If you want to know the truth—I know I presume—you must look into the technology of these matters." (167)

Throughout the book, this emphasis on technologies of death— especially the V-2 Rocket, and the nuclear rocket that it (pre)figures— is perhaps the ultimate marriage of dialectical thinking and killing, of end-oriented research and capitalism, of technology and "structures favoring death." Note the importance of research to Rathenau's corporate worldview, his interest in dialectical thinking, which is the "process" or "the technology" by which German cartels such as IG Farben hope to gain and maintain control. And it is this emphasis that poses a very difficult question to claims for humanist freedom made by the pluralists: how can this emphasis on ends and use not be a concomitant emphasis on a certain kind of manipulation and violence? How can this be taken into account? Again, I cite Rorty: "From a full-fledged pragmatist point of view, there is no interesting difference between tables and texts, between protons and poems. To a pragmatist, these are *all* just permanent possibilities for use, and thus for redescription, reinterpretation, manipulation" (*Consequences of Pragmatism* 153). Because it effaces differences among objects—or, better, because it treats everything as a potential object—this "full-fledged pragmatist point of view" shows itself to be in league with a manipulative, technological worldview; such a pluralist pragmatism, it seems, promotes the dialectical, end-oriented thinking that allows and promotes, in large part, the discovery of the war order's "structures favoring death," and the extension and refinement of those war structures into the peacetime life of multinational capitalism.

This relationship between dialectical thinking and death moves not only at the empirical level of invention, but indeed at the *structural* level that Rathenau points us to. Death can be seen as that which fuels dialectical thinking, that which allows the very movement of progress and history, "epoch on top of epoch, city on top of ruined city." In fact, as Hegel argues in the *Phenomenology of Spirit*, dialectical thinking cannot perform any useful work until it confronts and masters death. The dialectic moves forward only when it appropriates the negative moment of death, what Hegel calls "the tremendous power of the negative; it is the energy of thought, of the pure 'I' " (19). Hegel continues:

> Death, if this is what we want to call this non-actuality, is of all things the most dreadful, and to hold fast what is dead requires the greatest strength. . . . But the life of Spirit is not the life that shrinks from death and keeps itself untouched by devastation, but rather the life that endures and maintains itself in it. It wins its truth only when, in utter dismemberment, it finds itself. . . . Spirit is this power only by looking the negative in the face, and tarrying with it. This tarrying with the negative is the magical power that converts it into being. (19)

Hegel here makes it clear that dialectical thinking needs the negativity of death—the negativity of "non-actuality," of the unrealized or unrealizable.[12] In fact, the negative moment of the dialectic, the necessary "dismemberment" of totality or surety wherein truth "finds itself,"[13] is the only "productive" moment of thought. If thought were to "shrink from death," it would never experience this dismemberment, and hence never experience the higher unity

---

12. The following discussion of death and negativity owes a tremendous debt to Paul Davies's lectures on Blanchot and Hegel.

13. In fact, death is fundamental to Hegelian "Man," as Bataille points out: "If the animal which constitutes man's natural being did not die, and—what is more—if death did not dwell within him as the source of his anguish . . . there would be no man or liberty, no history or individual. In other words, if he revels in what nonetheless frightens him, if he is the being, identical with himself, who risks (identical) being itself, then man is truly a Man: he separates himself from the animal" ("Hegel, Death, and Sacrifice" 12).

that the dialectic allows, the "magical power which converts it [death, the negative] into being." In short, dialectical thought, which uncovers the technologies necessary to build death-favoring apparatuses, is *itself* a "structure favoring death," death in the form of the productive negativity necessary to dialectical sublation. The dialectic confronts death—the absolutely other that dismembers life—and masters it, thereby allowing thought to master anything else in its path. And it is this structure (or, as Derrida writes, this *stricture*) of dialectical thinking that must be accounted for in pragmatic-pluralist criticism. Such a pluralism rather naively argues that a unitary metaphysics cannot deal with any kind of uncertainty, dismemberment, or plurality, that uncertainty or freedom can simply be opposed to or "defeat" a totalitarian certainty.[14] For Hegel, giving up such certainty is, on the contrary, actually the productive moment of thought: "Thoughts become fluid . . . when the pure certainty of the self abstracts from itself—not by leaving itself out, or setting itself aside, *but by giving up the fixity of its self-positing*" (*Phenomenology of Spirit* 20, my emphasis). In *Gravity's Rainbow*, then, it seems one is compelled to analyze not only the death-dealing products of a certain technological worldview, but the *structure* of the worldview itself—the structure of the insidious movement(s) of the structures favoring death—and to ask if these movements and structures can be disrupted in any way.

Although the intervention of a thematizing or interpretive moment is necessary and inescapable in this inquiry, there must be an other moment in the postmodern economy of meaning if a pluralist economy of ends is to be disrupted. As Derrida writes:

The other relationship to competitive plurality would not be strictly and rightly through and through interpretive, even if it includes an interpretive moment. Without excluding the first interpretation, above all without opposing it, [this other relationship] would deal with the multiplicity which cannot be reduced to the order [of competitive plurality], be it a war order or not. It would deal with

14. See, for example, Slade's "Escaping Rationalization" and Leverenz's "On Trying to Read *Gravity's Rainbow*," both of which center on the opposition of reason and unreason—with unreason as the eventual winner—as the key to reading *Gravity's Rainbow*.

this multiplicity as a law of the field, a clause of nonclosure which would not only never allow itself to be ordered and inscribed, situated in the general *Kampfplatz*, but would also make possible and inevitable synecdochic and metonymic competitions: not as their normal condition of possibility, their *ratio essendi* or *ratio cognoscendi*, but as a means of disseminal alterity or alteration, which would make impossible the pure identity, the pure identification of what it simultaneously makes possible. ("Some Statements and Truisms" 72)

A "reading" of *Gravity's Rainbow* must be accompanied by an other reading, a second or double reading that "would deal with . . . multiplicity as a law of the field." This double reading could, in other words, deal with other readings as a structural necessity rather than a pragmatic consequence; it allows one to account for multiple readings as the consequence of a disseminated ground that must be attended to rather than as a series of determinate ends that must be fought for.

For all its discussion of multiplicity, a pluralist economy remains an economy of opposition because it does not consider the structure of the field or network in which truth arises. Its conception of multiplicity consists rather of (re)evaluating competing claims among opposing truths. A double reading necessarily begins in such an economy of interpretation, opposition, and thematization, but it moves from there to examine the ground of that economy itself, not as a foundation that could assure the ends of inquiry—"not as their normal condition of possibility, . . . but as a means of disseminal alterity or alteration, which would make impossible the pure identity, the pure identification of what it simultaneously makes possible." The structure of what I have been calling the "postmodern" field both makes thematization possible and makes it impossible for that thematization to cover or master the entire field, both makes relation possible and interrupts determinate relation through a disseminal otherness or alteration within the constituting space of relation. The discipline of literary criticism, as I have likewise argued, on the whole concerns itself solely with this first reading or economy; however, it is toward this other field or economy in *Gravity's Rainbow*

that we now turn, not to escape an economy of reading or interpretation, but rather to double this economy and disrupt it, to alter
its space and open it to its other.

The Structure of the "Structures Favoring Death"

One of the most compelling plot lines in *Gravity's Rainbow* revolves
around the Herero, the African tribe subjugated by the colonial
Germans and subsequently turned into death-worshipers, into a
people favoring death. We should note, however, that when the
Germans went to Africa to build colonies and subjugate the Herero,
the logic behind this movement was also dialectical: the other is
appropriated as a version of the same, to be studied, analyzed, and
used. In Hegel, for example, otherness is thought as "a *difference*
which is no *difference*, or only a difference of what is *self-same*, and
its essence is unity" (*Phenomenology of Spirit* 99). Otherness, in other
words, is only a necessary moment in the continuing movement of
the same. This is, I take it, Pynchon's point in his 1969 letter to
Thomas Hirsh, in which he writes: "I don't like to use the word but
I think what went on back in Südwest is archtypical of every clash
between west and non-west, clashes that are still going on right now
in South East Asia" (in Seed, *Fictional Labyrinths*, 242). Or, as *Gravity's
Rainbow* phrases the Herero's plight, "Europe came and established
its order of Analysis and Death" (722). This link between "Analysis"
and "Death" explains Tchitcherine's (and, one imagines, his
Schwarzkommando brother Enzian's) interest in dialectics: "Not till
recently did he come to look for comfort in the dialectical ballet of
force, counterforce, collision, new order—not till the War came and
Death appeared across the ring [. . .] only then did he turn to a
Theory of History—of all pathetic cold comforts—to try and make
sense of it" (704). The link between "Analysis" and "Death" is,
strictly speaking, an impossible one: when death, the absolutely
other, as that which cannot be experienced, thematized, or understood, appears and comes to thought, thought must find a way to
master that death, to find some way to make it productive, or at
least to obviate its potentially interruptive or dismembering effects.
Thought will "try and make sense of" death through the "comfort"

afforded by "the dialectical ballet of force, counterforce, collision, new order." But, insofar as death cannot be negated, used, understood, or even really chosen, it has the potential to cripple dialectical thought. For example, in a famous scene in Gravity's Rainbow, Tchitcherine and Wimpe discuss mystification and Marxist dialectics. Wimpe argues, in an eminently quotable passage: " 'Marxist dialectics? That's *not* an opiate, eh? [. . .] Die to help History grow to its predestined shape' " (701). Dialectics, here the Marxian variety (with its well-known debt to the Hegelian),[15] makes of death a productive moment within the narrative of history; it substitutes the narrative of History for the narrative of God, and does so with the fuel supplied by the negative moment of the dialectic.

But here a question remains: is death really so easily sublated, so easily mastered by a dialectic? Is death a simple, sublatable negativity? As Tchitcherine stumbles through the drug-induced argument with Wimpe, he becomes increasingly less sure; he goes on concerning death: " 'You don't know. Not till you're there, Wimpe. You can't say.' 'That doesn't sound very dialectical,' [Wimpe replies]. 'I don't know what it is' " (701). Indeed, death is not very dialectical: as Tchitcherine points out, one never "knows" about death until one "is there"; however, when one "is there," one is no longer in a position to "know" anything at all—one is dead, drawn out of the network of possible relations that constitutes the world of knowledge. In fact, death, insofar as it does not respond to a rational analysis, stands in a cripplingly neutral *non-relation* to thought: the inability to thematize death comes not from its potential richness or the plurality of relations that a being can have toward or with it, but rather from the fact that death shows itself in no determinate relation whatsoever to a being. "Analysis" and "Death" are, in a dialectical system, two terms that are impossible to think together—even though the negativity of "Death" fuels "Analysis."

To deal with this problem, as Hegel points out, there must be a double meaning to the negative. If there is to be sublation and

15. See Marx's introduction to the second edition of *Capital:* "The mystification which dialectic suffers in Hegel's hands, by no means prevents him from being the first to present its general form of working in a comprehensive and conscious manner. With him it [dialectic] is standing on its head. It must be turned right side up again, if you would discover the rational kernel within the mystical shell" (25).

mastery (analysis), the negative (death) must first disassemble or rend totality, but must then enter into a determinate relation with this fragmentation, saving it, in the process, from the status of a mere fragment. In other words, for the negative to be productive (indeed, for there to be production at all), the dialectic must grasp terms within a relation. It is, in turn, this relation that assures the subject that it can appropriate anything. As Hegel writes of this dual meaning, "Consciousness *distinguishes* something from itself to which, precisely, it *relates*" (in Hyppolite, *Genesis and Structure*, 21–22). But, again, as Wimpe and Tchitcherine's conversation points out, the subject cannot have a determinate relation with death, for death "is" the disruption or stoppage of life and the absence of all relationality. This non-relation of death to life is precisely why death has to be mastered by dialectical thought; it must be brought into a (productive) relation with life if there is to be any "progress." This conflation of life and death is the brilliance of the dialectic: it *acknowledges* the potentially dismembering effect of something other than thought (other than life and reason) but goes on to master that other (that fracturing irrationality) in an ever-stronger and more rational unity. This other-than-thought is trapped in a productive relation with thought and becomes other-*to*-thought, thought's opposite, dialectically contained *within* thought as thought's other, and can thereby be taken up in a philosophical relation and used toward the ends of thought. Institutions such as the White Visitation, then, strive to produce "rationalized forms of death—death in the service of the one species cursed with the knowledge that it will die" (*Gravity's Rainbow* 230). In short, they produce technologies that reassure comfort in the face of death, if in no other way than through the knowledge that humans can (re)*produce* death, control its randomness, make death's negativity productive, put it at the service of a cause or a useful end, in a determinate relation with life.

But perhaps there remains an other death, a death radically other to death as productive negativity, a death that stands in no determinate (and therefore no enabling) relation to technological thought. As Rilke, an important presence in *Gravity's Rainbow*,[16] writes, per-

<hr />

16. For a concise discussion of the secondary material on *Gravity's Rainbow* and Rilke, see Hohmann's "Pynchon and Rilke: A Survey of Criticism," in *Thomas Pynchon's "Gravity's Rainbow*," 271–82. John Stark, for example, writes that "information about Rilke is indis-

haps the problem is finding that which "permit[s] the reading of the word death *without* negation; like the moon, life surely has a side permanently turned away from us *which is not its counter-part*" (*Letters* 316, second emphasis mine). Heidegger glosses Rilke's strange formulation: "Within the widest orbit of the sphere of beings there are regions and places which, being averted from us, seem to be something negative, but are nothing of the kind if we think of all things as being within the widest orbit of beings.... The self-assertion of technological objectification is the constant negation of death. By this negation, death becomes something negative" ("What Are Poets For?" 124–25). Perhaps Heidegger's gloss here is stranger than Rilke's initial formulation, but both ask the same question: is there something that stands outside of the seemingly totalizing relation(s) of use, something that cannot simply be taken up by technological, dialectical thinking—something that is not simply "counter-part" or opposite? Technological thinking translates all things into a determinate, negative relation and thereby masters them dialectically by bringing them into a relation where their truth can be known. In *Gravity's Rainbow*, for example, the Herero myth of death and the hidden side of the moon is shot through with this technological relation: "It began in mythical times, when the sly hare who nests in the Moon brought death among men, instead of the moon's true message. The true message has never come. Perhaps the rocket is made to take us there someday, and then the Moon will tell us its truth at last" (322). Because the Herero have been "Europeanized in language and thought" (318), they are no longer able to think that perhaps the "moon's true message," as Rilke suggests, is that not everything exists to be appropriated by a technological worldview, that (like death and the other side of the moon) not everything exists in some determinate relation to technological thought. Likewise, the Herero stood in no determinate relation to Europe until its technological order of analysis and death was inflicted upon them and coerced them into believing there was a determinate "truth" to the moon and to death, a deadly truth that enslaved them to the project of the rocket.

---

pensable for a full understanding" of *Gravity's Rainbow* (quoted in Hohmann, "Pynchon and Rilke," 271).

All of this is not, of course, to argue that death is a wonderful thing; rather, it is to argue that death resists characterization, resists being opposed in any positive/negative way, resists being placed in any determinate relation at all. The fact that one hears (and Blicero and the Schwarzkommando read) a death-worshiping affirmation of dying in Rilke makes this very point: we have not learned to hear death (or anything else, for that matter) as other than simply negative or positive. We have not learned to think things, in short, as *other*, as standing in no determinate relation at all to humanity's technological worldview. As Rilke writes, we have yet to think the "open":

> You must understand the concept of the "open" . . . in such a way that the animal's degree of consciousness sets it into the world without the animal's placing the world over against itself at every moment (as we do); the animal is *in* the world; we stand *before it* by virtue of that peculiar turn and intensification which our consciousness has taken. . . . By the "open," therefore, I do not mean sky, air, and space; *they* too are "object." (In Heidegger, "What Are Poets For?" 108)

The "open" that Rilke speaks of stands in no relation to the circumspective consciousness of appropriating, technological subjectivity. It cannot be object for a subject, and hence cannot be thematized in terms of the relationality that pluralism posits as an alternative to a binary worldview. Rather, Rilke's "open" is the very opening of relationality itself—with which there can be no determinate relation. Everything in the technological world has become "object" to or for totalizing "subject," and must be drawn out from that relation and allowed to resonate in what Rilke calls the "open." Accomplishing this would seem to require, then, some notion of de-subjectification and impersonality. The determinate self, which experiences the world in relational terms, in terms of use, of short-term goals, must be somehow drawn out of the determinate relations of dialectical thinking.

This is precisely Slothrop's fate in *Gravity's Rainbow*. Slothrop's self—a self that is endlessly (but not end-lessly) tracked, charted, and probed—is consistently compared to an albatross, until it finally becomes "scattered": "He has become one plucked albatross.

Plucked, hell—*stripped.* Scattered all over the Zone. It's doubtful if he can ever be 'found' again, in the conventional sense of 'positively identified and detained' " (712). Slothrop's scattering is often treated in Pynchon criticism as a negative or lamentable situation. Mendelson, for example, argues that Mexico ends up as the novel's hero.[17] Slothrop, in his scattering, suffers a terrible fate; and although Mexico survives to form the Counterforce, "Slothrop will lose all real and potential relation to *any* world, whether of language or of act" ("Gravity's Encyclopedia" 191). Perhaps there is another way to read Slothrop's scattering—a way to read his scattering as other than involving a *lack* of wholeness or possibility. Perhaps the self is an albatross, one of "their" agents: "The man has a branch office in each of our brains, his corporate emblem is a white albatross, each local rep has a cover known as the Ego" (712–13). And Slothrop, even (perhaps *especially*) in drawing out of "their" world of determinate relations, *remains* involved in a power struggle, a power struggle not thematizable as a simple opposition—a "Counter-force"—but rather as a struggle against a more insidious kind of power. Perhaps Slothrop carries on the kind of struggle Foucault talks about in his late work, a struggle that sets out

> to attack not so much "such or such" an institution of power, or group, or elite, or class, but rather a technique, a form of power. This form of power applies itself to immediate everyday life which categorizes the individual, marks him by his own individuality, attaches him to his own identity, imposes a law of truth on him which he must recognize and which others have to recognize in him. It is a form of power which makes individuals subjects. There are two meanings of the word *subject:* subject to someone else by control and dependence, and tied to his own identity by a conscience or self-knowledge. Both meanings suggest a form of power which subjugates and makes subject to. ("Subject and Power" 212)

Slothrop's determinate relation to forces throughout this book—his individuality, his proper name—is what allows him to be " 'posi-

17. For Mendelson, Mexico represents the "affirmative and 'true' aspects" of *Gravity's Rainbow,* "almost all the book's moments of hope and love" ("Gravity's Encyclopedia" 186).

tively identified and detained' " and to be marked by "a form of power which makes individuals subjects." His proper name, however, shifts throughout the book only to disperse in his scattering, in what could perhaps be called his final heroic action—if it can be properly considered either "heroic," an "action," or even his "final" action in the (admittedly odd and unreliable) logic of *Gravity's Rainbow* itself.[18]

Language here becomes difficult, because it too depends on the categories (cause and effect, subjective intent and objective act) that Slothrop's scattering disrupts. It is not that Slothrop exactly *causes* this disruption.[19] Perhaps we should say that Slothrop brings about or calls for(th) a certain disruption: Slothrop's scattering disrupts a kind of subjectivity that is part and parcel of the contemporary war state, of the modern world of the subject and the state that depends on identity, property, statistics, and the individual. Slothrop's scattered state disrupts the worldview of the Nazis, who, he notices, are consistently "purifying and perfecting their Fascist ideal of Action, Action, Action, once his own shining reason for being. No more. No more" (266). Perhaps in posing a question to the "Fascist ideal of Action, Action, Action," Slothrop wages his own war, a war no longer waged, however, in the name of "liberation" or action. Perhaps Slothrop's agenda is not "liberation" of "self" at all; perhaps, as Foucault writes, "The political, ethical, social, philosophical problem of our days is not to try to liberate the individual from the state, and from the state's institutions, but to liberate us both from the state and the type of individualization which is linked to the

18. Slothrop continues to figure in the logic of *Gravity's Rainbow* even after his "scattering." For example, in mid-July 1945 (according to Weisenburger), Slothrop overhears a conversation among some reporters concerning the 1946 Miss Rhinegold beauty pageant, although we're told that it "will be months before he runs into a beer advertisement featuring the six beauties" (381). When he does run into the advertisement (and finds himself rooting for a Dutch woman who reminds him of Katje), it will be *after* his 6 August "scattering." Likewise, we are told that Slothrop may have played harmonica on an album by "the Fool," put out sometime after the Rolling Stones were famous (742). Slothrop does not, then, "simply" disappear in some mythic or messianic manner, but rather he becomes untrackable, untraceable, unidentified.

19. As the text informs us, this scattering has been a long time coming and has not exactly been Slothrop's choice: "Slothrop, as noted, at least as early as the *Anubis* era, has begun to thin, to scatter" (509).

state. We have to promote new forms of subjectivity through the refusal of this kind of individuality which has been imposed on us for several centuries" ("Subject and Power" 216). So Slothrop, when he scatters/is scattered, may indeed "lose all real and potential relation to *any* world," but he also opens up a gap—a resistance—in a world that thinks only in terms of "real" and "potential." Slothrop opens a space within the terms of dialectics, in which an actual world is consistently opposed to a coming world, in which the only relation among things is one of opposition, negation, sublation—in short, in which the only relation is a relation of control.

As I argued in Chapter 3, to grant a dialectical worldview is to lose to the status quo in a fixed game, the game of the negative. To disrupt this world, it must not only be negated or opposed, but also contested: an "absolute" gap of otherness must be opened up within the totality of the same. As Emmanuel Levinas writes, "What is absolutely other does not only resist possession, but contests it. . . . If the same would establish its identity by simple *opposition to the other*, it would already be part of a totality encompassing the same and the other" (*Totality and Infinity* 38). So Slothrop's scattering, which can be thematized as either active or passive (positive or negative), is properly neither, precisely because his scattering brings the rupture of the proper, the dependability of the sameness of the same. In short, Slothrop's scattering, by drawing him out of the determinate relations of the technological world, opens upon an otherness that is *not simply the opposite of sameness*, an otherness that breaches totality rather than allowing itself to be contained within it: in short, an otherness that is—to strain language—other to the relations of opposition. Slothrop's death as scattering approaches, in this way, Rilke's "open" or his "other" death—an end that is not properly an end at all, a continuing end that carries no relation to a totality, but is rather a disruption of totality itself.[20]

And this disruption—this drawing language itself out of work, out of a determinate relation with the traditional system(atic)s of meaning—is perhaps the postmodern "work" of *Gravity's Rainbow*, though it is a work that performs more than the thematizable work

20. See Blanchot's reading of Rilke and death in *The Space of Literature*.

of the negative, and hence creates a disruption of work. The systematics of work and ends have obtained throughout the history of Western thinking, a history that Levinas thematizes in terms of war: "The visage of being that shows itself in war is fixed in the concept of totality, which dominates Western philosophy" (*Totality and Infinity* 21). This disruption of the systematics of work and ends, of course, raises the question—a question I have emphasized throughout this book—of the *end* of totality, the question of post-war, the question of postmodern. What is the postwar relation to a war economy, to the language and concepts of the war, of totality? In *Gravity's Rainbow*, this question first comes up as Slothrop escapes the V-2, in liberated France on his furlough at the Casino Hermann Goering:

> The manager of the Casino Hermann Goering, one César Flebótomo, brought in a whole chorus-line soon as the liberators arrived, though he hasn't found time to change the place's occupation name. Nobody seems to mind it up there, a pleasant mosaic of tiny and perfect seashells, thousands of them set in plaster, purple, pink, and brown, replacing a huge section of roof (the old tiles still lie in a heap beside the Casino), put up two years ago as recreational therapy by a Messerschmitt squadron on furlough, in German typeface expansive enough to be seen from the air, which is what they had in mind. The sun now is still too low to touch the words into any more than some bare separation from their ground, so that they hang suppressed, no relation any more to the men, the pain in their hands, the blisters that grew black under the sun with infection and blood. (184–85)

Here we see worked out quite intricately the postwar relation to the "occupation name": the words "Casino Hermann Goering," once so pregnant with meaning for "a Messerschmitt squadron on furlough," now exist in no more "than some bare separation from their ground, so that they hang suppressed, *no relation any more* to the men," no determinate relation anymore to the war economy of totality in which they formerly functioned. Of course, this is not to say that the postwar name bears no connection at all to the war name; rather, it is to say that the postwar names do not exist in a properly philosophical relation, a relation that is part of a totality.[21] These words are now "separat[ed] from their ground," uprooted from their fixed place within totality—after the war, after the subject, after ontology—and bear no relation anymore to the painful work of the war. They are unable to explain the terror and horror of that economy, but do not simply stand outside it either, and are thereby able to open up a dissembling space within it.

The incommensurability of the war vocabulary and postwar vocabularies (one could say subjective and post-scattering vocabularies, or, following Levinas, ontological and post-ontological language) is a recurring concern of *Gravity's Rainbow*, and is not simply, I would argue, a "thematic" or "critical" concern, insofar as such a problem concerns the very (im)possibility of something like a theme or critique in a postmodern context. In fact, this incommensurability is first treated in the novel's famous opening lines, the always already underway (non)place where *Gravity's Rainbow* begins: "A screaming comes across the sky. It has happened before, but there is nothing to compare it to now. It is too late" (3). Note how the nonrelationality of the rocket—"there is nothing to compare it to now"—is phrased in temporal terms; the rocket's nonrelational "now" is, in Marc Redfield's words, "disturbingly sandwiched between competing temporal markers ('It has happened before'; 'It is too late')" ("Pynchon's Postmodern Sublime" 160). The rocket certainly refers to past occurrences, but these do not seem to be up to the task of describing it "now," of capturing this event in a properly philosophical relation: something like it may have happened before, but there is nothing to compare it to now, no context that can give it(s) meaning. Hence, this "nothing to compare it to now" is a reversal—a negation, an opposition—that can lead to a displacement: the present itself—the "now" in which there could be a relation—is exploded, and along

---

21. Again, Hegel: "Each extreme is a middle term for the other extreme, a middle term by means of which it enters into a relation with itself and gathers itself up. . . . [Each extreme] is for-itself only through this mediation [relation]" (in Hyppolite, *Genesis and Structure*, 165n).

with it goes the continuity between (and the ground for) the past and future. Under the postmodern logic of the rocket, the present, like Slothrop, becomes a perpetual crossroads that stands in no determinate relation to the known past or foreseeable future. It stands in relation only to the nonrelation of an indeterminate future characterized by the unthematizable approach of death. Each segment of the novel is, in turn, akin to this "beginning" undecidable screaming; past events or future promises cannot explain the events at hand: "now," postwar, postmodern, there is nothing to compare events with in order to reveal their hidden truth in the same way that one section of the novel cannot be appealed to in order to explain or ground all the others. *Gravity's Rainbow* is an exterior, flat network of statements, with all its sections on the same level, so to speak— with no secret message hidden below their surface. It has the structure of apocalypse without revelation.

This nonrelationality in or of the text can be discussed in other ways, and is "at work" in any number of the book's other "controlling metaphors." In fact, the very title of the book poses a question to the sublation of dialectical relations. When two nouns are placed together, one would expect an attempt at sublation; with *Gravity's Rainbow*, then, one would expect an attempt to think Newton's explanation of the rainbow together with the imaginative resonances of the rainbow for the poet, to bring the two to some synthesis.[22] But, as the possessive of the title suggests, the rainbow— even in its long symbolic history in poetic or imaginative writing— *always already belongs to a kind of scientific discourse,* insofar as even poetics is a subgenre of the discourse of truth, of philosophy. So the question posed even in the title of *Gravity's Rainbow* is not how to think the technological (gravity) in relation to the poetic (rainbow), but how to think the poetic in such a way as it is not simply a subset of a determining technologized philosophical discourse: this project becomes *not* the romantic project (an attempt to recuperate the primacy of the imaginative rainbow over the technological determinacy of gravity), but rather the postmodern project of drawing the rain-

22. For such a discussion in a general context, see Abrams, "Newton's Rainbow and the Poet's," in *The Mirror and the Lamp,* 303–12.

bow out of relation to the determining, technological world of gravity—of attending to its opaque alterity rather than attempting to render it transparent.[23]

23. It would be remiss of me to ignore a specific alterity to which *Gravity's Rainbow* is almost completely blind: gender. While the text is sensitive to the topic of alterity and to preterites of class and race, it is maddeningly—infuriatingly, at times—crass in its treatment of gender. There are, of course, spots in the book where sexism can be attributed to characters—for example, Bland's pinball machine, "a little hostile to the ladies, but *all in fun*" (583), and an anonymous soldier's view of freedom in the Zone, where "life is good, and nobody's much looking forward to redeployment. There are frauleins for screwing, cooking, and doing your laundry" (298).

Much more disturbing is the sexism of the narrative voice (see, for the most blatant example, 606). This voice that is careful enough to gesture to the alterity of pigs remains seemingly blind to its own sexist rhetoric: "Under the sign of The Gross Suckling. Swaying full-color picture of a loathsomely fat drooling infant. In one puddinglike fist the Gross Suckling clutches a dripping hamhock (sorry pigs, nothing personal), with the other hand he reaches out for a human Mother's Nipple that emerges out into the picture from the left-hand side, his gaze arrested by the approaching tit, his mouth open—a gleeful look" (707). While this picture of an "approaching tit" may not be necessarily sexist, one would think that some hesitation is in order here—some way to extend the discursive consideration ["(sorry pigs, nothing personal)"] shown here to barnyard animals.

There is perhaps no shortage of good intentions in this text on the topic of gender; for example, its treatment of the exclusionary nature of phallic techno-culture (see, for example, 521) and the mutating role of military-industrial power in sexual relationships—the way that secrets of the phallic rocket are "*won*, away from the feminine darkness" (324)—both point to an awareness of questions of gender. But, in the end, the text remains problematically blind to the force of these questions.

6 / Politics, Poetics, and Institutions: "Language" Poetry

A society which was really like a good poem, embodying
the aesthetic virtues of beauty, order, economy and subordination of detail to the whole, would be a nightmare of
horror, for . . . such a society could only come into being
through selective breeding, extermination of the physically
and mentally unfit, absolute obedience to its Director, and
a large slave class kept out of sight in cellars.

Vice versa, a poem which was really like a political democracy—examples, unfortunately, exist—would be formless, windy, banal and utterly boring.

—W. H. Auden
"The Poet and the City"

Academic colonization is contemporary poetry's fundamental social problem because it incorporates the politics
of culture into a process that can only be determined
institutionally.

—Ron Silliman
"Negative Solidarity"

Although historically self-defined within an "anti-academic"
tradition, its long-term engagement with social, aesthetic,
and linguistic theory provides language poetry with both a
vocabulary and potential mechanisms for posing the institutional question that, for example, the anti-theoretical college workshop tradition lacks.

—Ron Silliman
"Canons and Institutions"

Up to this (late) point, I have for the most part deferred overtly
posing the question of the political implications of the postmodern—

though, of course, the topic has come up in several different guises throughout this book. In the literary critical field at large, the political questions raised by postmodern thought and literature are certainly well commented upon.[1] Unfortunately, however, the arguments concerning the politics of postmodernism are often all-too-easily reduced to a kind of crude (self-)parody that betrays much of the complexity of the questions. Note, for example, how Jerome Mc-Gann formulates the question concerning the "heated controversy which has developed around the idea of the postmodern—is it or is it not a reactionary social phenomenon?" ("Contemporary Poetry, Alternate Routes" 627). McGann's phrasing of the question concerning the politics of the postmodern is typically inadequate, and for reasons other than its reductive either/or binary form: McGann's question presupposes, as so much of the secondary literature on the politics of postmodernism does, that the "idea of the postmodern" is somehow a unitary thing, and that this idea has some sort of monolithic consequences—reactionary or progressive—for a "society." The apotheosis of this kind of reasoning can be found in Fredric Jameson's "Politics of Theory: Ideological Positions in the Postmodernism Debate," in which he presents a table of six theorists of postmodernism with a " + " or a " − " (or both, as in the case of Lyotard) next to their names, "the plus and minus signs designating the politically progressive or reactionary functions of the positions in question" (111). I think we must remain wary of this approach to the complex question of postmodernism's political implications, and for several reasons: first, of course, because it reduces a highly complex and contested field to a simple binary skeleton; second, because such a phrasing of the question takes for granted either an unproblematic movement between aesthetic phenomena and political actions or, conversely, the clean separation of text and context, postmodern art and postmodern culture.

---

1. The amount of work done on this question is, in fact, staggering. Jameson's work is, perhaps, "seminal." See, in a similarly Marxist/Frankfurt School vein, the critiques of Huyssen and Habermas—both of whom react to the type of "poststructuralist" treatment found in Lyotard's *Postmodern Condition*. For feminist discussions of the politics of postmodernism, see the essays collected in Nicholson, *Feminism/Postmodernism*. See also the essay collections edited by Ross and Arac, *Universal Abandon?* and *Postmodernism and Politics*. This list, of course, only scratches the surface of a topic that is buried under scholarship.

In this literary critical parlance, "postmodern culture" most often means "fragmented culture." As I argued in Chapter 4, the one thing that various postmodernisms and postmodernists have in common is their assertion that a stable transcendental has withdrawn; therefore, the controversies surrounding the politics of postmodernism tend to focus on whether this fragmentation or loss of center can be seen as positive or negative, socially progressive or reactionary. As McGann writes:

> In postmodern work we become aware of the many crises of stability and centeredness which an imperial culture like our own— attempting to hold control over so many, and so widely dispersed, human materials—inevitably has to deal with. *The response to such a situation may be either a contestatory or an accommodational one*—it may move to oppose and change such circumstances, or it may take them as given, and reflect (reflect upon) their operations. ("Contemporary Poetry, Alternate Routes" 628, my emphasis)

Here again we see a familiar but problematic either/or. For McGann, who is engaging contemporary American poetics, any (poetic) response to the conditions of a seemingly monolithic postmodern existence can be categorized as "either a contestatory or an accommodational one"; a poet produces either a work that opposes the "capitalist empire" (624), or one which merely takes it "as given" and reflects upon bourgeois experience, thereby reifying and validating it.

The political problem that McGann names here is not, however, particularly conducive to the treatment he wants to give it: his problem *with* postmodernism as literature—"Which side are you on?"— is complicated by the general problem *of* postmodernism as a societal space or place in which such simple oppositions and outside supports have been called into question. This problem is one that we have touched upon continually throughout this book: how does one secure a position outside what McGann calls the "given" structures of a language or society in a postmodern situation, given that a postmodern situation is in large part *defined* by the absence of an outside, the absence of an uncontaminated theory that could ground a truly revolutionary practice? Likewise, couldn't it be argued—

despite McGann's condemnation—that reflecting on the operations of culture, on, for example, the operations of advertising or the State Department or the university, is far from a merely "accommodating" societal response, but rather a reflection that can carry with it a necessary questioning? In addition, it seems that McGann conflates rhetorical or formal experimentation—the devices by which contemporary poetry makes us aware of postmodern "crises of stability and centeredness"—with politics, making a mistake that Auden warns us against. Auden's (elitist) poetics and politics are certainly not laudable, but he does warn us about the dangers of simply equating poetic structure and political structure, of assuming a simple relation (or of assuming any relation at all, for that matter) between the structure of "society" and the structure of a "good poem."

I have no desire to endorse Auden's conception of poetry or of politics. His idea that all poetry involves the "aesthetic virtues of beauty, order, economy and subordination of detail to the whole" is certainly among the first casualties of both "New American" and "Language" poetics. Also, his contempt for a radically democratic rhetorical poetics seems quite obviously tied to his elitist politics. Nevertheless, I think it is important to keep in mind (as Auden reminds us) that anything written is necessarily structured; and, indeed, much of the literature that poses essential questions to Auden's conception of poetry is itself intricately structured, even if it is structured in such a way as to de-structure beauty, order, and economy. The question is, in other words, always one of structure(s)—in poetry as in politics—and not simply a matter of structure-order-totalitarianism versus anarchy-freedom-peace.

Language Poetry and Politics

It is against the backdrop of questions such as these—questions about the politics of postmodern poetic form and content, about the possibility of political and syntactic disruption from *within* a dominant discourse—that the debate over "language poetry" is being played out. Enough general accounts of the language poetry "movement" exist to justify making my introduction to it here brief.[2] Language poets take their name from the journal $L = A = N = G = U = A = G = E$, edited by Bruce Andrews and Charles Bernstein from 1978 to 1981. The term "language poetry" has come to indicate a loosely affiliated group of North American poets who are engaged in a radically heterogenous questioning of contemporary poetic syntax, theory, and politics, although the radicality of their critique makes grouping them under such a homogenous label quite difficult from the outset. In fact, the name "language" poetry seems to suggest an emphasis on language, hardly something new in the history of poetics, and an emphasis that does not—on the face of it—seem compatible with a "political" poetry.[3] As Lee Bartlett points out, however, the common thread among these heterogeneous poets is their interest in poststructuralist theoretical discourse about language ("What Is 'Language Poetry'?" 750); they share an interest in language as that which, in some senses, shapes experience and constructs the world, and an interest in the materiality and play of the signifier rather than in the meaning of the signified, in paratactic orders of poetic surface rather than in strictly hypotactic orders of subordination and depth. In this view, they draw connections between themselves and the radical modernist poetics of Stein, Williams, Zukofsky, Mallarmé, and even the Eliot of *The Waste Land*.[4]

Language poetry began as an "outsider" movement in American poetics, and it remains marginal to the "academic" or "workshop" poetics dominant in most MFA programs and prestigious poetry

2. For a general introduction to and evaluation of language poetry, see especially Silliman's introduction to *In the American Tree*. See also Bartlett, "What Is 'Language Poetry'?"; McGann, "Contemporary Poetry, Alternate Routes"; Hartley's introduction to *Textual Politics*; and Perloff, "The Word as Such: $L = A = N = G = U = A = G = E$ Poetry in the Eighties."

3. Indeed, as Greer points out, an emphasis on "language" is perhaps not what these disparate poets have in common at all: "The name 'language poetry' is a misnomer insofar as it suggests an organic or essentialist view of language. . . . [I]t seems one should argue instead that 'writing' rather than 'language' is the central term in this field of work—not poetry, politics, or theory as distinct fields of discourse, but writing as a space in which all of what were once distinct genres, forms, modes of address, may now intersect, undermine, reinforce, echo, contradict, restate, or transform one another" ("Ideology and Theory" 351).

4. See Silliman's "Negative Solidarity": "Like other avant-garde movements, 'language poetry' began by identifying its own distinctness, criticizing the naive assumptions of a speech-centered poetics. But, unlike many of its modernist ancestors, 'language poetry' also drew *positive* connections between itself and the work of preceding generations, most explicitly to the New American Poets of the 1950s and '60s: the projectivist or Black Mountain writers, the New York School, the San Francisco Renaissance and even the Beats" (170–71).

magazines. Language poetry remains at the margins of what Charles Bernstein calls "official verse culture" (*Content's Dream* 246).[5] Like any other avant-garde, however, language poetry is now moving from the margins toward the center as it gains more attention from academic critics and as more of its "practitioners" take jobs within the university.[6] And this attention has, not surprisingly, only gained them more scorn in the eyes of fellow poets and in the pages of *The American Poetry Review*. Language poet Ron Silliman summarizes the conflict over language poetry within the poetry community:

> The specific charges are the following: "language poetry" is alleged to be driven by theory; it is anti-speech and thereby anti-individual (sometimes this is extended to anti-democractic and elitist); it participates in self-conscious collective behavior; it valorizes the ugly and the unintelligible; its leftist politics are strident and didactic. Taken together, the implicit claim is that "language poetry" is a closet academic verse, seeking explicators rather than readers. ("Negative Solidarity" 171–72)

One is immediately struck by the fact that the "specific charges" leveled against language poetry are similar to those leveled against theoretical discourse in general: language poetry is accused—as is, say, deconstruction—of being at the same time impenetrable or elitist in its difficulty *and* ultimately frivolous or meaningless. Language poetry is accused of slashing and burning a speech-based poetic tradition in favor of an "unintelligible," "strident and didactic" writing process; and it is accused, like the theoretical discourse it often incorporates, of being a "collective behavior" produced solely for other insiders. As critic Eliot Weinberger writes, language writing is, for many, far too "jargon-enstrangled [*sic*]" ("Weinberger on Language Poetry" 181), characterized by "specialized language, self-referentiality, and disdain for the uninitiated" (182); however, according to Weinberger, all of this sound and fury signifies nothing

5. See, for example, David Shapiro's review in the *American Poetry Review*, in which he suggests that one could plausibly map the current poetic spectrum as a political one, with " 'Language' poetries as an infantile left" ("Salon of 1990" 37).

6. Bernstein, for example, has accepted the David Gray Chair in the Humanities—formerly held by Robert Creeley—at the State University of New York at Buffalo, where Susan Howe also teaches. Bob Perelman teaches at the University of Pennsylvania, and Barrett Watten is on the editorial board of *Representations*.

in the end: "The 'language' poets have exploded the myth of the whole, and what seems to be left is what television calls 'bites.' . . . A 'language' poem in perhaps its most typical form begins, ends, and goes nowhere" (184).

It will, of course, be difficult to assess these charges without examining an "actual language poem." Of course, doing that runs the converse risk of having any poem I cite taken for a (non)representative example of an extremely diverse and contested field of writing, but that is a risk that must be taken if I am to avoid obscuring in generalizations the heterogeneity and specificity that language writing stresses. So, with these caveats in mind, consider the (in some ways) arbitrary introduction to language poetry provided by Barrett Watten's long poem *Progress*, which begins:

> Relax,
>   stand at attention, and.
>   Purple snake stands out on
>   Porcelain tiles. The idea
> *Is* the thing. Skewed by design. . . .
>
> One way contradictory use is to
>   Specify empty.
>   Basis, its
>   Cover operates under insist on,
> Delineate. Stalin as a linguist. . . .
>
> I trust replication.
>   Gives,
>   Surface. Lights string
>   The court reporter, distances.
> That only depth is perfect. . . .
>
> Comes to the history of words.
>   The thought to eradicate
>   In him. The poetry,
>   by
> Making him think certain ways. . . . (1, ellipses Watten's)

The first thing we note about *Progress* is that it begins with a logical contradiction: the contradictory imperatives "Relax, / Stand at attention, and."[7] We note also that this opening sentence ends with "and."—another seeming paradox, insofar as the connector "and" should signal and/or promise syntactic continuation and continuity. Hope for or anticipation of an answer to the syntactically logical question " 'and' what?" is immediately disrupted by the period. The continuity of meaning that should be guaranteed by the syntactic bridge of the "and" is interrupted from the very beginning of the poem: the bridge that should guarantee intelligibility is destroyed from the outset. The opening sentence ends in mid-thought, without coming to a proper sublation or synthesis of meaning, without fulfilling the dialectical promise of the connector. The continuous movement of meaning is interrupted prior to the initial sublation necessary for progress (or for the poem *Progress*) properly to begin.

Progress continues (or does it begin again?): "Purple snake stands out on / Porcelain tiles. The idea / *Is* the thing. Skewed by design. . . . " These lines seem to engage the poetics of William Carlos Williams: "Purple snake stands out on / Porcelain tiles." may be a gentle parody of Williams's "Red Wheel Barrow," though the question posed to Williams's poetics becomes more pressing in the sentence "The idea / *Is* the thing." The emphasis here is shifted from Williams's "no ideas but in things" to an even more radical emphasis on the materiality of the poetic idea: "The idea / *Is* the thing." emphasizes an exteriorizing of the space within or behind things that could carry or protect their essence, and which poetry could make it its job to reveal. Rather, Watten's revision of Williams's dictum emphasizes repetition and surface as a kind of radically non-revelatory "essence": "I trust replication. / Gives, / Surface." Williams's "no ideas but *in* things" presupposes a depth—presupposes, as does "the court reporter," "That only depth is perfect. . . . " Watten suggests here that thinking in terms of depth may actually "eradicate" poetry, eradicate a type of poetic thinking that moves along the surface play of writing.[8] "[T]he history of words" thought as

7. I cite Watten's text complete with intra-line periods, ellipses, and other punctuation. This may require some patience on the reader's part: some of his periods will end some of my sentences, though any punctuation I add to a quotation will be placed in brackets.
8. See Watten's *Total Syntax*, in which he compares Williams's and Silliman's "insistence on the unheroic particulars . . . where the 'nonaesthetic' observed detail is the key to social insight": "In Williams . . . the inconsequential is dramatized in a single moment of truth

depth, "distances[,]" or meaning eradicates poetry "by / Making him think certain ways. . . . " and not others; but perhaps the idea here is *written as surface* (and the fragmentation thereof): "I write, as in a mirror, / This present." (4).

It should be noted, though, that in *Progress* this "I" which "writes" and "trust[s] replication" also places its "trust" in a lot more than replication: we find "I trust wheat. . . . " (2); "I trust the materials." (2); "I trust the thing itself. . . . " (3). "[R]eplication" here becomes essence or "the thing itself"—insofar as the thing itself can be reconstituted in or by any number of differing contexts. It seems that trusting replication is, in other words, trusting not "in" the idea *in* things, but rather trusting the necessary movement of or between things, the necessity of error, change, and the impossibility of static meaning: "Stasis is a pinball." (10). The "I" that "trusts" and "writes," then, is necessarily drawn into this drama of nonteleological movement: "I am otherwise." (69) because "I" is always part of this "replication[,]" of this linguistic network that "Gives, / Surface." The poem, then, becomes a matter of thinking and writing this surface—"Thinking on the planes / Of a building, / but in verse." (6)—rather than thinking toward a dialectic sublation that would reveal the stable essence of the thing.

For *Progress*, it is not simply a matter of employing words whose "contradictory use is to / Specify empty" the category meaning. Nor does *Progress* give in to the urge simply to "delineate[.]" Rather, *Progress* attempts to think an other notion of progress, an economy that is not simply found or represented, but haltingly, disruptively written from the ground up. *Progress* names its disruption as an "Aggressive neutrality." (6), a kind of writing that Bernstein characterizes as

> noninstrumental (a writing that does not carry a meaning along with it as information to take away, which would make the writing there primarily to serve up this information, a shell in itself) where language is not in gear, is idling. . . . Writing as stupor, writing as out-to-lunch. Writing as vacation. Writing degree zero. Idleness as antistatic (functionless, it becomes estranged). Writing as idled

that is also ironic, while in Silliman its use is in a much more radical, ongoing process of evaluation" (109).

thinking (not just the means to a displaced end . . .). (*Content's Dream* 83–84)

The intransitivity of writing named here seems to describe well Watten's *Progress*, and is, perhaps, characteristic of language poetry on the whole, much of which could be called "idled thinking (not just the means to a displaced end)." Although there certainly is a displacement that language writing creates, the writing and thinking of language poetry is "not *just* the means to a displaced end," but a bringing forth of this displacement coupled with a necessary displacement of end-oriented thinking itself—the disrupting of a larger, end-oriented economy of meaning.

But, even within this double economy of disruption, it is not a matter of being once and for all free of teleological meaning's economy. As Bernstein writes in the poem/talk/essay "Artifice of Absorption":

The designation of the visual, acoustic,
& syntactic elements of a poem as "meaningless,"
especially insofar as this is conceptualized as
positive or liberating—& this is a common habit
of much *current* critical discussion of syntactically
nonstandard poetry—is symptomatic of a desire to
evade responsibility for meaning's total, &
totalizing, reach; as if meaning was a husk
that could be shucked off or a burden that could be
bucked. Meaning is not a use value *as opposed to*
some other kind of value, but more like valuation
itself; & even to refuse value is a value & a sort
of exchange. Meaning is no where *bound*
to the orbit of purpose, intention, or utility.
(*A Poetics* 13)

For Bernstein, there certainly is a "positive or liberating" moment in language writing's "syntactically / nonstandard poetry," but this liberation of alternative syntactical meanings is not "just" the "displaced end" that language writing moves toward. Rather, there is a second necessary consideration for this writing, a consideration that makes it impossible to "evade responsibility for meaning's total,

& / totalizing, reach"; poetry, in other words, cannot be simply liberated from an economy of meaning, "as if meaning was a husk / that could be shucked off or a burden that could be / bucked." Meaning is not just one poetic value among others, but "more like valuation / itself"; hence, language writing, if it wishes to pose a question to this economy, cannot simply throw off meaning, but rather must disseminate meaning—disrupting it doubly: first, meaning must become "no where *bound* / to the orbit of purpose, intention, or utility"; second, this writing must somehow account for its disruptions as other than simply non-meaningful or non-sensical. As Bernstein writes, his interests lie in "a poetry that does not assume a measure but finds it" (*Content's Dream* 75), a writing that does not move toward the wholeness of a meaning but strives to find a measure for itself, a way to account for the surface play of the poem itself, rather than solely to refer to or to clarify some end or meaning "outside" of this play.

The politics of such a poetic project, however, seem unclear at best. In fact, for many commentators, language poetry comes dangerously close to reproducing an "art-for-art's-sake" aesthetic. Despite the overt political claims of the poets themselves,[9] a question is often posed to language poetry concerning the potential for a political praxis drawn from a poetics of "idleness," discontinuity, or disfunctionality. For example, Marjorie Perloff—summing up the critique of Jackson MacLow and others—writes that "if language were really stripped of its referential properties . . . 'language poetry' would be no more than a mandarin game, designed to entertain an elitist coterie" ("Word as Such" 233).[10] Such an equation of language poetry with an art-for-art's-sake aesthetic, however, seems to miss the essential questions posed by language writing. It seems odd, for example, that this line of reasoning would align language poetry with something like MacLeish's famous dictum "A poem should not

9. Silliman, for example, writes quite clearly and unambiguously: "Let us undermine the bourgeoisie" ("If By 'Writing' " 168). His essay is included in the second section of *The L=A=N=G=U=A=G=E Book*, in which more than twenty-five writers associated with language writing take up the question of writing and politics (119–92).

10. Perloff, however, goes on to argue that this impotent elitism is not necessarily the case in language poetry because much of its syntactically nonstandard work can empower or free the reader to see myriad connections between things. In the end, though, Perloff remains a bit skeptical: "The question remains whether the calling into question of 'normal' language rules . . . is a meaningful critique of capitalism" (233).

mean / But be." A conception of poetry like MacLeish's, in which the poem is mystifyingly wrenched out of the material networks of language and into the purity of the realm of being, is in fact the prime target of language poetics. Art-for-art's-sake aesthetics have always implied that the artistic object is to be somehow elevated above any networks of signification, placed at an unreachable aesthetic distance, and then contemplated in its being. But language poetry collapses this aesthetic distance. The language poem exists in a network where language and syntax cannot be separated from meaning and being. The language poem cannot be purified and held at a distance because no notion of disinterested aesthetic distance can continue to hold in language poetics. As I argue throughout this work, in a postmodern context no pure space outside the drama of signification can be secured, and language poetry is, if nothing else, an attempt to come poetically and politically to grips with that fact.

This repudiation of disengaged art is, however, no simple call for or validation of an "engaged art." As Emmanuel Levinas writes in a 1948 essay on Sartre's notion of engaged art, an art-for-art's-sake aesthetic certainly "is false inasmuch as it situates art *above* reality and recognizes no master for it" ("Reality and Its Shadow" 131); however, Levinas also asks, "Is to disengage oneself from the world always to go *beyond*, toward the region of Platonic ideas and toward the eternal which towers above the world? Can one not speak of a disengagement on the hither side—of an interruption of time by a movement going on on the hither side of time, in its 'interstices' " (131). Perhaps, as Levinas suggests here in the context of a similar argument, the interruptions of language poetry cannot be collapsed quite so easily into a hermetic "mandarin game." Perhaps there can be a disruption of meaning—a disruptive disengagement—that does not simply or necessarily elevate the work of art to the untouchable realm of being, but rather, attends to the discontinuous space *between* things, to the "interstices" of presence or experience rather than to the seemingly smooth continuities. Perhaps language poetry is attempting to bring about this disengagement on what Levinas calls the "hither side of time," an interruption on *this side* of transcendence—a disengagement that does not try to take the work of art beyond the world into a realm of purity, but rather attempts to create a disruption in the smooth functioning of *this* world's systems of meaning and being. This disruptive disengagement would deny itself what Levinas calls the "pretentious and facile nobility" (131) that characterizes the aesthetic distance engendered by an art-for-art's-sake theory.

Nevertheless, the politics of language poetry's poetics of disengagement, disruption, or discontinuity remain a sharply contested question. Perhaps the most famous academic critique of language poetry along these lines is contained in Jameson's "Postmodernism, or The Cultural Logic of Late Capitalism." For Jameson, language poetry is representative of the surface-obsessed, fragmentary, "schizophrenic" aesthetic of postmodernism, and of an aesthetic/cultural logic that, in its destruction of the autonomy of the subject and the continuity of history, cannot help but ruin any possibility for personal conviction or political change. As Jameson writes, a postmodern critique may liberate one from the bounds of an oppressive notion of subjectivity, but it also entails a "liberation from every other kind of feeling as well, since there is no longer a self present to do the feeling" (64).[11] Jameson, in fact, critiques a notion of postmodernism very much like the one I have been developing here; the "flattening of discourse," the absence of an outside or *hors-texte*, the (dis)locating of the subject within in a network of exteriority, these are precisely what Jameson attacks as "a new kind of superficiality in the most literal sense—perhaps the supreme formal feature of all the postmodernisms" ("Postmodernism" 60).

For Jameson, Warhol's work and language poetry are prime examples of this schizophrenic depthlessness and its emphasis on the surface or signifier. While discussing Warhol's "Diamond Dust Shoes," however, Jameson inadvertently makes a case for a kind of "depth" to Warhol's work—and to postmodern "fragmentation" on the whole. He writes "[In 'Diamond Dust Shoes'] it is as though the external and coloured surface of things—debased and contaminated in advance by their assimilation to glossy advertising images—has been stripped away to reveal the deathly black-and-white substratum of the photographic negative which subtends them" (60).

11. This type of critique animates many feminist and postcolonial critiques of postmodernism, which are less interested in "feeling" than in the oppositional power which seems to require a subject position. See the essays collected in Nicholson's *Feminism/Postmodernism*. Also see Minh-ha's *Woman, Native, Other*.

It seems that Jameson here (dis)misses the fact that Warhol's emphasis on something like a "photographic negative"—that which allows pictorial representation to take place but is not itself representative—is itself a kind of "depth" exploration, insofar as it explores the conditions of possibility for representation. But, as Jameson notes, Warhol's negative *subtends* the image, that is, it "underlie[s] as to enclose or surround" it (*American Heritage Dictionary*). So the subtending negative has no essential or philosophical depth-relation to the photograph; it is not simply *before or below* the photographic image, but rather is *both* before the image *and* contained within it, is a kind of always-already-divided ground.[12]

This emphasis on a peculiar kind of ground in Warhol's work helps bring us back to Derrida's thinking, which Gasché has written about in similar terms, in terms of the subtending, nonreflective back or "tain" of a mirror that makes reflection possible without itself being reflective. As Gasché puts it, "Derrida's philosophy, rather than being a philosophy of reflection, is engaged in the systematic exploration of that dull surface without which no reflection and no specular or speculative activity would be possible, but which at the same time has no place and no part in reflection's scintillating play" (*Tain of the Mirror* 6). Gasché here sums up many of the arguments I have been making concerning postmodernism and (the end of) philosophy: the emphasis on the play of surfaces or networks in the work of Derrida, Foucault, Pynchon, or the language poets is not simply a hedonistic, irresponsible reaction to an *ethos* of impossibility; rather, this confrontation with surface or depthlessness is, as I have maintained throughout, *necessary* insofar as it is part and parcel of the systematic and historical specificity of the postmodern situation. There simply is no outside to appeal to, no space that can be protected from the play of an exterior network; hence, thinking must proceed *differently*, in and through the thought of difference without reduction to sameness.

Of course, this recognition of the conditions of postmodernity does not stifle but rather amplifies the question of the politics of this kind of postmodern work—and specifically the politics of language

---

12. See, for example, my discussion of Heidegger, Derrida and "sending" in Chapter 4.

poetry. In "Postmodernism," Jameson criticizes language poet Bob Perelman's poem "China," which begins:

China
We live on the third world from the sun. Number three.
  Nobody tells us what to do.
The people who taught us to count were being very kind.
It's always time to leave.
If it rains, you either have your umbrella or you
  don't.
The wind blows your hat off.
The sun rises also. . . .
(Quoted in "Postmodernism" 73)

"China," we should note in passing, only gets increasingly discontinuous from here, and Jameson hails this emphasis on discontinuous, paratactic series as the "fundamental aesthetic" of "so-called Language Poetry" (73). For Jameson, this paratactic emphasis on the play of signifiers in the poem means that it "turns out to have little enough to do with that referent called China" (75). He goes on to argue that the poem's refusal to engage the real historical situation of third-world China ("the third world from the sun") robs it of any proper political significance that it might have had, leaving it instead merely as an example of late capital's "schizophrenic fragmentation" (73).[13] In Jameson's reading of "China," then, "the signifying chain . . . is reduced to an experience of pure material Signifiers" (72); the signified is "reduced" to the level of the signifier, and we are left with the materiality of language without any hierarchical order(ing) and with a world bereft, therefore, of history or praxis. In short, for

13. See Bernstein, who poses a question to Jameson concerning his totalization of the conditions of postmodernism and the artistic responses to it: "The 'same' artistic technique has a radically different meaning depending on when and where it is used. . . . [J]uxtaposition of logically unconnected sentences or sentence fragments can be used to theatricalize the limitations of conventional narrative development, to suggest the impossibility of communication, to represent speech, or as part of a prosodic mosaic constituting a newly emerging (or then again, traditional but neglected) meaning formation; these uses need have nothing in common. . . . Nor is the little-known painter who uses a Neo-Hellenic motif in her work necessarily doing something comparable to the architect who incorporates Greek columns into a multimillion-dollar downtown office tower. But it is just this type of mishmashing that is the negative horizon of those discussions of postmodernism that attempt to describe it in unitary socioeconomic terms" (A Poetics 91–92).

Jameson, language poetry's paratactic aesthetic of fragmentation cannot help but be reactionary because it simply mimics and thereby upholds the fragmentation and apathetic end-lessness promoted by the bourgeois ideology of late capitalism.[14]

George Hartley, in *Textual Politics and the Language Poets*, takes issue with Jameson's characterization of the politics of language poetry. Hartley argues that when Jameson reads Perelman's poem merely as a schizophrenic "breakdown of the signifying chain" ("Postmodernism" 72) and a reification of the logic of late capital, he misses the fact that "China" produces exactly the kind of powerful critique of bourgeois ideology that Jameson sees lacking in much postmodern art. For Hartley, Perelman's "China" is an example of language poetry's "deconstruction of the 'referential fetish'—and with it the bourgeois claim to 'natural' language" (*Textual Politics* 99). Language poetry performs this "deconstruction" through a "laying bare of the framing process" (99), through the exposure of the arbitrariness and multiplicity of any poetic order(ing). This being the case, Hartley writes,

> Ironically, Perelman and other so-called language poets can be seen to meet Jameson's call for a new political art whose "aesthetic of cognitive mapping" in this confusing postmodern space of late capitalism may achieve "a breakthrough to some as yet unimaginable new mode of representing [the world space of multinational capital], in which we may again begin to grasp our positioning as individual and collective subjects and regain a capacity to act and struggle which is at present neutralized by our spatial as well as social confusion." (52, quoting Jameson 92)

In Hartley's reading, Jameson misses the point of language poetry's "fragmentation"; Hartley argues that language poetry does the needed work of ideology critique so that, in Jameson's own words, "we may again begin to grasp our positioning as . . . subjects," begin

14. See, contra Jameson, Adorno's *Aesthetic Theory*: "Those who allege that art has no longer any right to exist because it upholds the status quo do no more than promote one of the stale clichés of bourgeois ideology. The latter has always been prone to frown and demand to know 'where all this is going to end.' Art, in effect, must escape from this sort of teleology. . . . The idea of destination or final end is a covert form of social control" (356–57).

once again to act and struggle against the forces of late capital.[15] In fact, Hartley argues that language poetry performs this progressive ideology critique in and through the very concepts that Jameson points to as the reactionary element in language poetry: its fragmentation of poetic form and its emphasis on the materiality of the signifier. Hartley writes, "In their questioning of the function of reference, the self-sufficiency of the subject, and the adherence to standard syntax of the closed text, some so-called Language poets have developed a poetry which functions not as ornamentation or as self expression, *but as a baring of the frames of bourgeois ideology itself*" (*Textual Politics* 41, my emphasis). So, in the end, for Hartley language poetry functions as a discourse that, far from simply reifying bourgeois (poetic) ideology, actually bares the ideological frame of bourgeois workshop poetics and its conception of poetry as a product or message simply to be consumed "as ornamentation or as self expression." And in laying bare this framing process, language poetry allows the reader to see and participate in the myriad possibilities for meaning that are covered over by a unitary poetic and sociological ideology of consumption.

So, in the end, Jameson and Hartley have less a disagreement on the proper ends of a politically engaged postmodern art than they do a disagreement over whether language poetry fits the bill. For both Jameson and Hartley, it is imperative that there be a postmodern art of critique, an art, in Jameson's words, that "explicitly foreground[s] the commodity fetishism of a transition to late capital" (60). In fact, among those academic critics sympathetic to language poetry, the thematization of its project as this kind of ideology critique has become the standard reading: for McGann, language poetry's project is to reverse or oppose that "deformed and repressive form of reference called referentiality wherein language is alienated from its use-functions" (640). Likewise for Perloff, who, when she is most sympathetic to language writing, argues that it helps us to see that "our words can no longer be our own but that it is in our

---

15. As Hartley writes, "It is to the ruling class's benefit that we do not recognize the socially-constructed nature of language, for if we did we might recognize that the hegemonic views of reality—such as that commodities are 'natural'—are to a certain extent arbitrary, and, therefore, open to questioning" (*Textual Politics* 35).

power to represent them in new, imaginative ways" ("Can(n)on" 654).

But, as compelling as it may be, this critical apology for language poetry remains itself problematic; these literary critical *readings* of language poetry seem rather *un*problematically to recuperate a proper "job" or brand of commodified "work" for language poetics: namely, the work of ideology critique. This work of ideology critique, it should be noted, is in large part a job *given* to language poetry by criticism. Many language poets in the late seventies and early eighties were quite comfortable with a poetry of ideology critique that attempted to restore to the reader and society a linguistic *use*-value rather than a deformed *exchange*-value. This project, however, has since come under scrutiny. Steve McCaffery, for example, writes, "In hindsight, I can admit to certain naiveties in that approach. This writing was all produced before any of us had discovered Baudrillard's seminal work *The Mirror of Production*. . . . In light of the Baudrillardian 'proof' that use value is but a concealed species of exchange value, I would say now that the gestural 'offer' to a reader of an invitation to 'semantically produce' hints at an ideological contamination" (in Bartlett, "What Is 'Language Poetry'?" 747n). If, as McCaffery argues, for language poetry "use value is but a concealed species of exchange value," there remain several pressing questions for the standard academic reading of this work: how, for example, is the politically engaged critic or poet to account for the end product or work performed by ideology critique itself? How, in other words, can a poetics of ideology critique pose a radical question to the drama of commodification if it too produces a circumscribed use- or exchange-meaning, if it reveals a consumable end? What happens, in other words, when ideology critique itself "hints at an ideological contamination"? In yet other words, one could ask whether reading language poetry as ideology critique doesn't allow or force language poetry to become simply another "bourgeois" poetry of reference in which the reader comes to a consumable poetic realization or epiphany—an epiphany concerning the poetic "framing process itself, and by extension the process of ideological framing, which is no longer taken for granted" (Hartley, *Textual Politics*, xiii). If language poetry moves in the service of the predetermined end of ideology critique, as so many critics assert, doesn't it then participate in a rationalist project that leaves it squarely within an enlightenment bourgeois ideology of truth as revelation? How can the project of "laying bare" the truth behind the ideology escape the very ideological fetish that language poetry would displace? How can such a project overturn the referential fetish that ignores the surface in favor of the revelation, that ignores the parataxis of material signifiers in favor of the hypotaxis of the signified. Indeed, language poetry's "political" import seems to lie precisely in its refusal to be such a commodifiable "project." As language poet P. Inman puts it, "Writing is inescapably political. It doesn't illustrate the bleakness of late capitalism. It can't get outside itself. It is, rather, amidst itself, made out of the societal world around it" ("One to One" 225).

This gap between the surface of language writing and its reception or thematization by certain literary critics seems yet another indication of the drive toward determination in the discipline of literary criticism, which must cut this estranging discourse down to fit a recognizable literary category. When language poetry becomes thematized as an engaged avant-garde, its politics and its styles become recognizable. Critics who laud or disparage language poetry's politics for the most part eschew the fact that, in Michael Greer's words, language poetry's " 'political' claims rest not so much on the expression of a 'position' or an agenda as they do on an effort to change the way we attend to texts, 'poetic' and otherwise" ("Ideology and Theory" 335). Language poetry, in other words, has no traditionally recognizable political "agenda" over and above its engagement with "texts"—with thinking and acting in the postmodern world. As Inman insists, the poem is "made out of the societal world around it."

In fact, as Greer argues, literary criticism's disciplinary drive to circumscribe language poetry and to assign it a task ultimately diffuses the disruptiveness of the writing, diffuses the potential radicality of its rethinking the terms of the poetic and the political. He writes, "The rethinking of subjectivity and authorship [in language poetry] is ultimately overshadowed by a competing impulse [in literary criticism] to *situate* 'language poetry,' to name and define its 'place' in contemporary poetry" (336). He goes on concerning McGann, Bartlett, and Perloff:

All of these critics share an impulse to characterize language poetry as the repressed "other" of a dominant "workshop" poetic, theoretically sophisticated where it is naive, philosophically skeptical where it is idealistic, and politically oppositional where it is accommodating. . . . Language poetry is, in effect, marginalized as part of an avant-garde "alternative" which functions merely as an "ongoing corrective" to an equally reified "dominant" poetic. It loses any political or aesthetic significance it may have had in its own right as this binary historical map is drawn, and it becomes merely a way of provoking or irritating some fictional "mainstream." (337, 340)

Greer argues that McGann, Bartlett, and Perloff de-radicalize the disruptions created by language poetry when they name it as simply the opposite of the mainstream workshop poetics—as "an avant-garde 'alternative' which functions merely as an 'ongoing corrective' to an equally reified 'dominant' poetic." By locating language poetry as the center's opposite and opponent, a determining binary map is drawn and the fragmented text of language poetry suddenly becomes easily readable—the location of the work and the intention behind it having been ascertained.

Literary critics likewise domesticate language poetry, I would argue, when they make claims for language poetry's status as ideology critique. When language poetry is thematized as performing ideology critique, this determination ends up collapsing it into a familiar role that allows its potential disruptions to become revelatory in a traditional or recognizable way. It seems that this is especially true for Jameson's and Hartley's readings of an engaged postmodernism: when Hartley argues that language poetry can actually assist in Jameson's project of cognitive mapping, he goes a long way toward domesticating language poetry as precisely the kind of anti-postmodern postmodernism that Jameson calls for throughout his essay, an art that involves "reconquest of sense of place" (89).[16] In

16. Again, see Adorno's *Aesthetic Theory*, in which, contra Jameson, an appeal is made to an authentic artistic "mode of experience that is able to overcome the tendency to resort to false immediacy. Immediacy is gone forever" (311). More recently, however, Jameson's work has been becoming a bit more sympathetic to "fragmentary" postmodernism. In "Spatial Equivalents," for example, he speaks approvingly of the necessity for "a new kind of sentence, a new kind of syntax, radically new words, beyond our own grammar" and

short, readings that prescribe such literary critical work for language poetry seem not to account for the *disciplinary* politics of positing recognizable labels such as "engaged avant-garde" or "ideology critique" for language poetry. Literary criticism reduces the complexity of language poetry to an accessible and commodifiable code or intention, just as workshop poetry reduces the complexity of poetic experience to the consumability of an epiphany. As Bernstein writes about the recognizable codes and epiphanies of workshop poetics:

> Experience dutifully translated into these "most accessible" codes loses its aura and is reduced to the digestible contents which these rules alone can generate. There is nothing difficult in the products of such activity because there is no distance to be travelled, no gap to be aware of and to bridge from reader to text: What purports to be an experience is transformed into the blank stare of the commodity—there only to mirror our projections with an unseemly rapidity possible only because no experience of *other* is in it. (*Content's Dream* 59)

When language poetry's intention is thematized as the *dialectical other* of academic workshop poetry's bourgeois poetics, the unthematizable experience of *other* in reading it is hypostatized, negated, and sublated: the dissembling experience of *other* in language writing is smoothed out of the work as it is given a determining intention and a job to do, as its heterogeneous surface "is transformed into the blank stare of the commodity."

Language Poetry and the Academy

Thematizing language poetry as the dialectical other of academic workshop poetry can cause a certain amount of semantic confusion: "academic poetry" is itself vehemently opposed to the academy; it sees itself as the protector of the values of the individual against the increasing institutionalization of modern life. It values the "naturalist" qualities that are summed up in a speech-based, subjectivist

---

likewise seems more sympathetic to a radical materiality, lauding architect Frank Gehry's "attempt to think a material thought" (147).

poetics: the priority of the human voice, the priority of nonlinguistic experience over abstract thought, the priority of individual freedom over institutional constraints.[17] As Charles Altieri writes, these "contemporary poets prefer the direct, the personal, the local, the antiformal, and the topical" ("From Symbolist Thought to Immanence" 605) over the more formalist and impersonal strategies of the modernists. This poetry's ground in "man's normal non-reflective experience of the world" (617) leads it into a deep "contemporary distrust of mediation" (630), a deep suspicion of language and institutions, and a concomitant valorization of the transformative power of the subject. And, ironically, it is clearly these recognizably "liberal" values that have led to the protective sheltering of this tradition within the university. That being the case, however, this tradition is left in something of an uncomfortable position, trapped within a language and a university structure it wants to question, *and* quite literally compromised by its position within that structure. The obverse of the "insider" dilemma is, of course, to remain "outside" the academic poetic establishment, but this likewise seems compromising, insofar as it effectively cedes authority to the status quo. The canons of poetry and the manner in which poetry is taught, read, and disseminated to the general public would remain untouched by following this "outsider" strategy; political purity would be purchased at the cost of impotence.

Weinberger's position in this regard is instructive; although certainly no friend of an apolitical workshop tradition, he also defends his leftist poetics against language poets and literary critics—both of whom, remember, he chastises for being too theoretical. He writes, "Unlike critics and 'language' poets, I have no agenda, and am opposed to all canon-formation" ("Weinberger on Language Poetry" 184). There is something strange about a critique like Weinberger's coming from the left, as it seems to depend on a disinterested notion of objective standards that is thoroughly conservative. Unlike critics and language poets, Weinberger seems quite naive in his belief in a such an uncontested place of objectivity, an outside where he can be unproblematically opposed to and un-

17. For a good—if polemical—summary and critique of workshop poetics from outside the language movement, see Dooley's "Contemporary Workshop Aesthetic."

touched by the politics of an "agenda" or a "canon." Indeed, it is precisely through their common engagement with theoretical discourse that both "critics and 'language poets' " would become suspicious of the agenda embedded in Weinberger's claim, "I have no agenda." Likewise, as Silliman notes, it is actually "its long-term engagement with social, aesthetic, and linguistic theory [that] provides language poetry with both a vocabulary and potential mechanisms for posing the institutional question that . . . the anti-theoretical college workshop tradition lacks" ("Canons and Institutions" 164).

That "institutional question," as I have emphasized throughout this study, is necessarily double: if a pure "outside" space must be found in order to pose a relevant question, it will go unasked because this kind of outsider distance has disappeared in a postmodern epoch; the "purity" of the outside shows itself as an illusion. It seems, then, that the great institutional lesson learned by marginal groups over the past twenty-five years has been the necessity of mediating institutions—the recognition that, despite the potential problem of cooptation, the presence of traditionally oppressed or excluded groups within society's institutions is absolutely necessary, as is a simultaneous and ongoing engagement with problems of institutionalism. There must be, as I argue concerning Derrida and Foucault, a double move: first, there is the necessary and indispensable critical move that intervenes and overturns a historical repression or exclusion, that promotes access by the excluded to traditionally insular societal and political institutions; but there must likewise be a second move, an ongoing reevaluation of the field itself, if this critical move is to avoid revisiting the very exclusion it seeks to redress.

As Silliman argues in "Canons and Institutions," each important social movement of the twentieth century gravitates toward institutions to sustain its victories, or it dies. The women's movement, for example, would likely die if there were no women serving as legislators and lobbyists. Feminism would exist in name only if there had been no concomitant institutional gains by women in political and professional life. As Silliman writes, "The history of movements like these is virtually unanimous on the point that all tend to gravitate over time toward mediating institutions, regardless of what their original stance toward them may have been, or else they suffer defeats and dissolve outright" (162). Generally speaking, institutions are at the forefront of visiting repression on marginal groups, which, of course, makes these groups wary of becoming institutionally involved; however, reification of this inside/outside distinction depends on a kind of atheoretical one-way logic, wherein institutions are simply and repressively "bad" and outsider status is liberating and "good." As Silliman writes, this one-way logic of institutional avoidance can no longer hold: "I have suggested throughout this talk that a feature of mediating institutions is in fact that they are inescapable. All forms of organization that attempt to bypass, deny or avoid them are, I believe, social forms of psychological denial built out of an inner need to reject internal conflict and complexity" (162). For Silliman, the question of marginal groups and institutions cannot be sufficiently posed within an "attempt to bypass, deny, or avoid" institutions, but rather must be posed within a network of "internal conflict and complexity," within a theoretical framework that refuses to think institutions such as the academy in simple good/bad terms. As he writes, "Rather than being reducible to any reified identity, for example that of 'the enemy,' the academy is a ground, a field for contestation" (165). This does not mean that language poetry is merely an academic apologist discourse; it is, rather, a discourse that recognizes a certain postmodern necessity in mediating institutions. It recognizes, in short, that there is no "outside."

The academic "field for contestation," however, still finds it very difficult to deal with the disruptions of language poetry. One gets the feeling that academics on both the right and left wish that language poetry would simply disappear. And, although this work is receiving a certain amount of *critical* attention, it is making very few other academic inroads. For example, although the survey-course bible *The Norton Anthology of Modern Poetry* does pay lip-service to a certain pluralism, there is no mention of language poetry in it, even though the text was updated in 1988. This omission is not particularly surprising, but what is surprising is the exclusion of language-oriented writing from the new *Heath Anthology of American Literature*, the aggressively multicultural and unapologetically leftist anthology of American literature that first appeared in 1990. In the unsigned introduction to the contemporary period in the *Heath Anthology*, we are told the story of the multicultural canon wars of recent years: with the breakdown of "presumptively 'universal' standards of value," we are now obliged to "examine a far wider range of texts, some of which may seem to the literary traditionalist as exotic as a real Hiawatha might have looked to Henry Wadsworth Longfellow" (1768).

This profession of diversity, however, is something of a bait-and-switch tactic. As the introduction to the *Heath Anthology* puts it, "Contemporary literature demands some change in Williams's familiar phrase, 'No ideas but in things.' That principle today might better be stated 'No ideas but in feelings' " (1767). The diversity hailed by the *Heath Anthology*, then, seems to rest in opening up a kind of epiphanic white experience to many other groups. What is diversified here are the groups who can legitimately express a similar experience of personal feeling: such a poetry would, presumably, give "a real Hiawatha" the shared vocabulary in which to relate his otherwise "exotic" feelings to a white westerner like Longfellow. If this is the case, however, one is then left to negotiate two seemingly paradoxical ideas—in Bernstein's words, the "twin ideas of diversity and the common reader" (*A Poetics* 5). One is left, in other words, with a diversity that shows itself through the easily consumable sameness of a kind of subjective metagrammar. For example, according to the *Heath Anthology*, relating experiences of diversity requires "relentless clarity of . . . word choice" (1767); the literature of diversity may occasionally create an effect that will seem strange, but it is "always cohesive in the long run" (1767). Indeed, this smoothness of technique is first and foremost: "Contemporary writers may use innovative methods of expressing their subjects, but they may just as often insist on seemingly simple techniques. *Readability is their primary consideration*" (1769, my emphasis).

If a consumable "readability" and emphasis on "expressi[on]" is the ante to get into the game, it's not surprising that language poetry isn't asked to play, though, again, it seems that language poetry can in some ways account for its own exclusion even from the discourse of diversity: language poetry calls into question the modes by which the continuity of experience itself, the ground of the *Heath Anthology's* notion of diversity, is represented in poetry. Bernstein writes:

Too often the works selected to represent cultural diversity are those that accept the model of representation assumed by the dominant culture in the first place. "I see my grandpa on the hill / next to the memories I can never recapture" is the base line against which other versions play: "I see my yiddishe mama on Hester street / next to the pushcarts I can no longer peddle" or "I see my grandmother on the hill / next to all the mothers whose lives can never be recaptured" or "I can't touch my Iron Father / who never canoed with me / on the prairies of my masculine epiphany." Works that challenge these models of representation run the risk of becoming more inaudible than ever within mainstream culture. (*A Poetics* 6)

Bernstein here argues that pluralism's "diversity" of experience can quickly become standardized by a certain type of representation: the highly discontinuous experience of Jews, women, and Native Americans takes on a sameness imposed by the banal and predictable baseline of bourgeois white male experience. Literature is supposedly democratized by an emphasis on experiential diversity, but the representational standard by which valid experience is judged or adduced goes untouched.

In short, *difference is, once again, judged by the horizon or the ultimate possibility of sameness;* something like a discontinuous diversity is contained by reference to a discourse outside or not subject to the conflicted surface of contemporary American culture. Again, the *Heath Anthology,* "The most profound change that has occurred during the past twenty years is . . . that literature can no longer be divided into 'mainstream' and 'marginal.' Readers can choose from a wide variety of *good* fiction, poetry, and drama, being published and distributed by both commercial and more specialized presses" (1785, my emphasis). This seems like a plausible enough statement at first, but on further examination it becomes strange. It seems that the categories mainstream and marginal no longer obtain *not* because a white male standard arrogantly masquerading as universal has been successfully called into question, but because other groups have "risen" to that standard: " 'marginal' and 'mainstream' " are no longer operative because the reader can now "choose from a wide variety of *good* fiction, poetry, and drama." The word "good" here rather obviously functions as a code word for the type of subjective literature of feelings that the *Heath Anthology*'s editors find representative of "today's literary scene" (1768). And if the standard of "good" literature is the revelation of subjective experience, language poetry is clearly no damn good. And it is, needless to say, ironic that in a "scene" in which the center/margin dichotomy supposedly no longer obtains, language poetry remains so far from this non-existent center that it is not even mentioned.[18]

I suspect that this is the case not only because language poetry irritates the ruling orthodoxy of the academic poetry world (as McGann and Perloff rightly say it does), but because language poetry—like the theory it is often accused of resembling—calls into question the entire balkanizing logic of consensus pluralism and its dreams of a transparent language and a kind of universal poetic or academic community. As Bernstein puts it:

> The insidious obsession with mass culture and popularity, . . . translated into the lingo of a unified culture of diversity, threatens to undermine the legitimacy of working on a small, less than mass and, yes, less than popular scale. . . . When we get over this idea that we can all speak to each other, I think it will begin to be possible, as it always has been, to listen to one another, one at a time and in the various clusters that present themselves. (*A Poetics* 6, 8)

A radically plural or diverse community, an academic, poetic, or societal community based on difference within and among itself, is the promise and the project of language poetry; and it entails, as Bernstein argues, first and foremost that "we get over the idea that we can all speak to each other" in some kind of metalanguage of communion. What "we"—whoever this "we" might be—have in common is that we have little or nothing in common, and to attempt to smooth out these differences on or into a preexisting horizon of

18. "Experimental" writing, of course, is often left out of these schematic summaries, but not so in the *Heath Anthology*, in which we are informed about "new currents in highly experimental fiction—by less established white male writers like Ronald Sukenick, Raymond Federman, Walter Abish, Steve Katz, Gil Sorrentino, [etc.]." Such writing is actually—if left-handedly—praised as "a truly innovative kind of text that might be at variance with some critical theory of the time, but was finding an apt readership whenever it was published" (1785).

sameness is to doom ourselves to more of the same lack of understanding.

Instead, we need always to remember the difference that actually constitutes any "we"—the dispersion that we actually are, rather than a "unified diversity" that we supposedly have in common. And this is the difference that language writing attends to in its dual focus: there certainly are and need to be communities built on consensus and openness, but these communities always run the risk of replicating the exclusionary logic that they are formed to combat. Hence, again, there are two movements: certainly there needs to be a continued opening up of what Bernstein calls the narrow "racist reading habits engendered by the educational system and the media" (4), certainly the gains of multiculturalism need to be continually expanded. But, at the same time, there needs to be an ongoing reconsideration of the field of the political and institutional itself, a field much wider and more diverse than the intersubjective networks of individuals and their personal experience. If our notion of "diversity" merely rests in a watered-down sameness of expression, that notion of diversity likewise needs to be disrupted and opened up: the initial call for difference needs to be heard again. But this call may have to come in a voice that is difficult to recognize and assimilate—a voice that is not so much a voice, but the proliferating network of discourses that is the forgotten ground of "our" society.

7 / By Way of a Conclusion: Three Words for Derrida

Yes and no (what else?)
> —BARBARA JOHNSON
> *Personal correspondence (a postcard,*
> *no less) in response to a question*
> *concerning this project*

Derrida apparently wants to have it both ways: to undermine all logocentric concepts and yet to continue to use them for his own purposes. The tactic of using them "under erasure" strikes me as less like being "suspended over an abyss" than like trying to be on both sides of a fence.
> —THOMAS McCARTHY
> "The Politics of the Ineffable:
> Derrida's Deconstructionism"

Even while remembering all we have said about ends, here at the end of this work perhaps a question remains: are we, despite everything, left with a version of what we began to study? Are we, after the deconstruction of an end-oriented economy, left simply with another, more pernicious and ethically dangerous impasse? The question of deconstructive ethics—what's left for action or politics after the end of end-oriented thinking—is wide-ranging, hotly debated, and positively buried under scholarship.[1] Rather than merely rehearse the polemics surrounding this subject, I'd like to

---

1. Rather than cite the mass of material on the subject, let me recommend an incisive recent treatment of the literature in the field, Paul Jay's "Bridging the Gap: The Position of Politics in Deconstruction." I quibble with Jay's conclusions, but I find his analysis of the subject both comprehensive and insightful.

look specifically at three words that have, I think, come to characterize deconstructive decision: yes and no. These are three words that are expected from a "deconstructionist." Whether one finds them rhetorically evasive (a sign of deconstruction's endless ethico-political waffling) or philosophically necessary (a necessarily complex rewriting of the transcendentalist "yes *or* no"), these three words are, at least, a familiarly deconstructive response to a pointed question.

But how can we understand these three words that deconstruction offers in response to pointed ethico-political questions—and here we should keep in mind that, as I argue in Chapter 2, there is no undecidability in general. "Yes and no" obtains *only* in relation to a specific situation, a pointed question; it is not, in other words, the blanket deconstructive answer to *any* question. Still, what kind of "ethics" or "politics" can be based on or drawn out of such equivocation? In "The Politics of the Ineffable," Thomas McCarthy poses just such a question. For McCarthy, Derrida's "yes and no" is a symptom of deconstruction's wanting to have its cake and eat it too. As he puts it, "Derrida apparently wants to have it both ways: to undermine all logocentric concepts and yet to continue to use them for his own purposes" (154).

In short, McCarthy attacks the double gesture that I see at the heart of Derrida's project. McCarthy reads the double gesture as an equivocation that offers convenient rationalizations rather than firm positions, leaving deconstruction inexorably "on both sides of a fence" concerning ethico-political issues. McCarthy sums up quite succinctly many critiques of deconstruction when he writes that Derrida "has been rather evasive about just which politics, or approach to politics, it involves. . . . [One] cannot turn to Derrida's political 'theory' to settle the issue, for he has not offered one, and indeed regards the whole genre as eminently deconstructible. . . . Thus, the debate concerning deconstructionist politics stems in no small measure from Derrida's unwillingness or inability to 'decide' it by word or example" (146). McCarthy points to what he sees as the paradox of deconstruction: Derrida seems to want to make political decisions and make a case for a deconstructive political intervention; but at the same time he wants to deconstruct the recognized codes of political discourse, to show that all political decision must go through the trial of the undecidable. For McCarthy and many other critics, however, this tactic is severely limited and limiting for ethics or politics, and it leaves deconstruction mired in an intra-philosophical game—a ceaseless testament to the "unwillingness or inability to 'decide.' " For McCarthy, deconstruction remains a critique that has "very little to offer in the way of positive ethico-political proposals" (153–54) largely because such "positive ethico-political proposals" would inexorably smack of dialectical calculation, and therefore, on McCarthy's reading, they would certainly have to fall prey to the second movement of the double reading— a movement that, in Derrida's words, "remains *heterogeneous* both to the dialectic and to the calculable" (*Limited Inc.* 116). This radical heterogeneity of the double reading's second move is where McCarthy locates deconstruction's "politics of the ineffable."

McCarthy cites Derrida's article "The Laws of Reflection: Nelson Mandela, In Admiration" as an example of deconstruction's ethico-political fence-sitting. As McCarthy points out, Derrida's political writings have spoken in the name of many causes; his writings on apartheid, the law, the press, sexual difference, educational institutions, and a host of other recognizably political topics "have shown him to be generally on the 'progressive' side" (146), but McCarthy is quick to point out what he perceives to be an inconsistency in Derrida's political writings:[2]

> All of the analytic and critical work is done via "logocentric" concepts and norms, from which Derrida is at the same time obliged to distance himself. . . . [O]ne cannot help but notice that he has no other means of conveying the power of Mandela's witness than those same concepts and norms. Mandela is said to have turned "the very logic of the law" against those who wrongfully and scornfully usurped it, . . . to have brought its true force to bear against them. ("Politics of the Ineffable" 154)

McCarthy here offers an example to back up his argument that double reading is double dealing: deconstruction first allows itself

---

2. On apartheid, see "Racism's Last Word"; on the law, in addition to the Mandela article, see "Force of Law"; on the press, see *The Other Heading*; on sexual difference, see "Geschlecht"; on educational institutions, see "On Colleges and Philosophy," "Sendoffs," and "The Principle of Reason."

the luxury of logocentrism's "concepts and norms" in making its critiques of apartheid, and then denies that very logocentrism; it uses an end-oriented economy of meaning when it wants to be political or critical, only to deny such an economy's validity when it wants to be properly deconstructive. In the Mandela essay, for example, McCarthy locates the power of Derrida's defense and admiration of Mandela's actions in a thoroughly humanistic and logocentric appeal to the real and true spirit of the law, which Mandela turns against the unjust and therefore unlawful hypocrisy of apartheid. Here, McCarthy argues, Derrida is appealing to a very traditional formulation: Mandela shows us how the just metaphysical law has been mistranslated into an unjust code of laws, and, in his long captivity, Mandela continually bears witness to that more excellent transcendental law. Such logocentric appeals are Derrida's only available "means of conveying the power of Mandela's witness," and the necessity of such ethico-political logocentricity only further points out deconstruction's impotence when considering "its translation into a philosophico-political program" (151).[3]

Derrida, for his part, does indeed write about Mandela (who was still imprisoned at the time) as a "man of the law" ("Laws of Reflection" 26) who draws upon and reflects the law in the face of his captors. Mandela writes that he admires Western law, but Derrida is quick to point out that, in Mandela's admiration, he does not draw upon it merely as a reserve of normative constraints, as his captors do:

> If he admires this tradition, does it mean that he is its inheritor, its simple inheritor? *Yes and no*, depending on what is meant here by inheritance. You can recognize an authentic inheritor in one who conserves and reproduces, but also in the one who respects

3. For Derrida, there is perhaps a problem with McCarthy's word "translation." As any number of critics have pointed out, one of the things that Derrida ceaselessly shows us is that the supposedly "ontological" realm of thinking is always already the realm of the "political," and hence this talk of translating one into the other depends on a very traditional distinction between thought and action. Although this is true, it strikes me that the question posed to McCarthy by deconstruction can be heard in a somewhat different register. It seems that Derrida teaches us not merely that the ontological is political and vice versa, but rather that both ontological and political discourse emerge within and from a common network that I've been calling here the "postmodern," but that Derrida calls "deconstruction."

the *logic* of the legacy enough to turn it upon occasion against those who claim to be its superior guardians, enough to reveal, despite and against the usurpers, what has never yet been seen in the inheritance: enough to give birth, by the unheard-of *act* of a reflection, to what has never seen the light of day. (17, first emphasis mine)

McCarthy is clearly correct when he argues that Derrida shows Mandela to be turning the logic of the law against his captors. But his claim concerning the "logocentric" nature of Derrida's concept of law is more suspect. There could be no simply normative concept of law that exists to protect the radical alterity of "the unheard-of *act* of a reflection"—an act that in turn could bring about "what has never seen the light of day." As Derrida points out, Mandela admires the normative laws of Western tradition enough to take them seriously, both to reflect upon this tradition and to reflect it. But that does not make him "its inheritor, its simple inheritor," because, in the eyes of this tradition, he is an outlaw. Even if he were a law-abiding South African, this tradition would deprive him of basic privileges, and would certainly never allow a man or woman from a native African tradition to be white South Africa's "simple inheritor."

So when one asks if Mandela is an inheritor of this tradition—if Mandela is a "man of the law"—the *necessary* answer is Derrida's "yes and no." Such an answer is not, as McCarthy would have it, a matter of being evasive concerning this eminently decidable situation, of trying to be on "both sides of a fence" concerning the brutal regime of apartheid; rather, if one is adequately to account for Mandela's imprisoned status—and, I would argue, even his status as the free leader of the ANC, holder of a certain recognized position within South Africa—one *cannot* simply say "yes, he is" or "no, he's not" inheritor and protector of a Western conception of law: such a yes or no is simply not adequate to Mandela's situation.

Mandela's relation to this tradition, to this law, is *necessarily* double; he bears witness to it, as well as to what is beyond it or what remains unthought by it: Mandela's admiration of the law reveals a "conscience" or witness that is "not only memory but promise" (38), a "recognition" of one's duty not only to a preexisting tradition of normative law, but a simultaneous duty to the promise of what is not yet, to the future transformation of that tradition. But here again McCarthy's ear for logocentrism pricks up:

> The "promise" is itself identified, however, in terms of a traditional notion of "conscience": it arises from placing "respect for the law which speaks immediately to conscience" above "submission to positive law." The residual undecidability amounts, it seems, to nothing more than our inability to say today how Mandela will be understood in the future. But we do not need the apparatus of deconstruction to make us aware of that. ("Politics of the Ineffable" 154–55)

McCarthy here again claims that deconstruction is necessarily logocentric when it is political: the first, intervening reading of a double reading is the only one that accomplishes anything, and the second reading merely gestures toward an ineffable "undecidability" that, in actuality, is "nothing more than our inability to say today how Mandela will be understood in the future." This summary is, I think, rather inadequate, and does not pay sufficient attention to the supplementarity of the ethical *logic* at work here. Derrida argues that Mandela's relation to the law is double, but he is not merely opposing a normative "positive law" to a transcendental "higher" law of conscience. Occupying a position that is "not only memory but promise," not only inside a tradition, but also bearing and attesting to the trace of something beyond it, is a constant concern of Derridean discourse. To understand how it is deployed here, we need to look more closely at Derrida's notion of the "law," and how it is that Mandela both reflects and protests this law, how it is possible (indeed, how it is *necessary*) for Mandela to be both inside and outside the law.

According to Derrida, Mandela can be both inside and outside the law because of the structure of the law itself—because the law is already, necessarily multiple. As Leonard Lawlor writes in "From the Trace to the Law":

> Derrida designates the minimal sameness of the law as the law's "structure." It is necessarily a part of the law's structure to have

a scope of application. Although the law is always empirically and historically determined, located in particular cases and documents, the law must cover an indefinite number of cases. The law does not and cannot *belong* to any particular case in which it is found. The law must remain minimally the same and yet be open to indefinite extension or differentiation. The law must therefore possess the possibility of being iterated. Iterability opens the law and enables it to protect diverse instances and persons, even deviant or heterogeneous instances. (10)

According to Lawlor, the term "law" in Derrida's discussion of Mandela is similar in function to a range of other Derridean "undecidables"; his work on Mandela and the law mirrors the logic that one sees throughout Derrida's work on, for example, the signature, the inscription of writing, the new Europe, and the university.[4] These analyses attempt to deal with the necessity of a concept's singularity or uniqueness coupled with the necessity that the concept be open to a wide variety of applications or contexts. They deal with the ways in which a radically specific analysis opens onto a larger field without becoming merely generalizable. Like a signature, for example, the law must be a radically specific guarantee within a certain "empirically and historically determined" context and, at the same time, be infinitely repeatable in a range of other potentially dissimilar contexts. As Lawlor writes, the law "must remain minimally the same and yet be open to indefinite extension or differentiation." The law, then, by its very structure, must be open, different from itself; it cannot rest in a single past interpretation of tradition (as it does for Mandela's captors), but must rather gesture toward "the promise of what has not yet ever been seen or heard" ("Laws of Reflection" 38), toward the future democratic South Africa of Mandela, where only totalizing systems such as apartheid will be excluded. Such is the law that Mandela witnesses before his captors, the law that does not rest in a singular interpretation, but in the structure of the law itself, whose iterability over a number of dissimilar contexts serves "to protect diverse instances and persons, even deviant or heterogeneous instances."

4. See, for example, "Signature, Event, Context," "Plato's Pharmacy" in *Dissemination, The Other Heading*, and "The Principle of Reason."

So here again Derrida's work shows us what we have come to expect from him, the insight, in McCarthy's words, that "every contextualization is open to recontextualization" ("Politics of the Ineffable" 155). McCarthy, however, chastises Derrida for merely stating this fact ceaselessly, and ignoring the pragmatic task of rebuilding concepts that can account for this state of affairs. He writes that "rather than meditate at the edge of the abyss, pragmatically inclined thinkers have tried to reconstruct the notions of reason, truth, objectivity and the like in non-foundationalist terms" (156). It is, however, difficult to see how Derrida, in the Mandela essay and elsewhere, is merely "meditat[ing] at the edge of the abyss." Derrida is almost fanatically interested in "reconstructing" a logic wherein words such as "reason, truth, objectivity and the like" could be accounted for in other than transcendental terms. Indeed, one could argue that for Derrida it is *always* a matter of a structuration that can account for difference as other than lack of sameness; it is, indeed, a matter of building a logic that holds "for thought and for the relation to the other, the two of which I do not separate" (*Limited Inc.* 117). Derrida writes, for example, that

a theory of non-marginal cases is only possible, interesting, and consistent if it can account, in the structure of those cases said to be nonmarginal, for the essential possibility of cases interpreted as marginal, deviant, parasitical, etc. How are the latter possible? What must the structure called "normal" or "normative" be, what must the structure of the field where it inscribes itself be, for the deviant or the parasitical to be possible? (*Limited Inc.* 126)

Here we clearly see, in the context of his reading of speech-act theory, Derrida's interest in building a coherent logic in what McCarthy calls "non-foundationalist terms." According to Derrida, the normative (a general law of interpretation) must be able to account for the other acts or interpretations ("the deviant or the parasitical") that could likewise be produced from the same situation or data: "Every contextualization is open to recontexualization" is not, for Derrida, merely a hypothesis or one view among others. It is, rather, the law of possibility that obtains in our historical space or time, and one is obliged to construct a logic to account for it—to render reasonable this postmodern situation, from which ground has been withdrawn.[5]

Because every context is subject to recontexualization, undecidability becomes necessary and inescapable: the existence of other or excluded contexts must necessarily complicate a normative theory of decision. One is unable *simply* to choose among the wide range of possible contextualizations for a specific decision without somehow taking into account, rather than merely ignoring or discounting out of hand, other possible conclusions. As Derrida writes:

> In accordance with what is only ostensibly a paradox, *this particular* undecidable opens the field of decision or of decidability. It calls for decision in the order of ethical-political responsibility. It is even its necessary condition. A decision can only come into being in a space that exceeds the calculable program that would destroy all responsibility by transforming it into a programmable effect of determinate causes. There can be no moral or political responsibility without this trial and this passage by way of the undecidable. Even if a decision seems only to take a second and not to be preceded by any deliberation, it is structured by this *experience and experiment of the undecidable*. (*Limited Inc.* 116)

For Derrida, to decide merely with easy reference to an existing norm is not to decide at all. Such "decision" is nothing other than a "programmable effect." This is, of course, *not* to say that decisions are *simply* impossible, that decision is merely halted or stifled; it is, however, to insist that the "deliberation" necessitated by the myriad decisions that are possible and consistent—the "experience and experiment of the undecidable"—is absolutely unavoidable. This fact, about which I suspect there is little disagreement, leads to an obvious paradox: one must continue to make decisions when standard norms of decision making have shown themselves to be open to multiple recontextualizations and, thus, have ceased to provide univocal guidance. And this situation just as necessarily calls for an ostensibly

5. Cf. *Limited Inc.*, in which Derrida thematizes quasi-transcendental undecidability as "a proposition that can appear paradoxical, even contradictory in the eyes of common sense or of a rigid classical logic. It is perhaps unthinkable in the logic of good sense. . . . It is of this too that we are speaking when we say 'margin' or 'parasite.' It is of this as well that an accounting, and a reason, must be rendered" (127–28).

paradoxical theory of decision, a theory of decision in McCarthy's "non-foundationalist terms": a traditional yes-or-no decision is necessary but, strictly speaking, impossible.

Determinate decision, then, remains just as important and necessary for Derrida as it is for McCarthy; they part ways not concerning this necessity of decision, but rather concerning how one accounts for other potential decisions. For Derrida, even though decision necessarily begins and ends in an argumentative economy of "yes or no," other decisions ultimately cannot be accounted for simply as mistakes, miscalculations, or rival interpretations. To do so would be merely to dismiss them. Rather, Derrida's "yes and no" is a necessary response if one is to *experience* the radical plurality of otherness, if one is to take into account the network of alterity in which decisions arise. In fact, normative, determinate, or calculable decision is made possible by such a "space that exceeds the calculable."

And this problem of accounting for other decisions brings us to another of the double characters of deconstruction: it is at once an interventionary "theory" and, as Derrida insists, that which gestures beyond all theories toward a network that can reinscribe and account for them. As Derrida puts it, "What we call deconstruction in its academic or in its editorial form is also a symptom of a deconstruction at work elsewhere in society and the world" ("On Colleges and Philosophy" 222). Or, as he rather puzzlingly writes, "Deconstruction is neither a theory nor a philosophy. It is neither a school nor a method. It is not even a discourse, nor an act, nor a practice. It is what happens, what is happening today in what they call society, politics, diplomacy, economics, historical reality, and so on and so forth. Deconstruction is the case" ("Some Statements and Truisms" 85). For McCarthy, I suspect, this is Derrida at his obscurantist best (or worst)—wanting deconstruction both to be a traditional normative discourse, and the logic of discourse itself; however, the two senses of deconstruction outlined here are perfectly consistent with Derrida's emphasis on the double gesture, the necessity to think from within a language or a tradition, even as one attempts to think what is repressed within that tradition or what is beyond it. Deconstruction is a " 'thought' [that] requires *both* the principle of reason *and* what is beyond the principle of reason, the *arkhe* and an-archy"

("Principle of Reason" 18–19). This formulation, as I have argued throughout this book, names the postmodern situation, the need to think and act rationally, decisively, and ethically without transcendental support for reason, decision, and ethics. We as postmoderns are *necessarily* both inside a tradition (its language, its concepts, its institutions, its norms) and outside it (beyond its unitary epiphanic or revelatory logics). This is, as Derrida insists, "the case"; it is "what happens," "what is happening" in a postmodern world where there is no foundational extra-text.

And this situation carries with it new codes of ethico-political responsibility. For example, as Derrida writes concerning the role of the university scholar (using the very line of reasoning followed in "Laws of Reflection"), the "provocation to think brings together in the *same* instant the desire for memory and exposure to the future, the fidelity of a guardian faithful enough to want to keep even the chance of a future, in other words, the singular responsibility of what he does not have and what is not yet" ("Principle of Reason" 20). Here we see Derrida outlining a deconstructive "responsibility" toward the alterity that is quite literally the groundless ground of postmodern logic, the expropriative responsibility of the ethical subject toward what he or she "does not have and what is not yet." I think we can see concretely what this means for teaching and research within the university—where one must teach and uphold a certain tradition with a perhaps greater respect for what is beyond that tradition, what remains unthought by it, the ways it will necessarily have to be transformed in the future. And, in retrospect, according to this same logic we see how Mandela is a "man of the law" for Derrida: he bears witness to the law of reinscription and possibility that makes normative law possible. On the empirical level—which remains, always, equally a necessary one—Mandela reflects this other law by calling for democratic law that is "true" to the deconstructive law of possibility. Mandela's responsibility, then, is at every moment both to enact a normative law of respect and constraint *and* simultaneously to preserve the possibility of the future, the possibility of an other context that would require a rethinking of this normative law. This other law would keep open other contexts in which questions concerning the normative law (*how* to enact *what* constraints to guarantee *whose* respect?) would always need to be raised. Mandela's responsibility both reflects and reflects upon the law, and thereby mirrors the deconstructive notion of an ethical responsibility that remains (always, even in the "present," at the level of the empirical) double.

If McCarthy's first objection to deconstruction's ethics or politics concerns its logocentric inconsistency, certainly his larger objection concerns the ethical responsibility that deconstruction posits. He writes:

> It is sheer romanticism to suppose that uprooting and destabilizing universalist structures will of itself lead to letting the other be in respect and freedom rather than to intolerant and aggressive particularism, a war of all against all in which the fittest survive and the most powerful dominate. Enlarging the social space in which otherness can be, establishing and maintaining a multifarious and spacious pluralism, seem, on the contrary, to require that we inculcate universalistic principles of tolerance and respect, and stabilize institutions that secure rights and impose limits. Otherwise, how is the tolerance of difference to be combined with the requirements of living *together* under *common* norms? And, in justifying such norms, is there any alternative superior to free and open discussion of matters of public interest? ("Politics of the Ineffable" 158)

Here McCarthy poses a series of most troubling questions to deconstruction: doesn't deconstruction's openness to the undecidability of the other and the future also open the door for an "intolerant and aggressive particularism"? Doesn't protection from such an unpleasant future "require that we inculcate universalistic principles" in order to live peacefully together? And, in creating our future society, "Is there any alternative superior to free and open discussion of matters of public interest?" These are all difficult questions, yet deconstruction offers a concrete answer: yes and no.

Yes, it certainly is necessary for there to be "free and open discussion," and there must be concrete laws of some wide application enacted to protect marginal groups in addition to merely philosophically "accounting for" them. But, at the same time, there needs to be a hesitation here—another set of concerns to tarry with the normative: how, for example, does one "inculcate"—to teach or impress by forceful urging or frequent repetition," from the Latin meaning "to trample"—a "spacious pluralism"?[6] Likewise, McCarthy's notion that deconstruction cannot protect us from future ethico-political backsliding seems a bit odd. Could Marxism have predicted or prevented the crimes committed in its name? Can a Habermasian communicative rationality? Indeed, can any ethical or political system predict the future? The deconstructive law, for its part, attempts to protect the promise of the future by insisting on normative laws that respect other contexts, laws that keep the future open to further expropriative transformations, and thereby keep a vigilant eye out for repression. As Derrida maintains, the only thing that deconstruction excludes is totalization.

In addition, we need to question whether the "free and open discussion" that McCarthy celebrates has not led to precisely the "intolerant and aggressive particularism" that he worries about deconstruction fostering. Such a pluralism, insofar as it depends upon a very traditional philosophical and cultural economy of competitive mastery, certainly has its limitations, and, in fact, it seems to open the door quite nicely for a "war of all against all in which the fittest survive and the most powerful dominate." Indeed, it seems "sheer romanticism" to think that there has ever been anything like "free and open discussion," and it seems likewise a romantically traditional ruse to argue that such discussion is a community's common heritage and will actually solve its societal problems.

Of course, for McCarthy the ideal of rational consensus is just that, a regulative ideal that has little or no chance of ever being realized. As he writes about Habermas's work, this ideal "has to be understood in process terms, that is, not as an actually realizable state of affairs but as an orientation for what must always be an ongoing effort" (*Ideals and Illusions* 194). As McCarthy writes about such "idealizing presuppositions," "Without that idealizing moment there would be no foothold in our accepted beliefs and practices for the critical shocks to consensus that force us to expand our horizons and learn to see things in different ways. It is precisely this context-transcendent—in Kantian terms, this 'regulative'—surplus of meaning in our notion of truth that keeps us from being locked into what

6. Definition from the *American Heritage Dictionary*.

we happen to agree on at any particular time and place, that opens us up to the alternative possibilities lodged in otherness and difference" (*Ideals and Illusions* 33–34). For McCarthy, the regulative ideal of uncoerced consensus holds open the possibility of critique: the "foothold" for "critical shocks to consensus" is secured by the fact that any particular consensus in this or that culture will always and everywhere fall short of ideal consensus. The regulative ideal exists literally nowhere; nevertheless, positing the ideal allows one to pose a question to (necessarily non-ideal) consensus everywhere, to question the ruling ideology in the name of another, excluded point of view. This openness to other points of view, in fact, is the primary guarantee of otherness in McCarthy's Habermasian paradigm of intersubjectivity; as Habermas writes, "As soon as linguistically generated subjectivity gains primacy, . . . [the] ego stands within an interpersonal relationship that allows him to relate to himself as a participant in an interaction from the perspective of the alter" (*Philosophical Discourse of Modernity* 297). In other words, the regulative ideal of communication or consensus forces reasonable participants to put themselves in the other's shoes, to weigh the other's point of view toward the end of rational consensus. But, as McCarthy himself writes, "The success of Habermas's universalization principle in getting from multifarious 'I want's to a unified 'we will' depends on finding 'universally accepted needs'" (*Ideals and Illusions* 191), and there is certainly no guarantee of reasonable participants coming to some consensus concerning those needs. McCarthy seeks to remedy this problem in Habermas by expanding the Habermasian model of uncoerced rational agreement to take into account more pragmatic "elements of conciliation, compromise, consent, accommodation, and the like" (197); he softens Habermas's too-ideal insistence on rational consensus by including "strategically motivated compromise of interests" (196) as a satisfactory outcome for societal discourse. This is a necessary revision because, as McCarthy puts it, "citizens may enter public debate with a variety of expectations, of which the possibility of unanimity is only one" (198–99).

McCarthy, however, remains committed to Habermas's vision of intersubjective or perspectival alterity, where each reasonable discursive participant is committed to seeing things from various other points of view. It seems, however, that this vision of intersubjectivity is doomed to heighten the very violence, solipsism, and indecision it is meant to combat. As Anthony Cascardi writes, such a vision of intersubjective alterity "in essence reduce[s] the Other to a merely empirical or 'perspectival' variation of the self, and this reduction is in turn symptomatic of the Habermasian attempt to reconstruct the totality of knowledge based on the accessibility of practical 'rules' to rational consciousness" (*Subject of Modernity* 271). Cascardi argues that the seemingly generous gesture to see through the other's eyes is in fact a thoroughgoing appropriation of the other—a projection of the other that is merely a fantasy of the subject. Here the other exists only as not-yet-same, always on the way to (and always just short of) consensus or sameness. And, as Cascardi adds, "since the needs of the Other are the same as mine, the demand for recognition as expressed in the intersubjective realm *is also a recipe for perpetual struggle, and so a ceaseless war*" (273–74, my emphasis).

Indeed, a pluralist discourse puts interpretations into competition for a truth that, as McCarthy admits, has disappeared in our epoch. Because of this disappearance, "the political stakes between the competing interpretations are quite high" ("Politics of the Ineffable" 157). In other words, truth is open to a process of societal definition wherein the best argument will hopefully win the day. Such a system keeps open the future by always allowing a competing consensus or interpretation to shake the prevailing wisdom. But the fact of the matter is that mere dependence on the pluralist system of parceling out truth to the strongest claim *is* an appeal to the status quo: this is *already* how things are dealt with in our dominant political and societal discourses. As Theodor Adorno writes, such competitive pluralism is "popularized materialism" (*Aesthetic Theory* 36). In addition, the picture of society as a war of competing interpretations actually condemns societal discourses to the very inability to decide that McCarthy accuses deconstruction of bringing about. As de Man's work clearly shows us, more than one "valid" interpretation can be produced in most any situation; and, as I argue concerning de Man, without some other economy, without some way to account for these multiple valid contexts as other than error or mistake, a singular economy of argumentation is doomed to self-canceling chiasmic reversal. In an economy of competing interpretations, no one interpretation can account for another except in reference to itself, and then only as "wrong" or "incorrect," as falling short of the horizon of sameness that the privileged interpretation would comprise. In such a competitive economy, the interpretation at hand comprises, de facto, a fairly traditional philosophical ground. If the privileged interpretation generously gives up its grounding privilege, however, it then opens the economy to a pernicious undecidability in which ground is merely endlessly reconstituted in and for the benefit of differing contexts. Without a double movement of some kind, our "non-foundationalist" discourses are, then, doomed to indecision; without some way to account for a number of valid contextualizations and thereby to enable a different kind of decision among them, the necessary economy of argumentation leads to an impasse among competing "true" alternatives.

Deconstruction and/of Competing Interpretations

So, we have seen the negative case that deconstruction makes vis-à-vis an ethico-politics of competing cultural interpretations, but the question concerning deconstruction's potentially positive role remains unanswered. Does or can deconstruction play a role in a discourse in which daily decisions are made concerning the directions and attitudes of a culture—in, for example, the press? Derrida writes, "Let us not forget the constraints of the press, which are not only quantitative: they also impose models of readability.... Can one speak seriously of the press in the press? Yes and no, in contraband" ("Call It a Day for Democracy," in *Other Heading* 97). As Derrida unequivocally answers, "yes and no" (leave aside for the moment the odd qualifier, "in contraband"). Deconstruction's famous "yes and no," however, brings with it a different set of concerns when brought to bear on something other than a philosophico-literary discourse. Indeed, the seemingly paradoxical complexity of deconstruction's "yes and no" points to a problem faced by any largely academic discourse: these three words play out the drama or spell out the difficulty of constructing a relation between an "academic" discourse such as deconstruction and a "popular" discourse such as the daily press. The jargon-laden complexity of any theoretical academic discourse—even those which are at odds with de-construction—and the lack of publishing venues for such a possible discursive intervention between the academic community and the community at large make any direct relation between deconstruction and the press a difficult one to construct.[7]

Having said that, however, I find it curious that the press has of late been expending considerable energy discrediting deconstruc-tion—or, as it is more commonly known, deconstruction*ism*. For example, we read the following in the *Tempo* section of the 4 October 1991 Chicago *Tribune:* "Liberal arts faculties are mesmerized by de-construction, a voguish, nihilistic philosophy that proclaims the Great Books no better than Harlequin Romances, given that truth is but a figment of our imaginations" ("Thanks" 1–2). It is painfully obvious that the journalist writing this, Ron Grossman, has no in-terest in actually engaging deconstruction; he is, rather, interested in characterizing it quickly and dismissing it out of hand. He is not, in fact, even consistent in his characterizations of deconstruction's itinerary. In the *Tribune* of 5 May 1991 we read the following about Derrida's visiting lectures at the University of Chicago, under Gross-man's byline and the headline "Academia's Anarchist a Hit in Hyde Park": "Deconstruction involves the painstaking rereading of classic literary texts, tearing down accepted interpretations in favor of a nearly infinite number of alternatives" (1).

One could, of course, note any number of inconsistencies in Gross-man's two characterizations: deconstruction is literary criticism in May, but it's philosophy in October; it's interested in "classic literary texts" one time, in "proclaim[ing] the Great Books no better than Harlequin Romances" five months later; truth is a mere subjective projection ("but a figment of our imaginations") in October, al-though it rested in a process ("a nearly infinite number of alterna-tives") in May; deconstruction is "voguish [and] nihilistic," yet "painstaking." One could, it seems, pose any number of straight-forward journalistic questions (yes-or-no questions) to Grossman: Is

7. The best treatment of the topic I've encountered is Stephens's "Deconstruction and the Get-Real Press," in which he writes: "The major source of journalistic intolerance for the contemporary theoretical work in the humanities . . . may be just simple late-twentieth-century, information-overloaded, get-to-the-point impatience . . . an impatience with thoughts that cannot be summed up in a newspaper-length paragraph" (42).

deconstruction philosophy? Is deconstruction another name for canon reform? Is deconstruction mere subjectivism? Is deconstruction rigorous? The journalist, in response to such pointed questions, is forced to respond: "Yes and no; yes and no."

There is, of course, a sizable difference between Derrida's "yes and no" and Grossman's "yes and no"—the difference between a deconstructive characterization of the press and the press's characterization of deconstruction. Grossman can account for his "yes and no" only as a mistake—a momentary miscalculation or misrepresentation that could be cleared up, allowing him to rest on either yes or no. For Derrida, however, this "yes and no" is, as I argue above, a postmodern necessity, one inscribed in the very (im)possibility of decision, and one that must be accounted for in a horizon other than the horizon of sameness—the horizon of "yes or no."

As Derrida argues in "Call It a Day for Democracy," the press in large measure produces the public opinion that it supposedly merely reflects, but it also produces and bolsters something much more sinister: "the form of *judgment that decides* (yes or no) and that is produced in a *representation*" (in *Other Heading* 92). To use a sinister but pervasive idiom, common sense *dictates* that one cannot respond "yes and no." The ethical hesitation of undecidability, if it exists, cannot be accounted for within the horizon or purview of the press, which can only entertain the argumentative conclusion of yes or no. That being the case, Derrida asks,

> What then becomes of this reserve of experience, evaluation, and even determination (the "trends," "tastes," and "customs") that is not of the order of judgment (yes or no) and representation, in any sense of this word? It is here that one can question the authority of opinion—not in its content but in its form as pre-electoral judgment; and one can even question the distinction public/private whose rigor will always be threatened by language. . . . What public—and thus political—place is to be made for this kind of question? (93)

Here Derrida poses a specific question to the "authority of opinion," the argumentative rationality that the press bolsters through its insistence on nothing other than a yes or no: what, Derrida asks, becomes of the deliberation of the undecidable, of the "pre-electoral judgment" in which various conflicting decisions are considered? In the daily press, how does one report on decisions *not* made? Indeed, how does one account for the "trends," "tastes," and "customs" that are not of a yes-or-no order? According to Derrida, the press cannot account for such phenomena as long as it is tied to this notion of "opinion," and to the picture of society as the war of opinions. The upshot of Derrida's analysis is a call to recognize and "fight against" what he calls a "new censorship" carried out by the press, a censorship that attempts to "marginalize or reduce to silence anything that cannot be measured on their scale" (99).

It is not, however, simply a matter of saying "yes" to the press, of entering the fray of "yes or no," of merely offering the press a better or truer representation of deconstruction in the hopes of combating and triumphing over its rivals. To do so would be to lose to the status quo in a fixed game:

> The "new censorship"—and this is the strength of its ruse—combines concentration *and* fractionalization, accumulation *and* privatization. It de-politicizes. This terrible logic is not restricted to the "audiovisual," though it is more perceptible there. It is at work as soon as an interpretation, that is to say, a selective evaluation, informs a "fact." No information escapes it. . . . [The press] dogmatizes, no matter what its real eclecticism or facade of liberalism. (100–101)

Derrida thematizes the supposed argumentative rationality of the press as a "new censorship" because it quite literally reduces everything to its parameters. In the seemingly generous argumentative discourse of "yes or no" is embedded this more sinister truth: that the horizon of this "yes or no" swallows up everything in its path, and, no matter how liberal a discourse of competing opinions might seem, the press reduces the potential complexity of an issue to its horizon, to its "selective evaluation." Not only is "yes or no" a totalized theory of decision, but it has come to totalize the whole of Western societal discourse. Any discourse that would pose a question to this "facade of liberalism" is dismissed as a chimera or intellectual game.

If deconstruction cannot simply cede the power of discourse to the war of opinion, and if it cannot in good conscience submit or reduce deconstruction to a yes or no, what, then, is to be done? Perhaps to answer that question we need to return to Derrida's question and answer, "Can one speak seriously of the press in the press? Yes and no, *in contraband*" (97, my emphasis). The strategy that Derrida outlines to break the totalizing logic of the yes or no follows a logic of contraband: one must smuggle into the press's argumentative discourse that which this discourse normally does not allow. Words, ideas, idioms, styles, and themes that are contraband to the press must nevertheless be smuggled into its discourse—not to merely present themselves or announce their arrival, but to attest to that which such discourse excludes. In this way, Derrida's work on the "yes or no" of the press is very similar to his work on dialectical metaphysics, a metaphysics that can, in turn, be read as the unsaid (the "common sense") that informs much of the press's coverage of issues. Can one speak of seriously of metaphysics in metaphysics? Yes and no. Recall Derrida on Hegel's dialectic, a passage I quote in Chapter 3:

There is no choosing here: each time a discourse *contra* the transcendental is held, a matrix—the (con)striction itself—constrains the discourse to place the nontranscendental, the outside of the transcendental field, the excluded, in a structuring position. The matrix in question constitutes the excluded as transcendental of the transcendental, as imitation transcendental, transcendental contra-band. The contra-band is *not yet* dialectical contradiction. To be sure, the contra-band necessarily becomes that, but its not-yet is not-yet the teleological anticipation, which results in it never becoming dialectical contradiction. The contra-band *remains* something other than what, necessarily, it is to become.

Such would be the (nondialectical) law of the (dialectical) stricture, of the bond, of the ligature, of the garrote, of the *desmos* in general when it comes to clench tightly in order to make be. Lock of the dialectical. (*Glas* 244a)

Derrida argues that something like contraband, an excess that univocal meaning cannot account for, quite literally makes a discourse of conflicting opinions possible, but this contraband itself is not merely locatable within an economy of argumentative rationality. Such an argumentative discourse reduces the radical heterogeneity of a culture to the horizon of consensus, and in the process protects an economy of sameness.

The press—like metaphysics—cannot adequately answer the question of its own (im)possibility. Hence, for Derrida, one both can and cannot speak seriously of the press in the press. Here then is a way to understand deconstruction's "yes and no": *yes*, it is necessary to participate in the dominant yes-or-no discourse, but it is just as incumbent upon a participant to offer a *no* to the limiting horizon of that discourse, to mark its limit in hopes of opening up the "lock of the dialectical"—the lock of thinking that thematizes all decision as yes-or-no decision, and all societal discourse merely as the discourse of competing (and ultimately self-canceling) truths.

And, although the press is certainly nothing like an ideal speech community, this brings us back to the question that Derrida poses to McCarthy's society of "discursive competition." McCarthy writes, "Large-scale sociopolitical views and analyses of our present situation are not the special province of philosophical insight. They have entered into discursive competition with other accounts—which often have the virtue of laying their empirical, theoretical, and normative cards on the table for everyone to see and challenge" ("Politics of the Ineffable" 160). This is an enticing formulation, but it seems that in a postmodern context this picture of society as the site of competing truths is difficult to uphold in practice. How can the best interpretation objectively win out if any interpretation can be infinitely recontextualized? Certainly, and I cannot stress this point enough, societal argument, judgment, and decision are necessary; but in *addition* to judging competing claims, the network in which these interpretations arise and fight it out in a supposedly free and open forum—the ideological, philosophical, and institutional frameworks of postmodern culture—must be taken into account somehow if we are not to fall into a merely obfuscatory undecidability. Take the following example from the Chicago *Sun-Times*, 19 June 1991: "The first federal court trial over Boy Scout membership and religious beliefs wound up Tuesday with appeals for freedom by both sides. Richard Grossman, lawyer for an agnostic Hinsdale [Illinois] boy barred from the Cub Scouts, urged the judge to 'strike a blow for freedom of conscience.' George A. Davidson, attorney for the Scouts, said they can keep out nonbelievers in God because 'Any group is free to define its own values'" (10). How does one consistently decide between the two contexts employed for the word "freedom" here—between a personal freedom to believe as one wishes and a group's freedom to define itself in certain ways? Each argument, whether or not one finds it compelling, is at least consistent: "freedom of conscience" certainly has a long and illustrious history in American law; however, the rights of a nongovernmental group—marginal or otherwise—"to define its own values" is likewise well recognized in institutions as disparate as churches and women's colleges. How does one decide between these two perfectly consistent contextualizations of the word "freedom"?[8] One could travel the path of an argumentative pluralism, and further submit this discourse to what McCarthy calls "the procedures of evidence, argument, criticism and the like" ("Politics of the Ineffable" 161), but that seems destined only to add to the recontexualizing undecidability, and to maintain the status quo. *Without a double gesture,* I would argue, McCarthy's dependence on "competing interpretations" (157) is doomed to a mere undecidability (to something like de Man's "inability to choose") and/or to a continued bolstering of the status quo amid the sound and fury of the "intolerant and aggressive particularism" of warring opinions.[9]

In fact, it is deconstruction's question to an economy of argumentative pluralism that McCarthy is at greatest pains to discredit. It is strange that he is not particularly concerned that his theory will be jeopardized by deconstruction as a competing theory—insofar as McCarthy's theory could account for and could actually be borne

8. This Illinois case was decided in favor of the Scouts, but the Scouts have since lost a similar case—involving the membership of twin agnostic Scouts—in California.

9. McCarthy would perhaps counter with the assertion that deconstruction's undecidable law of expropriation cannot decide in the Boy Scout case either; however, within a deconstructive notion of law, this is an eminently decidable case—the appeal to "freedom" here which actually opens up other contexts is the lawful freedom. From a deconstructive vantage point, this case is not primarily one dealing with the rights of an individual's "conscience" or a group's "self-definition"; it is, rather, decidable by an appeal to the necessity of an openness to other so-called deviant or heterogeneous contexts.

out by the argumentative triumph of a competing theory. Perhaps McCarthy's larger worry is that the entire institutionalized enterprise of something like "social theory"—thematized as the continuing argumentative conversation among competing theories—will be disrupted by deconstruction. He writes, for example, about Derrida's contention that "any determination of context involves 'force or irreducible violence' ": "To use 'power,' 'force,' and 'violence' in this way—to color everything from mutual agreement and negotiated compromise to false consciousness and open repression—is to go into the night in which all cows are black, *that is, to go back behind all the differentiations so crucial to social and political theory*" (156, my emphasis). McCarthy here criticizes Derrida's insistence on the necessity of a certain kind of violence hidden in the supposedly benign movement of reason. For McCarthy, such a view makes differentiation impossible, and makes us all settlers down on the nihilist dairy farm. I have treated this reading of power as an undifferentiating mass at some length in Chapter 3, but I am interested here in the *upshot* of McCarthy's "night in which all cows are black." Nihilism is defined here *not* as a tragic or destructive social phenomenon, but as something that poses a dangerous or unanswerable question to the institutional enterprise of social theory. Deconstruction is dangerous not so much because it is an inadequate social theory— though McCarthy clearly feels that it is—but because it threatens to "go back behind all the differentiations so crucial to social and political theory," because it threatens to rethink the ruling institutional, philosophical, and ideological field in which the game is played, rather than to continue to play by the rules of competing interpretations. It seems, then, that nihilism per se—the specific charge leveled at Derrida—is not so much the problem for McCarthy; rather, deconstruction's crippling interruption or questioning ("go[ing] back behind") of McCarthy's "theory" ends up to be the real worry— and, conversely, it seems that McCarthy is most interested in protecting the whole enterprise of institutionalized sociopolitical discourse thematized as the war of competing interpretations, an economy of single reading. From within the singular logic of the war, a double reading—a gesture toward anything other than or beyond this war of interpretations—is necessarily a mere specter, an "ineffable" nothing.

Conclusion: Ends

In *Aesthetic Theory* Adorno writes, "Two propositions seem to me to have continued validity: that the strictly technical work of art has failed, and that the opposing route of arresting technique arbitrarily leads to indifferent results. While technique is the epitome of the language of art, it also liquidates that language. This is art's inescapable dilemma" (310). In this passage Adorno outlines what I've called the question or impasse of postmodernism, the impasse of a language whose end-oriented economy of meaning as technique has "failed," but a language that needs this economy in order that it not lead merely to "indifferent results." For Adorno, these "indifferent results" are brought about whenever one tries to pose a question to an end-oriented economy of technique; "indifferent results" are, then, the inexorable upshot of taking "the opposing route of arresting technique arbitrarily," of attempting to question the functioning of meaning. According to Adorno, because of the postmodern disruption or alteration of an end-oriented economy of meaning, the language of art cannot hope to lead to anything other than these indifferent results. Because art is left with nothing other than this failed language, it too must fail. He writes, "While technique is the epitome of the language of art, it also liquidates that language." For Adorno, this double bind is "art's inescapable dilemma."

This dilemma could, of course, also be posed within the question of the theoretical or societal ends of discourse in general—that is, if Adorno does not pose it in these terms already. Insofar as determinable ends in a postmodern economy seem both necessary and impossible, the dilemma of societal ends *is* the dilemma of the language of art. In fact, these dilemmas are tied together by the question of language, by the inescapability of language, the necessary mediating role that language plays in society's discourses—a role that, in a frustrating turn, makes determinate ends both possible and *im*possible. Language holds out the promise of an end, while simultaneously sweeping the ends of determinate meaning away; and this would seem to leave us squarely within another impasse, as deep if not deeper than the institutional impasse with which we started.

Throughout this work, however, I have tried to articulate an other economy of meaning, one that does not depend on traditional notions of opposition, possibility, ends, or language, an economy of meaning that is not simply stifled by the closure or radical alteration of these philosophical problematics. Note that I do not write, as Adorno does, about the "failure" of philosophy, language, or thinking; as I argue concerning de Man, to talk in terms of failure is to grant the validity of a philosophical economy of ends. To talk of failure (or, for that matter, to talk of pluralism) is to remain always within reach of the end, always having to account for the nonexistence of an end as the *lack* of an end (or the *multiplicity* of many ends), in short, always having to account for difference in terms of the ultimate possibility of sameness. It has been my contention here that there is a thinking that, although not wholly or simply outside or beyond the problematics of this discourse, remains other to the discourse of opposition, lack, or plurality, other to Adorno's choice between a feeble discontinuity and an iron-fisted control.

Adorno's impasse is located at the impossible choice between two untenable opposites: the uncertain "route of arresting technique arbitrarily" and the stifling oppression of a "strictly technical work of art." Perhaps Samuel Beckett offers us an other way to think this opposition when he writes, "These few general remarks to begin with. What am I to do, what shall I do, what should I do, in my situation, how proceed? By aporia pure and simple? Or by affirmations and negations invalidated as uttered, or sooner or later? Generally speaking. There must be other shifts" (*The Unnamable* 291). His passage begins by taking up Adorno's problematic of two impossible ways to proceed: merely discontinuously ("by aporia pure and simple") or simply within the language of argumentative, dialectical philosophy (by "affirmations and negations invalidated as uttered, or sooner or later"). But he concludes with what I have been trying to reach throughout this book. Specifically, *after* the impossible (non)choice or opposition we seem to be left with, *after* the recognition of an impossible postmodern decision between a seemingly nonsensical progression and a wholly untenable and manipulative fall back into tradition, in this time or space we call the postmodern, "There must be other shifts."

Works Cited

Abrams, M. H. *The Mirror and the Lamp.* New York: Oxford University Press, 1953.

Adorno, T. W. *Aesthetic Theory.* Translated by C. Lenhardt. London: Routledge & Kegan Paul, 1984.

Althusser, Louis. *Lenin and Philosophy and Other Essays.* Translated by Ben Brewster. New York: Monthly Review Press, 1971.

Altieri, Charles. "From Symbolist Thought to Immanence: The Ground of Postmodern American Poetics." *boundary 2* 1, no. 1 (1973): 605–41.

American Heritage Dictionary. Edited by William Morris. Boston: Houghton Mifflin, 1980.

Ames, Christopher. "Power and the Obscene Word: Discourses of Extremity in Thomas Pynchon's *Gravity's Rainbow.*" *Contemporary Literature* 31, no. 2 (1990): 193–206.

Arac, Jonathan. *Critical Genealogies.* New York: Columbia University Press, 1987.

——. "To Regress from the Rigor of Shelley: Figures of History in American Deconstructive Criticism." *boundary 2* 8, no. 3 (1980): 241–57.

——, ed. *Postmodernism and Politics.* Minneapolis: University of Minnesota Press, 1986.

Bartlett, Lee. "What Is 'Language Poetry'?" *Critical Inquiry* 12 (Summer 1986): 741–52.

Bataille, Georges. "Hegel, Death, and Sacrifice." Translated by Jonathan Strauss. *Yale French Studies* 78 (1990): 9–28.

Beckett, Samuel. *The Unnamable. Three Novels.* New York: Grove Press, 1965: 290–414.

Bennington, Geoff. "Aberrations: De Man (and) the Machine." In Waters and Godzich, *Reading De Man Reading,* 209–21.

——. "Cogito Incognito." *Oxford Literary Review* 4, no. 1 (1979): 5–8.

Bernasconi, Robert. "Deconstruction and the Possibility of Ethics." In *Deconstruction and Philosophy*, ed. John Sallis, 122–39. Chicago: University of Chicago Press, 1987.

Bernstein, Charles. *Content's Dream*. Los Angeles: Sun & Moon Press, 1986.

——. *A Poetics*. Cambridge: Harvard University Press, 1992.

Bérubé, Michael. *Marginal Forces/Cultural Centers: Tolson, Pynchon, and the Politics of the Canon*. Ithaca: Cornell University Press, 1992.

Blanchot, Maurice. *The Space of Literature*. Translated by Ann Smock. Lincoln: University of Nebraska Press, 1982.

Bloom, Harold, et al., eds. *Deconstruction and Criticism*. New York: Seabury Press, 1979.

Boly, John R. "Deconstruction as a General System: Tropes, Disciplines, Politics." *Cultural Critique* 11 (Winter 1988–89): 175–201.

Bové, Paul. *Intellectuals in Power: A Genealogy of Critical Humanism*. New York: Columbia University Press, 1986.

Brainard, Marcus, ed. *Heidegger and the Political; Graduate Faculty Philosophy Journal* 14–15 (1991).

Carroll, David. *Paraesthetics: Foucault, Lyotard, Derrida*. New York: Methuen, 1987.

Cascardi, Anthony J. *The Subject of Modernity*. Cambridge and New York: Cambridge University Press, 1992.

Clerc, Charles, ed. *Approaches to "Gravity's Rainbow."* Columbus: Ohio State University Press, 1983.

Comay, Rebecca. "Gifts without Presents: Economies of 'Experience' in Bataille and Heidegger." *Yale French Studies* 78 (1990): 66–89.

Cowart, David. *Thomas Pynchon: The Art of Allusion*. Carbondale: Southern Illinois University Press, 1980.

Culler, Jonathan. *Framing the Sign: Literature and Its Institutions*. Oxford: Basil Blackwell, 1988.

——. *On Deconstruction*. Ithaca: Cornell University Press, 1982.

Deleuze, Gilles. *Foucault*. Translated and edited by Seán Hand. Minneapolis: University of Minnesota Press, 1988.

de Man, Paul. *Allegories of Reading*. New Haven: Yale University Press, 1979.

——. *Blindness and Insight*. Minneapolis: University of Minnesota Press, 1983.

——. "An Interview with Paul de Man." Edited by Stefano Rossi. *Nuova corrente* 31 (1984): 303–13.

——. "Shelley Disfigured." In Bloom et al., *Deconstruction and Criticism*, 39–73.

Derrida, Jacques. *Acts of Literature*. Edited by Derek Attridge. New York: Routledge, 1992.

——. "The Age of Hegel." Translated by Susan Winnett. In *Demarcating the Disciplines*, ed. Samuel Weber, 3–35. Minneapolis: University of Minnesota Press, 1987.

——. "Biodegradables: Seven Diary Fragments." Translated by Peggy Kamuf. *Critical Inquiry* 15 (Summer 1989): 812–73.

——. "But, beyond . . . (Open Letter to Anne McClintock and Rob Nixon)." Translated by Peggy Kamuf. *Critical Inquiry* 13 (Autumn 1986): 155–70.

——. "Cogito and the History of Madness." In Derrida, *Writing and Difference*, 31–65.

——. "Différance." In Derrida, *Margins of Philosophy*, 1–28.

——. *Dissemination*. Translated by Barbara Johnson. Chicago: University of Chicago Press, 1981.

——. "Force of Law: The 'Mystical Foundation of Authority.' " *Cardoza Law Review* 11, nos. 5–6 (1990): 919–1045.

——. "Geschlecht: Sexual Difference, Ontological Difference." *Research in Phenomenology* 13 (1983): 65–83.

——. *Glas*. Translated by John P. Leavey, Jr., and Richard Rand. Lincoln: University of Nebraska Press, 1986.

——. "The Laws of Reflection: Nelson Mandela, In Admiration." Translated by Mary Ann Caws and Isabelle Lorenz. In *For Nelson Mandela*, ed. Jacques Derrida and Mustapha Tlili, 13–42. New York: Seaver, 1987.

——. "Letter to a Japanese Friend." In *Derrida and Difference*, ed. Robert Bernasconi and David Wood, 1–8. Coventry, U. K.: Parousia Press, 1985.

——. "Like the Sound of the Sea Deep within a Shell: Paul de Man's War." Translated by Peggy Kamuf. *Critical Inquiry* 14 (Spring 1988): 590–652.

——. *Limited Inc*. Translated by Samuel Weber. Evanston: Northwestern University Press, 1988.

——. "Living On—Border Lines." Translated by James Hulbert. In Bloom et al., *Deconstruction and Criticism*, 75–176.

——. *Margins of Philosophy*. Translated by Alan Bass. Chicago: University of Chicago Press, 1982.

——. *Memoires: For Paul de Man*. Translated by Eduardo Cadava et al. New York: Columbia University Press, 1986.

——. "No Apocalypse, Not Now." Translated by Catherine Porter and Philip Lewis. *Diacritics* 14 (Summer 1984): 20–31.

——. "Of an Apocalyptic Tone Recently Adopted in Philosophy." Translated John P. Leavey, Jr. *Oxford Literary Review* 6, no. 2 (1984): 3–37.

——. *Of Grammatology*. Translated by Gayatri Chakravorty Spivak. Baltimore: Johns Hopkins University Press, 1976.

——. *Of Spirit*. Translated by Geoffrey Bennington and Rachel Bowlby. Chicago: University of Chicago Press, 1991.

——. "On Colleges and Philosophy." In *Postmodernism: ICA Documents*, ed. Lisa Appignanesi, 209–28. London: Free Association Books, 1989.

——. "On Reading Heidegger: An Outline of Remarks to the Essex Colloquium." Edited by David Farrell Krell. *Research in Phenomenology* 17 (1987): 171–85.

——. *The Other Heading: Reflections on Today's Europe*. Translated by Pascale-Anne Brault and Michael Naas. Bloomington: Indiana University Press, 1992.

——. *Positions*. Translated by Alan Bass. Chicago: University of Chicago Press, 1981.

——. *The Post Card*. Translated by Alan Bass. Chicago: University of Chicago Press, 1987. Originally published as *La carte postale* (Paris: Flammarion, 1980).

——. "The Principle of Reason: The University in the Eyes of Its Pupils." Translated by Catherine Porter and Edward P. Morris. *Diacritics* 12, no. 3 (1983): 3–20.

——. "Psyche: Inventions of the Other." Translated by Catherine Porter. In Waters and Godzich, *Reading De Man Reading*, 25–65.

——. "Racism's Last Word." Translated by Peggy Kamuf. *Critical Inquiry* 12 (Autumn 1985): 200–99.

——. "The *Retrait* of Metaphor." Translated by Frieda Gardner et al. *Enclitic* 2, no. 2 (1978): 3–33.

——. "Sending: On Representation." Translated by Peter and Mary Ann Caws. *Social Research* 49, no. 2 (1982): 295–326.

——. "Sendoffs." Translated by Thomas Pepper. *Yale French Studies* 77 (1990): 7–43.

——. "Some Statements and Truisms." Translated by Anne Tomiche. In *The States of "Theory,"* ed. David Carroll, 63–94. New York: Columbia University Press, 1990.

——. *Writing and Difference*. Translated by Alan Bass. Chicago: University of Chicago Press, 1978.

Dooley, David. "The Contemporary Workshop Aesthetic." *The Hudson Review* 43 (Summer 1990): 259–81.

Dreyfus, Hubert, and Paul Rabinow. *Michel Foucault*. Chicago: University of Chicago Press, 1982.

Duyfhuizen, Bernard. "Taking Stock: 26 Years since *V.*" *Novel* 23, no. 1 (Fall 1989): 75–88.

——, ed. Deconstructing *"Gravity's Rainbow:" Pynchon Notes* 14 (1984).

Eagleton, Terry. *Literary Theory: An Introduction*. Minneapolis: University of Minnesota Press, 1983.

Earl, James W. "Freedom and Knowledge in the Zone." In Clerc, *Approaches to "Gravity's Rainbow,"* 229–50.

Educational Testing Service. *GRE Literature in English Test, Descriptive Booklet, 1989–91*. Princeton: ETS, 1989.

Fish, Stanley. "Anti-Professionalism." *New Literary History* 17, no. 1 (1985): 89–112.

——. "Commentary: The Young and the Restless." In Veeser, *The New Historicism*, 303–16.

——. *Is There a Text in This Class?* Cambridge: Harvard University Press, 1980.

——. "A Reply to Gerald Graff." *New Literary History* 17, no. 1 (1985): 119–27.

——. "What Makes an Interpretation Acceptable?" In Fish, *Is There a Text in This Class?* 338–55.

Foucault, Michel. *The Archaeology of Knowledge* and *The Discourse on Language*. Translated by A. M. Sheridan Smith. New York: Pantheon, 1972. Originally published separately as *L'archéologie du savoir* (Paris: Gallimard, 1969) and *L'ordre du discours* (Paris: Gallimard, 1971).

——. *Foucault Live*. Translated by John Johnston, edited by Sylvère Lotringer. New York: Semiotext(e), 1989.

——. *The Foucault Reader*. Edited by Paul Rabinow. New York: Pantheon, 1984.

——. *Language, Counter-Memory, Practice*. Translated by D.F. Bouchard and Sherry Simon. Ithaca: Cornell University Press, 1977.

——. "My Body, This Paper, This Fire." Translated by Geoff Bennington. *Oxford Literary Review* 4, no. 1 (1979): 9–28.

——. "Nietzsche, Genealogy, History." Translated by Donald Bouchard and Sherry Simon. In Foucault, *The Foucault Reader*, 76–100.

——. *The Order of Things*. New York: Vintage Books, 1970.

——. *Power/Knowledge*. Translated by Colin Gordon et al., edited by Colin Gordon. New York: Pantheon, 1980.

——. "The Subject and Power." In Dreyfus and Rabinow, *Michel Foucault*, 208–26.

——. *The Use of Pleasure*. Translated by Robert Hurley. New York: Vintage, 1986.

——. "What Is an Author?" Translated by Josué Harari. In Harari, *Textual Strategies*, 141–60.

——. "What Is Enlightenment?" Translated by Paul Rabinow. In Foucault, *The Foucault Reader*, 32–50.

Friedman, Alan J. "Science and Technology." In Clerc, *Approaches to "Gravity's Rainbow,"* 69–102.

Fynsk, Christopher. "A Decelebration of Philosophy." *Diacritics* 8 (Summer 1978): 80–90.

Gasché, Rodolphe. "Deconstruction as Criticism." *Glyph* 6 (1979): 177–215.

——. "In-Difference to Philosophy: De Man on Kant, Hegel, and Nietzsche." In Waters and Godzich, *Reading De Man Reading*, 259–96.

——. "Postmodernism and Rationality." *The Journal of Philosophy* 85, no. 10 (1988): 528–38.

——. *The Tain of the Mirror*. Cambridge: Harvard University Press, 1986.

Godzich, Wlad. "Afterword." In Weber, *Institution and Interpretation*, 153–66.

Gottlieb, Anthony. "Heidegger for Fun and Profit." *New York Times Book Review*, 7 January 1990, 1, 22–23.

Graff, Gerald. *Literature against Itself*. Chicago: University of Chicago Press, 1979.

Greenblatt, Stephen. *Shakespearean Negotiations*. Berkeley and Los Angeles: University of California Press, 1988.

Greer, Michael. "Ideology and Theory in Recent Experimental Writing or, The Naming of 'Language Poetry.' " *boundary 2* 16, no. 2/3 (1989): 335–56.

Grossman, Ron. "Academia's Anarchist a Hit in Hyde Park." *Chicago Tribune*, 5 May 1991, Section 5: 1, 8.

——. "Thanks, Mr. Chips." *Chicago Tribune*, 4 October 1991, Section 5: 1–2.

Habermas, Jürgen. *The Philosophical Discourse of Modernity*. Translated by Frederick G. Lawrence. Cambridge: MIT Press, 1990.

Harari, Josué, ed. *Textual Strategies: Perspectives in Poststructuralist Criticism*. Ithaca: Cornell University Press, 1979.

Hartley, George. *Textual Politics and the Language Poets*. Bloomington: Indiana University Press, 1989.

Hartman, Geoffrey. Preface to Bloom et al., *Deconstruction and Criticism*, vii–ix.

Harvey, Irene. "The *Différance* between Derrida and de Man." In *The Textual Sublime: Deconstruction and Its Differences*, ed. Hugh Silverman and Gary Aylesworth, 73–86. Albany: SUNY Press, 1990.

Hassan, Ihab. "Making Sense: The Trials of Postmodern Discourse." *New Literary History* 18, no. 2 (1987): 437–59.

——. *The Postmodern Turn: Essays in Postmodern Theory and Culture*. Columbus: Ohio State University Press, 1987.

The Heath Anthology of American Literature, Volume 2. Edited by Paul Lauter et al. Lexington, Mass.: D.C. Heath, 1990.

Hegel, G.W.F. *Phenomenology of Spirit*. Translated by A. V. Miller. New York: Oxford University Press, 1977.

Heidegger, Martin. "The Age of the World View." Translated by Marjorie Grene. *boundary 2* 4, no. 2 (1976): 341–55. Originally published as "Die Zeit des Welt-bildes," in *Holzwege*, 69–104 (Frankfurt am Main: Vittorio Klostermann, 1950).

———. *The Basic Problems of Phenomenology*. Translated by Albert Hofstadter. Bloomington: Indiana University Press, 1988.

———. "The End of Philosophy and the Task of Thinking." Translated by David Farrell Krell. In *Basic Writings*, ed. David Farrell Krell, 369–92. New York: Harper & Row, 1972. Originally published as "Das Ende der Philosophie und die Aufgabe des Denkens," in *Zur Sache des Denkens*, 61–80. (Tubingen: Max Niemeyer Verlag, 1969).

———. *On Time and Being*. Translated by Joan Stambaugh. New York: Harper & Row, 1972. Originally published as "Zeit und Sein," in *Zur Sache des Denkens*, 27–60. (Tubingen: Max Niemeyer Verlag, 1969).

———. "What Are Poets For?" Translated by Albert Hofstadter. *Poetry, Language, Thought*, 89–142. New York: Harper & Row, 1971. Originally published as "Wozu Dichter?" in *Holzewege*, 248–95. (Frankfurt am Main: Vittorio Klostermann, 1950).

Hite, Molly. *Ideas of Order in the Novels of Thomas Pynchon*. Columbus: Ohio State University Press, 1983.

Hohmann, Charles. *Thomas Pynchon's "Gravity's Rainbow": A Study of Its Conceptual Structure and of Rilke's Influence*. New York: Peter Lang, 1986.

Hume, Kathryn. *Pynchon's Mythography*. Carbondale: Southern Illinois University Press, 1987.

Huyssen, Andreas. *After the Great Divide: Modernism, Mass Culture, Postmodernism*. Bloomington: Indiana University Press, 1986.

Hyppolite, Jean. *Genesis and Structure of Hegel's "Phenomenology of Spirit."* Translated by Samuel Cherniak and John Heckman. Evanston: Northwestern University Press, 1974.

Inman, P. "One to One." In *The Politics of Poetic Form*, ed. Charles Bernstein, 221–25. New York: Roof Books, 1990.

Jameson, Fredric. "The Politics of Theory: Ideological Positions in the Postmodernism Debate." In *Ideologies of Theory*, vol. 2, 103–13. Minneapolis: University of Minnesota Press, 1988.

———. "Postmodernism, or The Cultural Logic of Late Capitalism." *New Left Review* 146 (1984): 53–92.

———. "Spatial Equivalents: Postmodern Architecture and the World System." In *The States of "Theory,"* ed. David Carroll, 125–48. New York: Columbia University Press, 1990.

Jay, Paul. "Bridging the Gap: The Position of Politics in Deconstruction." *Cultural Critique* 22 (1992): 47–74.

Johnson, Barbara. *A World of Difference*. Baltimore: Johns Hopkins University Press, 1989.

Jones, Gerard, Ron Randall, and Randy Elliott. *Justice League Europe 37: Doomed by Deconstructo.* New York: DC Comics, 1992.

Kaufmann, David. "The Profession of Theory." *PMLA* 105, no. 3 (1990): 519–30.

Keesey, Donald. *Contexts for Criticism.* Palo Alto, Calif.: Mayfield Press, 1987.

Kristeva, Julia. "Postmodernism?" In *Romanticism, Modernism, Postmodernism,* ed. Harry Garvin, 136–41. London: Associated University Press, 1980.

Kuberski, Philip. "Gravity's Angel: The Ideology of Pynchon's Fiction." *boundary 2* 15, no. 1 (1986–87): 135–51.

Lacoue-Labarthe, Philippe. "The Fable (Literature and Philosophy)." Translated by Hugh Silverman. *Research in Phenomenology* 15 (1985): 43–60.

———. *Heidegger, Art, and Politics.* Translated by Chris Turner. London: Basil Blackwell, 1990.

Lawlor, Leonard. "From the Trace to the Law: Derridean Politics." *Philosophy and Social Criticism* 15, no. 1 (1989): 1–15.

Lehan, Richard. "The Theoretical Limits of the New Historicism." *New Literary History* 21, no. 3 (1990): 533–54.

Lentricchia, Frank. *After the New Criticism.* Chicago: University of Chicago Press, 1980.

———. *Ariel and the Police.* Madison: University of Wisconsin Press, 1988.

———. "Foucault's Legacy—A New Historicism?" In Veeser, *The New Historicism,* 231–42.

Leverenz, David. "On Trying to Read *Gravity's Rainbow.*" In *Mindful Pleasures,* ed. George Levine and David Leverenz, 229–49. Boston: Little, Brown, 1976.

Levinas, Emmanuel. "Reality and Its Shadow." Translated by Alphonso Lingis. In *The Levinas Reader,* ed. Seán Hand 129–43. London: Basil Blackwell, 1989.

———. *Totality and Infinity: An Essay on Exteriority.* Translated by Alphonso Lingis. Pittsburgh: Duquesne University Press, 1969.

Lodge, David. *The Modes of Modern Writing.* Ithaca: Cornell University Press, 1977.

Lyotard, Jean François. *The Postmodern Condition.* Translated by Geoff Bennington and Brian Massumi. Minneapolis: University of Minnesota Press, 1984.

McCarthy, Thomas. *Ideals and Illusions.* Cambridge: MIT Press, 1992.

———. "The Politics of the Ineffable: Derrida's Deconstructionism." *The Philosophical Forum* 21, nos. 1–2 (1989–90): 146–68.

McGann, Jerome J. "Contemporary Poetry, Alternate Routes." *Critical Inquiry* 13 (Spring 1987): 624–47.

McHale, Brian. "Telling Postmodernist Stories." *Poetics Today* 9, no. 3 (1988): 545–69.

McHoul, Alec, and David Wills. *Writing Pynchon.* Urbana: University of Illinois Press, 1990.

McKenna, Andrew. "Postmodernism: Its Future Perfect." In *Postmodernism and Continental Philosophy,* ed. Hugh J. Silverman and Donn Welton, 228–42. Albany: SUNY Press, 1988.

Marx, Karl. *Capital.* Edited by Friedrich Engels. Translated by Ernest Untermann. New York: Random House, 1906.

Mazurek, Raymond. "Courses and Canons: The Post-1945 U.S. Novel." *Critique* 31, no. 3 (1990): 143–56.

Mendelson, Edward. "Gravity's Encyclopedia." In *Mindful Pleasures,* ed. George Levine and David Leverenz, 161–95. Boston: Little, Brown, 1976.

Merod, Jim. *The Political Responsibility of the Critic.* Ithaca: Cornell University Press, 1987.

Miller, J. Hillis. "The Critic as Host." In Bloom et al., *Deconstruction and Criticism,* 217–53.

——. "The Search for Grounds in Literary Study." In *Rhetoric and Form: Deconstruction at Yale,* ed. Robert Con Davis and Ronald Schleifer, 9–36. Norman: University of Oklahoma Press, 1985.

Minh-ha, Trinh T. *Woman, Native, Other.* Bloomington: Indiana University Press, 1989.

Mitchell, W.J.T., ed. *Against Theory.* Chicago: University of Chicago Press, 1985.

Modern Language Association. *Introduction to Scholarship in Modern Languages and Literatures.* Edited by Joseph Gibaldi. New York: MLA Press, 1981.

Moore, Thomas. *The Style of Connectedness: "Gravity's Rainbow" and Thomas Pynchon.* Columbia: University of Missouri Press, 1987.

Nicholson, Linda J., ed. *Feminism/Postmodernism.* New York: Routledge, 1990.

Nietzsche, Friedrich. *The Gay Science.* Translated by Walter Kaufmann. New York: Vintage, 1974.

Norris, Christopher. *Deconstruction: Theory and Practice.* London: Methuen, 1982; revised 1991.

Perloff, Marjorie. "Can(n)on the Right of Us, Can(n)on to the Left: A Plea for Difference." *New Literary History* 18, no. 3 (Spring 1987): 633–56.

——. "The Word as Such: L = A = N = G = U = A = G = E Poetry in the Eighties." In *The Dance of the Intellect: Studies in the Poetry of the Pound Tradition,* 215–38. Cambridge: Cambridge University Press, 1985.

Plato. *Phaedrus.* Translated by H. N. Fowler. In *Plato,* vol. 1, Loeb Classical Library, ed. T. E. Page et al., 405–580. Cambridge: Harvard University Press, 1914.

Porter, Carolyn. "History and Literature: 'After the New Historicism.' " *New Literary History* 21, no. 2 (1990): 253–70.

Pynchon, Thomas. *The Crying of Lot 49.* New York: Bantam, 1967.

——. *Gravity's Rainbow.* New York: Viking Press, 1973.

Rapaport, Herman. *Milton and the Postmodern.* Lincoln: University of Nebraska Press, 1983.

Redfield, Marc. "Pynchon's Postmodern Sublime." *PMLA* 104, no. 2 (1989): 152–62.

Rilke, Rainer Maria. *Letters.* Vol. 2. Translated by Jane B. Greene and M. D. Norton: New York: W. W. Norton, 1948.

Rorty, Richard. *Consequences of Pragmatism.* Minneapolis: University of Minnesota Press, 1982.

——. "Foucault/Dewey/Nietzsche." *Raritan* 14, no. 4 (1990): 1–8.

——. *Philosophy and the Mirror of Nature.* Princeton: Princeton University Press, 1979.

Ross, Andrew, ed. *Universal Abandon? The Politics of Postmodernism.* Minneapolis: University of Minnesota Press, 1988.

Said, Edward W. *The World, the Text, and the Critic.* Cambridge: Harvard University Press, 1983.

Sallis, John. *Delimitations: Phenomenology and the End of Metaphysics.* Bloomington: Indiana University Press, 1986.

Saussure, Ferdinand de. *Course in General Linguistics.* Translated by Wade Baskin. New York: McGraw-Hill, 1966.

Schaub, Thomas H. *Pynchon: The Voice of Ambiguity.* Urbana: University of Illinois Press, 1981.

Schürmann, Reiner. *Heidegger on Being and Acting: From Principles to Anarchy.* Translated by Christine-Marie Gross. Bloomington: University of Indiana Press, 1987.

Seed, David. *The Fictional Labyrinths of Thomas Pynchon.* London: Macmillan Press, 1988.

Selden, Raman. *A Reader's Guide to Contemporary Literary Theory.* Lexington: University of Kentucky Press, 1985.

Shapiro, David. "A Salon of 1990: Maximalist Manifesto." *American Poetry Review* 20 (January/February 1991): 37–44.

Shuger, Debora K. *Habits of Thought in the English Renaissance.* Berkeley and Los Angeles: University of California Press, 1990.

Silliman, Ron. "Canons and Institutions: New Hope for the Disappeared." In *The Politics of Poetic Form,* ed. Charles Bernstein, 149–74. New York: Roof Books, 1990.

——. "If By 'Writing' We Mean Literature (if by 'literature' we mean poetry (*if* . . .))." In *The L = A = N = G = U = A = G = E Book,* ed. Charles Bernstein and Bruce Andrews, 167–68. Carbondale: Southern Illinois University Press, 1983.

——. "Negative Solidarity: Revisionism and 'New American' Poetics." *Sulfur* 22 (Spring 1988): 169–75.

——, ed. *In the American Tree.* Orono, Me.: National Poetry Foundation, 1986.

Slade, Joseph. "Escaping Rationalization: Options for the Self in *Gravity's Rainbow.*" *Critique* 18, no. 3 (1977): 27–38.

Spivak, Gayatri Chakravorty. "New Historicism: Political Commitment and the Postmodern Critic." In Veeser, *The New Historicism,* 277–92.

Stephens, Mitchell. "Deconstruction and the Get-Real Press." *Columbia Journalism Review* (September/October 1991): 38–42.

Sukenick, Ronald. *The Endless Short Story.* New York: Fiction Collective, 1986.

Tölölyan, Khachig. "War as Background in *Gravity's Rainbow.*" In Clerc, *Approaches to "Gravity's Rainbow,"* 31–68.

Tompkins, Jane P. "The Reader in History." In *Reader-Response Criticism,* ed. Jane P. Tompkins, 201–32. Baltimore: Johns Hopkins University Press, 1980.

Ulmer, Gregory. *Applied Grammatology.* Baltimore: Johns Hopkins University Press, 1985.

Veeser, H. Aram, ed. *The New Historicism.* New York: Routledge, 1989.

Waters, Lindsay, and Wlad Godzich, eds. *Reading De Man Reading.* Minneapolis: University of Minnesota Press, 1989.

Watten, Barrett. *Progress.* New York: Roof Books, 1985.

——. *Total Syntax*. Carbondale: Southern Illinois University Press, 1985.

Weber, Samuel. *Institution and Interpretation*. Minneapolis: University of Minnesota Press, 1987.

——. "The Vaulted Eye: Remarks on Knowledge and Professionalism." *Yale French Studies* 77 (1990): 44–60.

Weinberger, Eliot. "Weinberger on Language Poetry." *Sulfur* 22 (Spring 1988): 180–86.

Weisenburger, Steven. "The End of History? Thomas Pynchon and Uses of the Past." In *Critical Essays on Thomas Pynchon*, ed. Richard Pearce, 140–56. Boston: G. K. Hall, 1981.

——. *A "Gravity's Rainbow" Companion*. Athens: University of Georgia Press, 1988.

Wolfley, Lawrence. "Repression's Rainbow: The Presence of Norman O. Brown in Pynchon's Big Novel." In *Critical Essays on Thomas Pynchon*, ed. Richard Pearce, 99–123. Boston: G. K. Hall, 1981.

Index

Library of Congress Cataloging-in-Publication Data

Nealon, Jeffrey T. (Jeffrey Thomas)
   Double reading : postmodernism after deconstruction / Jeffrey
T. Nealon.
      p.   cm.
   Includes bibliographical references and index.
   ISBN 0-8014-2853-X (alk. paper)
      1. American literature—20th century—History and criticism—
Theory, etc.   2. Postmodernism (Literature)—United States.
3. Deconstruction.   I. Title.
PS228.P68N43   1993
801'.95'09730904—dc20   93-636

ACP-8505   2/4/94

PS
228
P68
N43
1993